David Coa...

TECHNICAL AND INDUSTRIAL
ADVERTISING AND MARKETING

TECHNICAL AND INDUSTRIAL
ADVERTISING AND MARKETING

P. I. SLEE SMITH

LONDON
BUSINESS PUBLICATIONS LIMITED

First published 1963

© PAUL IGNATIUS SLEE SMITH, 1963

No part of this book may be reproduced, except for normal review purposes, without permission.

This book has been set in 12 on 13 pt. Bembo: printed in England by Cox and Wyman, Limited, London, Reading and Fakenham, for the publishers Business Publications Limited (registered office: 180 Fleet Street, London, E.C.4) publishing office: Mercury House, 103–119 Waterloo Road, London, S.E.1.

MADE AND PRINTED IN GREAT BRITAIN

CONTENTS

ILLUSTRATIONS

ILLUSTRATIONS

PREFACE

THIS BOOK is an attempt to describe the mechanics of industrial advertising and marketing from the viewpoint of the manufacturer who uses these services. It is contended that publicity and marketing are complementary subjects and should not be divorced, and the author has tried to present a carefully integrated and yet balanced treatment in which both of them are made to play their correct roles.

In modern industry there is a tendency for over-capacity to be met with inadequate marketing. This inadequacy is reflected in several ways, but notably by a general disinclination on the part of the industrialist to 'prepare the market' by means of market research, product planning and advertising. Although these are acknowledged to contribute substantially to the success of every campaign designed to sell consumer goods to the mass market, they are not always considered to be applicable to the marketing of industrial goods.

The innate mistrust of market research existing in the minds of manufacturers is made evident in several ways. First of all there is still a reluctance to employ professional market researchers in providing basic information upon which market forecasts are made, secondly, there is a strong disinclination to release statistics relating to exports, imports, home production, capital investments, etc. Indeed, throughout industry and the Government, very little enthusiasm is shown in the collection and publication of statistics. Yet without such data the work of the market researcher becomes more difficult, and his interpretation of results more uncertain.

It is not always appreciated that market research is not only of value in assessing the sales potential of a product, but also in helping to evaluate a process before the actual plant is built. This view is not always accepted by industrial leaders, many of whom still regard market research as a 'gimmicky' business applicable only to consumer goods and the mass market. The author believes that the responsibility for making major decisions involving heavy capital investment should lie with the more enlightened sections of higher management who employ the divining rods of modern research.

Advertising is a marketing function and, as such, it can contribute substantially to the promotion of an industrial product. This statement is not, however, generally believed, although lip service may be paid to it by higher management.

In a way this attitude is understandable because the advertising executive in industry, unlike his colleague on the consumer side, cannot readily justify expenditure on publicity in terms of 'measurable', increased sales. Industrial advertising becomes, therefore, an act of faith! Higher management in the non-consumer section of industry cannot yet appreciate the fact that the real function of technical advertising is not to sell industrial goods but to build up interest in them and to 'soften up' the market.

Advertising, if well planned and properly focused, can definitely assist the manufacturer, but to be really effective it needs to be integrated with the marketing section of the organization. Alone and isolated from the commercial interests there is no doubt that advertising is of doubtful value to any industrial company. It would appear to matter very little whether the marketing department has within its boundary an advertising section, or whether marketing and advertising run in harness as two departments, the vital consideration is that advertising should never be divorced from marketing.

The importance of Trade and technical publicity cannot, unfortunately, be accurately gauged by reference to the published figures on advertising expenditure. The only relevant figure that emerges from the official statistics is 30·5 million pounds on Trade and technical advertising for 1961. It is, apparently, impossible to disentangle other items of Trade and technical publicity from the gross figures which include consumer expenditure. However, a very rough approximation would appear to indicate that the yearly expenditure on all forms of Trade and technical publicity exceeds 60 million pounds a year.

The author owes a debt of gratitude to his friends at S. H. Benson Limited, who have read many of the chapters and given him a great deal of most valuable advice. In particular, he would like to acknowledge the help of Mr. J. H. Mackenzie for his critical and yet always helpful comments. Prominent in this list of acknowledgement should be a reference to Mr. J. Ball of Albert Reed Limited, for his contributions to the chapter on 'Industrial Market Research', to Mario Armengol for his striking advertisement designs and Miss Doris Burgess for reading the proofs. In conclusion the author would like to thank his colleagues in I.C.I. Central Publicity Department for their encouragement and advice.

February, 1963   P. I. SLEE SMITH

1

WHO BUYS, HOW AND WHEN?

EXHAUSTIVE STUDIES have been undertaken about the buying habits of consumers, but comparatively little has been published about the pattern of buying raw materials and manufactured industrial products and goods. Yet this is a subject of great significance to all those engaged in marketing and advertising non-consumer goods. The industrial buyer differs radically from the consumer buyer, and the motivating forces which apparently play an important part in helping to influence buying habits in the mass market do not play such an important part in modern industry.

In some instances, such as the buying of primary raw materials, advertising has no influence whatever on decisions. Here the buying is in the complete control of specialists who base decisions on purely technical considerations and are governed entirely by quality, price and delivery. Indeed, it is feasible that instead of assisting the supplier, the presence of advertising could, in some instances, actually lessen his chances of business by giving the impression that money was being spent on promotion that could have been used to lower the price of the product. This, indeed, is the attitude of some of the nationalized industries towards advertising by their major suppliers of basic raw materials. This does not mean that the industrial buyer is completely unaffected by advertising pressures, indeed, there is plenty of evidence to support the view that he is susceptible to the persuasive arguments of the advertiser and that advertising and all the supporting forms of promotion can play a useful part in helping to influence buying decisions. It has to be realized, however, that the industrial buyer is economically more rational than the consumer buyer, and more critical in his appraisement and judgement.

DEFINITIONS

Are the three functions – buying, purchasing and procurement one and the same thing? According to the dictionary they have much the same meaning and throughout this chapter the writer regards buying and purchasing as interchangeable. It should, however, be stated that in the language of modern purchasing, each is claimed to have a special significance. Buying is usually taken as the simple exchange of goods for an agreed sum of money, whereas purchasing is an exchange for a negotiated amount of money. The key to the difference between the two verbs is negotiation. This is the vital function of a purchasing officer whose special responsibility it is to buy on the most advantageous terms, taking into account such factors as a technical knowledge of the goods being bought, markets, prices, discounts and price trends.

Procurement is mainly used as a term contractually; when a contractor or agent acts on behalf of the principal to purchase equipment or materials to incorporate in the project for which the contractor is responsible. The principal usually pays a procurement fee which includes the cost of buying, inspection and progressing – usually the main contractor assumes all risks in respect of quality, delivery and performance of the item supplied.

WHO DICTATES BUYING POLICY?

There are many forms of industrial buying, each one requiring its own brand of specialized knowledge and having its own procedure. There is, for instance, the bulk purchasing of primary raw materials, such as tobacco, wool, cotton, chemicals, hides and skins, and rubber. Then there is the buying-in of materials and manufactured goods for use within the organization in the running of its business, such as the bulk purchases of steel and timber by nationalized industries running into many millions of pounds annually. The broad avenue of industrial buying covers the purchase of a very wide range of manufactured or processed goods for inclusion in or conversion into industrial and consumer products.

2

In smaller companies, the commercial director might take on the role of chief purchasing officer; in medium-sized concerns the purchasing is usually divorced from the selling although there is close liaison between the two sections, whilst in large companies the buying is delegated to a central purchasing agency or department. The overall responsibility for expenditure on raw materials and goods being bought is taken by the head of the concern. It is his job to see that the cash flow into the company as represented by sales more than balances the money being spent on goods, labour and overheads, particularly those that are used internally and represent capital investment. A saving effected in purchasing is generally reflected in a substantial increase in profits, indeed, with shrinking profit margins this offers the best prospect of a reasonable return on capital. Realization of the tremendous importance of wise buying is causing many commercial concerns to overhaul their purchasing machinery to see if it is up-to-date in the way in which it operates and if it works in harmony with the commercial organization.

If higher management is responsible for the sanction of expenditure on purchases, the actual job of purchasing is left to the specialist. He may operate alone or be a member of a team. Generally speaking, the purchasing officer is in constant touch with those sections of the organization that are expected to use the goods he intends to buy. If, for instance a buyer were negotiating the purchase of a machine for use in the works, he would first make sure that the technical, engineering, production, maintenance and safety departments were fully consulted and their general recommendations would influence him in reaching a decision on the type and source of the machine. Generally, the buyer would require the technical and engineering departments to provide him with a specification sufficient to cover the company's requirements, in so far as performance of the machine were concerned. He would also expect to receive from these departments recommendations as to firms who should be invited to tender, and also some general comments on their technical ability. On receipt of the tenders, a technical and commercial appraisal would be made of the offer which would take account of initial cost, technical

3

suitability of the machine for the work it is expected to do and operating and maintenance costs. As a result of this appraisal a buying decision would be made.

Similarly, the buyer who was concerned with the purchase of raw materials would make certain they were able to meet the rigid specifications laid down by the production side of the organization. Having decided on the nature of the goods to be purchased, it would be left to the buyer to work out the most advantageous terms of purchase and to ensure that the specification provided was sufficient to ensure that his firm's requirements were met in terms of quality, design and performance and the contractor had a clear idea of what was expected of him. Actual choice of contractor is determined by several factors. If we take as an example the purchase of valves, the selection of a suitable manufacturer could only be made by the buyer taking note of the following considerations:

(1) The reputation and financial stability of the supplier and his rating in the particular industry.

(2) Suitability of his plant and quality of his design staff to produce the goods in the quality and quantity required.

(3) The effectiveness of his quality control arrangements, inspection and testing facilities and the degree of independence enjoyed by his inspectorate.

(4) Previous experience of the supplier and first hand knowledge gained of the technical performance of the valves under both normal and abnormal conditions of use.

(5) Trading terms offered by the supplier and his ability within his own trading group to offer special discounts, etc.

(6) Effect, if any, of reciprocal trading arrangements, e.g. where the supplier is also a customer.

(7) Readiness and ability of the supplier to modify goods to meet certain domestic specifications where his own specifications are unacceptable and there is no relevant or acceptable British Standard on competitive terms.

(8) Delivery of goods to prearranged key points at prearranged times, in suitable packs. This is a vital factor, as it could hap-

pen that unless the supplier were prepared to keep to a strict time-table of deliveries, serious dislocation could occur in the factories when new valves were required to be installed immediately. It could, and frequently does happen, that suppliers are expected to hold stocks of purchased goods against delivery instructions, or emergencies, and the ability of a supplier to give warehouse facilities could be important.

These are the tangible factors, but alongside there are the intangible ones. There is, for instance, the personality of the supplier as represented by his salesman and there is the image of the company as represented by its publicity. Although intangible they cannot be dismissed lightly. A buyer, no matter how experienced and 'hard-boiled', has his likes and dislikes, and although he may be largely governed by a regimented purchasing procedure there is always some room for manoeuvre. All things being equal, the supplier whose representative is readily acceptable to the buyer must receive preferential treatment. To deny this is to deny the existence of human emotions.

BUYING RESEARCH

This is a somewhat unfamiliar term, but it has been well defined by Albert Kreig (*A Growing Concept: Purchasing Research, U.S.A.*) as 'the systematic, in-depth investigation undertaken by a staff group to improve purchasing performance'.

It is particularly applicable in the chemical industry where substantial savings may be effected in raw material costs by scientific purchasing. In the U.S.A. several of the largest and most successful chemical companies employ highly qualified purchasing researchers whose objective it is to investigate and advise on buying policy. They appear to have a wide remit and are qualified to advise top management of any changes in buying procedure that could lead to worthwhile economies, and also to negotiate with suppliers when material specifications have to be overhauled.

The new researchers are really the back-room boys of the purchasing department. Their job is to study the manufacturing process in reverse, in other words, to concentrate on the raw material that goes into the plant rather than the product that comes out of it. In the main, the efforts of any team concerned with rational purchasing are concerned with trying to answer such questions as:

(a) Are the most economical raw materials being used in manufacture?
(b) Have all sources of supply been examined?
(c) Is it possible to use another type or another form of raw material?
(d) Are the specifications for the raw material too high?

A similar kind of practice has been introduced into the British motor industry where special investigators are employed to review buying decisions made by purchasing officers. The management justification for this system is that it keeps the purchasing officers on their toes, as the primary function of the investigator is to find cheaper and better alternative sources of supply.

STANDARDS AND SPECIFICATIONS

The adoption of standards in industry makes possible greater economy of productive effort and materials and ensures a high degree of adaptability in use, as well as better quality control during manufacture. From the consumer angle, the recognition and acceptance of standards affords a protection of buying quality and this ensures better value for money. It has also to be realized that without standards the buyer's company is inevitably faced with expensive inspection and quality control to ensure suitability of the product for use.

It is true to say that the industrial buyer has now come to accept standardization as an instrument of quality and, indeed, welcomes it as a convenient means of controlling the purchase of a widening range of goods. In the western world there are a number of organizations, some sponsored by government bodies and others by private concerns, who issue standards of both quality and per-

6

formance for the consumer and industrial goods which enjoy general acceptance by manufacturers and the public. In Great Britain the British Standards Institution is the recognized body. It was set up in 1901 to prepare standards for goods acquired by industry and is independent of both government and industry, being non-profit making and non-political. Its primary function is to draft and to publish British Standards, and each one is drawn up by general agreement among representatives of makers, distributors and users of the articles, meeting in B.S.I. committees, most of whom are sponsored by the relevant trade organizations.

In considering British Standards and also Company Standards, it has to be appreciated that those who draw them up must influence actual purchasing decisions. There is a growing tendency by large undertakings, such as nationalized industries, to use branded goods of established quality rather than to have such commodities made up specially to their own specification – paint and automotive lubricating oils are good examples. By accepting standard production lines the buyer can take advantage of a nation-wide distribution, technical and warehousing service and the knowledge that the manufacturer's reputation backs the quality of the product. The prudent buyer does not, however, leave the matter there. Before deciding on the list of branded products of a particular commodity he will buy, he will set a standard of quality or performance to which the products must conform; such standards are usually based on a cross section of the products offered. Based on the restricted list of approved branded items, selection is made by competitive tenders.

Of interest to the advertiser is information about the type of person who is responsible for drawing up standards and particularly his susceptibility to advertising pressure. Committees who frame British Standards are drawn from the technical echelons of industry and are usually engineers, chemists and technologists. These men are nominated by their respective firms to serve on committees jointly organized by the Trade Federation and the British Standards Institution. The framing of a British Standard may take months, or even years, depending largely upon how much the particular industry wants the specification and how easy it is to reconcile the conflicting commercial arguments put forward by the trade representatives.

It is interesting to note that over 3,000 British Standards have been issued for goods produced in engineering, electrical, building, chemical and other industries. Since the end of the war a large number of standards for consumer goods has also been issued. Apart, however, from standards issued by the Institution, many companies issue their own specifications, either because there is no B.S.S. to meet the case, or the B.S.S. does not go far enough to satisfy the company's technical requirements. The preparation of such specifications by individual companies involves them in considerable expenditure and takes a great deal of time, as the work entails very close liaison with outside suppliers and users. Company specifications, once produced, are regarded as confidential documents. Because of the high cost of preparing such specifications, there is a general feeling in British industry today that, wherever possible, use should be made of British Standards in preference to company standards, and where the former do not exist, then energetic measures should be taken to ensure that they are drawn up by the Institution working alongside the particular industry.

Whilst acknowledging the growing importance of specifications, there is a danger of becoming too 'specification minded', and this can be very costly, e.g. if a company insists on all goods being made to their domestic specifications failing the existence of a British Standard, then purchasing can easily become unrealistic. Take, for instance, an ordinary galvanized bucket, which might be readily available ex factory at say 7s. 6d., and when made to a firm's specification costs 15s. Yet the cheaper article could easily satisfy all normal requirements and be a reasonable 'buy'. The extra quality required by the specification at double the price cannot be justified as the 15s. bucket will not give double the life of the one at 7s. 6d. This is just an over-simplified example, but it does illustrate the point that specifications can sometimes be carried to the extreme and involve the issuing company in a great deal of unnecessary expenditure.

APPROVED LIST OF SUPPLIERS

Purchasing departments frequently operate on the basis of 'Approved Lists of Suppliers' and it is, of course, the ambition of every potential supplier to qualify for inclusion on such lists. These are made up of suppliers who are well known to the firm, whose goods conform to the required standards, whose delivery, price, inspection arrangements and after-sales service are satisfactory and whose terms of business are acceptable. The list may also include 'reserve' suppliers who have a high reputation, but are not actually selling to the company at the time the list is compiled. A buyer will always endeavour to secure the long-term position often at the sacrifice of immediate advantages.

If a supplier fails to maintain the required standard, falls down on delivery, or in some way does not give satisfaction, then sanctions can be brought to bear against him and if he continues to cause dissatisfaction after being warned, his name is withdrawn from the list. It will be appreciated that an 'Approved List' is of vital importance to a supplier and could mean the difference between solvency and bankruptcy. The list is also of considerable significance to the advertiser who is concerned with general buying procedure and the kind of thinking that governs its compilation and use by suppliers. Advertising that really has to pull its weight should be directed mainly to firms who figure largely on 'Approved Lists'. For this reason a study of the whole mechanism of purchasing is well worthwhile.

THE ROLE OF THE HEAD BUYER

Having chosen the most suitable supplier, it is the responsibility of the chief buyer or purchasing officer to negotiate the best possible terms for buying, and to set in motion the normal purchasing machinery. It is not the purpose of this book to study general purchasing procedure, but rather to determine how the buying of raw materials and industrial goods is integrated with marketing and advertising policy. Whilst the primary function of the buyer is to control the whole complex process of industrial purchasing, he has to do a great deal more than to buy the right goods at the right price.

As a preliminary to the placing of any long-term contract, the buyer needs to be able to forecast price movements and trends so as to time his purchases to the best possible advantage to his company. Buying is always highly sensitive to selling and attention has to be drawn to the possible effect of sales forecasts on the control of purchases. This, of course, is an internal matter; something that has to be reconciled within the company. What is probably of equal importance is the possible effect of external market, labour and political conditions on prices. The buyer, if he is to be really successful, needs to be able to prophesy with reasonable accuracy the timing of major fluctuations that are likely to take place, so that he can buy at the right time on the most advantageous terms. Timing becomes a critical factor in any major buying operation and the buyer in the very large organization is only too well aware of this. That is why he finds it so necessary to reinforce his own departmental knowledge with intelligence drawn from the commercial sides of the organization. By using such well established divining rods as market research it is now possible to locate some of the vital facts upon which buying decisions can be based. The pattern of modern business is now so complex that a buyer, no matter how experienced and qualified he may be, must lean heavily upon the information supplied him by all those sensitive to purchasing.

The executive in any company who is responsible for buying, wields considerable power, as upon his judgement depends to a large extent the profit margin in any venture. The fact that so many buyers migrate to the Board is some indication of the importance being attached to his position in modern industry today.

The industrial buyer is usually regarded as a hard man to influence, and there is abundant evidence to support this view. Not only is he difficult to influence, but his approach to advertising is one of suspicion, not unmixed with hostility. Whilst it is recognized that in the main the buyer is largely unaffected by the kinds of pressure that are known to influence buying decisions in the consumer market, he is susceptible to the type of informative advertising that gives him alternative sources of supply or supplies new technical information. The buyer of citric acid for the soft drink trade would be completely unmoved by advertisements in the trade press which stated that Firm A made citric acid of superb quality in the most hygienic factory in the world. He would, however, be extremely interested to see an advertisement which announced that Firm A was now using a new type of synthesis for the production of citric acid. Such an announcement would satisfy him in two respects; first of all, it would put him fully in the technological picture and secondly, it could open up some very interesting possibilities of price reduction due to improvements in manufacture.

RECIPROCAL TRADING

Where suppliers are also customers, there is frequently pressure exerted by the sales side of the company to persuade the buyer to show partiality in giving out contracts. Generally speaking, reciprocal trading is detested by the buyer who, quite rightly, regards it as a pernicious practice which can only lead to uneconomical buying as it destroys or minimizes his bargaining position. Despite this attitude – and the justice of it is seldom contested – it is a fact that efforts are constantly being made to exert pressure on the buyer to favour the company's customers. It becomes impossible to ignore this pressure where the firm relies for the bulk of its turnover on a few very large accounts, one of whom is the potential supplier. On the face of it there is nothing to prevent a customer from meeting all the specifications demanded and providing in all respects the kind of service required.

The difficulty is not here, but in negotiating a contract. This is where the buyer often finds himself in an impossible position because, in his efforts to secure the most advantageous prices, he may weaken arguments put forward by his colleagues on the sales side when they are trying to effect a substantial deal. Even if heavy sacrifices have to be made, it would appear to be well worthwhile to reject any form of reciprocal trading and to divorce customers from suppliers. It is sometimes argued that reciprocal

11

trading provides an opportunity for the buyer's firm to sell their own products and so put pressure on the supplier to become a customer. On examination, this practice will be seen to be open to considerable abuse as the necessity for special inter-trading terms may tend to make such deals unprofitable.

WHAT DO BUYERS READ

Buyers as a class of specialized readers are mainly interested in commercial-cum-financial intelligence, such as:

Commodity market reviews
Company reports
Labour rate revisions and awards
Changes in Trade Union Practices, hours of work, condition of employment, etc.
Mergers
Board of Trade indices and industrial cost indices
Productivity trends
New processes, inventions and ideas.

Much of this kind of information is given in the financial papers and in the city columns of the daily and sometimes the provincial Press. In addition, such highly reputable and authoritative journals as *The Board of Trade Journal* and *The Economist*, also deal in great detail with some of the issues raised. The trade and technical Press, much of it monthly, comments at length on all these matters where they effect their particular trade, and it is these well informed comments that are of great interest to manufacturers. Apart, however, from this highly specialized type of intelligence, the trade and technical Press offers the buyer a great deal of useful background information upon which he can draw for news of interesting technological developments, alternative sources of supply as shown in the advertising sections, changes in personnel in the companies he deals with on a day to day basis and news of price changes.

As regards the technologist who may influence buying decisions or be responsible for 'buying research', there is evidence to support the view that on the whole they read the trade and technical Press for news and stimulation rather than for assistance in their work. This is borne out by the Social Survey carried out in 1956 on behalf of the D.S.I.R. when 1,082 technologists were interviewed to discover what use they make of technical literature. Although the investigation was confined to the electrical and electronics industries, which are known to consume a large amount of literature, the implications are very much wider and might well apply to the whole field of trade and technical journals. In this survey it is revealed that most technologists regularly see five journals or less and more than one third of these readers do not acknowledge ever having obtained useful information from an article or a trade journal! The corresponding number for learned society journals is 61 per cent.

2

INDUSTRIAL MARKET RESEARCH

IN THE sales promotion of consumer goods, research is commonly accepted as being indispensable to the creation of effective advertising. Product research, market research, media research and research into buying habits, attitudes and motives are regularly carried out in order to provide clients with the basic information upon which campaign-planning can be undertaken. The vast majority of these clients are engaged in the manufacture or sale of consumer goods and only a few of them are what might be termed industrial accounts.

It is often assumed, although quite wrongly, that because a manufacturer makes conveyor belting and not silk stockings, research is not applicable to his particular marketing problems. It is argued by the industrial manufacturer that as he knows the market, both present and potential, the customers and the competitors, he is in a far better position to forecast sales and market trends than some cranky researcher. This kind of reasoning hardly seems logical if one remembers the pattern of modern industrial progress where scientific research – chemical, physical, engineering and technological, all play a vital part in the discovery and development of every major product known to men. It is, therefore, surely unreasonable to suppose that marketing cannot also benefit from research.

Industrial research is the other side of the marketing penny, differing in design from consumer research, but serving the same general purpose, namely to assess the size and conditions of the market for any given product. The modern researcher tends to look upon the consumer market very much as a mathematician regards an algebraic problem, whilst with industrial research it is less a scientific investigation than an exercise in objective reasoning. If one looks at a survey of the market for a new type of general purpose liquid detergent, once all the necessary field work has been carried out, using a sample of say 5 or 10,000, according to the type of research being undertaken, it is possible by employing established statistical techniques to interpret the results in terms of the entire population. Such a survey would be expected to indicate to the manufacturer the size and pattern of the consumer market and enable him to start planning a selling campaign with reasonable confidence.

On the other hand, an industrial survey, which may only involve a fractional sample of a few hundred, or even less, depends largely for its usefulness on the framing of the questions asked and the skill shown in the interpretation of the answers. In the industrial field, the consumer is several stages removed from the manufacturer, and each stage may have several areas of uncertainty. This remoteness from the market place tends to make the manufacturer of industrial goods less sensitive to new ideas and new trends in design than his counterpart who produces manufactured goods for the mass market. It also renders him a good deal more conservative and less inclined to make changes in production techniques and marketing methods.

The general pattern of the industrial field differs radically from the consumer market. In the former, for instance, there is considerable 'weighting' in most trades by very large concerns, who may represent as much as 70 per cent of the purchasing power. Another difference is seen in the actual make-up of a sample. In the consumer trade, the units are not grossly dissimilar and their answers to cleverly phrased questionnaires follow a recognized pattern. This is not the experience of researchers in industry, where the answers given to questions put to business executives vary widely according to the position held in the firm by the person being interviewed. Such a wide difference would hardly be found when carrying out a consumer survey. It would, for instance, be reasonable to expect similarly 'typed' answers from a débutante in Mayfair and a shop assistant in Kilburn when asked for their opinion of a new lipstick.

One comfort to the industrial researcher is that, provided the right kind of person is approached for the information, it may be assumed that, whereas in the consumer field behaviour is motivated to a large extent by non-economic factors, the buyer of industrial goods can usually be trusted to arrive at decisions which are rational economically. This is very important, because it does mean that the reasons which actually motivate purchasing decisions are basically honest, and that the factors of major importance in specifying are price and quality.

There is a great dearth of information on industrial markets and very few manufacturing concerns are actually applying the basic principles of market research, as developed in the consumer field, to their own particular marketing problems. It is no exaggeration to say that with the production of industrial goods as distinct from manufactured goods intended for retail sale, there are many dangerous 'sales voids' where the companies concerned are not fully aware of what actually happens to their products once they have left their customers' works. Take as an example the case of a manufacturer of plastic moulding powder who sells to the moulding trade; whilst he may be thoroughly familiar with all the available moulding outlets, their potentialities and their problems, he could well be abysmally ignorant of the final destinations of the mouldings themselves. Yet this ignorance might at some future time be of very serious consequence to him. He could, for instance, make a heavy investment in new plant to increase his capacity in reasonable expectation of a rising market, only to find that influences quite unknown to him at the consumer end prejudice the choice of plastics and indicate a strong consumer preference for metal and ceramics. This ignorance of what the ultimate user thinks about an industrial product could not only adversely affect the fortunes of the manufacturer of industrial goods, but also his customer, the moulder, who is really much closer to the retail trade.

Prior to carrying out any serious piece of industrial market research there must be an analysis of the market; this is a preliminary essential to any survey. This exercise would, in effect, prepare a working brief for the researcher by describing the market to be investigated and, by fixing the goal posts, limit the extent of any inquiry. If we take, for instance, a survey to be carried out by a manufacturer of computers, a preliminary analysis could show that the bulk of his sales were made to 10 or 11 types of user, all of whom were very familiar with the simple punched card systems produced by the company. The analysis could also disclose where maximum sales resistance was being experienced and where lay the large but relatively unknown new product areas. It is on the basis of such an analysis that a market survey would be considered and eventually planned.

Following on this analysis, the market researcher would then plan a campaign in which each of these sectors would be studied in detail. Without the preliminary analysis a great deal of effort would undoubtedly be wasted and instead of an investigation being aimed fairly accurately at a number of clearly recognized targets, each one carefully defined, there would be a wild fusillade of researchers' bullets, a lot of noise and fuss, but no tangible result. An analysis of the market can be of the greatest assistance in making known to the research team the clear distinction between established sales areas and the new product areas where future growth is likely to be found.

OBJECTIVES

The successful marketing of a product, whether it is phosphates or baby food, depends on the availability of precise background information on a number of marketing factors relating to the goods being sold, the markets, the customers, the competitors, the price factor, the relevant economic trends and, perhaps, the advertising. Although it is difficult to define the kind of market research likely to be useful to the industrialist, the following broad objectives might be set out:

(1) To assess the size of the market.
(2) To determine the location and the number of customers.
(3) To study their requirements.
(4) To find out who actually specifies and why he buys the company's products in preference to those of anyone else.

(5) To secure reasons why some customers prefer goods made by competitors.

(6) To see what kind of price structure is generally favoured by the trade.

(7) To find out the kind of promotional material that tends to influence business.

Apart, however, from the more obvious objectives there are also the intangibles, some of which may be of very considerable importance to the industrialist. A manufacturer of glass bottles might feel worried about the inroads made into his business by moulded plastic containers and commission an independent organization to carry out some research to find out the true facts. In its final report the research team might comment on the general unreliability of information provided by the company's sales representatives who are in daily touch with customers. Such an observation, whilst outside the general remit of the researchers, could have a significance of far reaching importance. To an astute executive it might indicate one of several things:

(1) The salesmen are under such heavy pressure that they have not the time, or perhaps the inclination, to carry out their own market appraisals.

(2) The salesmen are contacting customers at too low a level of management so that any news of market trends which they obtain is likely to be uninformed.

(3) The representatives are of such poor calibre that they are not capable of assimilating worthwhile intelligence or, if they do, they are not able to assess its true value.

This kind of reasoning might trigger off further research to determine which diagnosis was the correct one. As every manufacturer, faced with either a manufacturing or a marketing decision, must depend a great deal on the facts provided by his field force, his decisions might be faulty if these are suspect! Here the intangibles assume a great deal more importance than the tangibles.

18

WHO CARRIES OUT RESEARCH?

Generally speaking, only the very large industrial concerns carry out complete market surveys within their own organizations, although a considerable number of medium-sized and large-sized companies regularly undertake desk research based on available information and sub-contract out any field research that may be necessary. The trend in modern industry is towards the formation of marketing departments operating within the commercial organization who are responsible both for research and planning. Less use is being made of the services of the advertising agency which, until a few years ago, was regarded as the obvious and, in some instances, the only source of research data. There is certainly a growing feeling within industry that agents should concern themselves exclusively with the creative side of sales promotion and not meddle with research. Far better to employ an independent organization with no obvious 'axe to grind' where this is necessary, and it is only really necessary where field work has to be carried out. It is a fairly safe prediction to make that within a few years most industrial concerns with a publicity budget exceeding £100,000 will have their own marketing and research departments.

Although it was suggested that when agencies carry out research for clients it might be difficult to avoid some bias there is, perhaps, a greater danger that where the research becomes the responsibility of a marketing manager, the temptation to provide conclusions in line with Board policy might prove too strong. This could be disastrous and lead the company into real danger. The ideal arrangement would appear to be that thoroughly reliable and independent research organizations should be employed to do any sampling necessary and to give general advice on the planning and, maybe, interpretation of all important researches to be carried out.

One of the chief difficulties experienced in commissioning outside concerns to do market research is that most investigations in the industrial field involve a fairly intimate knowledge of the product, and it may need weeks, if not months, for a newcomer to absorb this before undertaking a survey. Although market researchers are very versatile, it is a little too much to expect a man who has been spending three months examining the market potential of bacon slicers to become knowledgeable on stainless steel condenser tubing without undergoing a time-consuming and expensive apprenticeship – first of all to learn something about stainless steel and then about its application. Time is a vital factor in any survey, the results of which are usually required in a hurry by the commercial interests of a company. For this reason it is always an advantage if the work can be carried out within the company itself.

Whilst realizing that something like 73 per cent of the factories in the United Kingdom employ less than 100 people, and therefore the personnel resources of the majority of companies are very restricted, it should be possible for the sales manager to learn sufficient about market research techniques to employ them to advantage for his employers. After all, market research cannot pretend to be an exact science, and in the ultimate it is mainly a question of applying common sense to marketing problems. There is no doubt that such a recommendation will upset most professional market researchers who believe that without the expertise of the experienced investigator, the amateur in this field may do more harm than good. Whilst it would be foolish to expect to derive the same benefits from an unprofessional survey as one conducted by experienced researchers, at least the investigation should provide data of sufficient commercial value as to make the initial inquiry worthwhile, and possibly encourage the company to have it re-examined professionally.

WHEN IS RESEARCH NEEDED?

Research can be very expensive and manufacturers are somewhat critical of the high cost involved in some research exercises. They are also aware that many research campaigns have, in the past, been of extremely doubtful commercial value and resulted merely in the accumulation of a vast amount of useless information. This is undoubtedly true. The fault, however, lies not with the actual practice of market research, but with the lack of a clearly defined objective. Without adequate preparatory work and a well conceived plan, every market research exercise is almost bound to be a failure. The concept of market research as something which is done only when sales are falling and competitors gaining ground is, of course, entirely false. If the research is left until the company is almost on the rocks, then the chances are that it is too late in any event!

Defining the problem for the research team is of tremendous importance and it has been suggested by more than one eminent authority that more time should be spent on this aspect of an operation than the actual research itself. Defining the problem will not only cover the actual objectives of the research, but the type of research necessary to provide the most valuable kind of data; when it should be carried out and how the exercise is to be conducted. The next query arises as to the identity of the person who is to define the problem. He should preferably be the managing director or commercial director of a company and not the sales manager or advertising manager. The last two are unlikely to present a marketing problem without bias.

It is useful to consider the kind of brief that a manufacturer might want to discuss either with his own marketing manager, or an outside research company. Let us suppose he made conveyor belts of various kinds – mother belts, slope belts, boom belts, overland belts, etc. His business was generally good and customers appeared satisfied, but an analysis of sales over the last six months revealed a new and rather puzzling pattern. New accounts were not being added as regularly as they were twelve months ago, moreover 85 per cent of the entire orders placed for belting were now from very large concerns, whereas a year ago this figure was 70 per cent, with 30 per cent from small users. So radical a change of sales pattern certainly requires investigation and in this instance it might indicate one or more of several factors, e.g.:

(1) It could indicate that the sales policy had been altered.
(2) It could mean that the old sales force had been replaced by a new one with different ideas and with different direction.

(3) It could be the result of less effort on the part of the outside sales force, who were no longer prepared to spend as much time on small orders and new accounts as they were a year ago.

(4) The new sales pattern might possibly stem from a new attitude of the production department which was streamlining manufacture and concentrating on fewer grades and types of belting; extension of the range increased production costs and tended to make manufacture uneconomical.

The sales brief could take the following form: 'Examine the reasons why the pattern of sales as existing today differs so markedly from that existing twelve months ago.'

DESK RESEARCH

This is now being carried out by a large number of industrial concerns and is based on available information obtained from the company's own records, Board of Trade results, figures provided by Trade Associations and Federations, trade journals, foreign agencies and even competitors. This internal data is, of course, of great interest as it can provide material of immense value to the commercial departments of an organization. For example, a manufacturer of sulphuric acid can quickly determine with great accuracy the total production of acid in the United Kingdom; the main users and the tonnage taken by each one of them; the profitability of sulphuric acid manufacture by each of his competitors and, from the pattern of sales over the last five years he is able to forecast a sales curve for the next two or three years. Data of this kind, when considered in the light of knowledge about the national trends in trade and the economic position of the country, can provide the higher management with a reliable marketing picture. Here desk research, perhaps supplemented with information obtained by means of a few telephone calls, can provide the manufacturer with all the information he requires and there will be no need for him to use an outside research organization to provide external data obtained from a sampling exercise.

Where a field force becomes necessary is when the manufacturer wants to determine the likelihood of a diminution in the volume of business due to the lesser use of sulphuric acid. This could happen if an alternative process had been discovered which did not involve the use of acid, e.g. if dry car batteries, instead of accumulators, were used throughout the transport industry, or if pickling and cleaning of metal no longer required an acid bath. Another factor of importance to the manufacturer might well be the handling of acid – use of tankers, carboys, etc., and the reaction of the user trades to the present methods. It might well be that following a market research survey there could follow an exercise in operational research to determine the attitude of the trade towards the size of purchase, and to examine the policy governing the actual issuing of orders by customers.

The weakness of desk research is that it has no reliable yardstick with which to measure its usefulness and in some instances this can only be supplied by carefully planned and well directed field work. There is, however, a marked and perhaps quite natural inclination on the part of certain research organizations to advise clients of the necessity or advisability of carrying out sampling to supply additional information, when such information can be made available without actually employing a field force. It has to be remembered in this context that research companies make a living by operating a field force and there must therefore be a not unexpected bias towards sampling as distinct from desk research.

SAMPLING METHODS

The success of any sampling exercise depends to a very large extent on the kind of questions asked, the skill of the interviewers and the selection and number of the persons interviewed. In the consumer field it might well be that 2,000 is the right size of sample, whereas to provide the right kind of data for a purely industrial piece of research 300 might be quite adequate. For some industrial exercises it could happen that a census is possible, e.g. if a survey were required involving lifebelt and buoy manufacturers it would be possible to go round and interview the entire 25 of them. Information obtained as the result of a census should be more reliable than that secured by any sampling method but everything, of course, depends on the size of the industry being studied. There are only 11 lithographic machinery manufacturers, and all of these could be interviewed in two or three days, whereas the 1,398 lithographic and colour printers would present something of a problem. A sample of say 250 of these could, if carefully selected, give a very balanced viewpoint.

The size of sample is largely determined by the degree of accuracy required in the research. It does not follow, however, that the larger the sample, the better the accuracy. There is in all audiences to be tested a straightening out of the curve so that between a sample size of say 2,000 and 10,000 there is an appreciable difference in the response. This is where expert advice from experienced researchers can help in arriving at the best possible sample for any given exercise.

Sampling need not, of course, involve actual interviewing. Very useful work can sometimes be done by postal questionnaires and even by telephoning, depending on the kind of problem being studied. If the questionnaire is prepared by the company's own marketing staff without consultation with the actual organization which is going to carry out the field work, then there is a risk that it might have an undesirable bias and the answers to this questionnaire could therefore be suspect. Questions should be framed by impartial experts, preferably by experienced professional researchers working with the client's own marketing staff.

The next problem arises in the selection of the sample. If the investigation is concerned with the actual sales of a product, difficulties are likely to arise in determining who in an organization, particularly a very large one, are the officials who actually influence decisions on the purchase of raw materials, engineering supplies, etc. Having found out the identity of these men, the next thing to worry about is the best means of canvassing their opinions.

In carrying out an industrial survey, complications can arise in connection with security rulings, real and imaginary. Many firm both in the United Kingdom and on the Continent are still not prepared to provide the most elementary statistics to their own trade associations, even though they are assured that such information will be treated as highly confidential. It is only to be expected therefore that such concerns should be hostile towards researchers and most unwilling to co-operate. This is probably one of the most frustrating aspects of the business. The reception given to a potential interviewer depends largely on the company that employs him. If this is a very large concern with an internationally famous name, then the interviewer is likely to be given a much better reception than if he came from a small advertising agency. Market researchers do treat all information as confidential and it is never disclosed to anyone but the client who sponsors the investigation.

PILOT STUDY

Before carrying out any serious market research programme involving sampling it is essential that a pilot scheme should be undertaken. This may be carried out on a small number of selected people, as few as 50, all very carefully chosen. The object of the pilot study is to test out the questions and the method of carrying out the main exercise. As a result of the pilot it might be found that the questions are unsuitable and need re-framing in order to provide the right kind of information. It could also be indicated that the questions are such that only a very small percentage of people could ever be found to answer them. A decision will then have to be reached as to whether the questionnaire is to be overhauled or the entire research abandoned. In effect, the pilot study has for its chief objective the determination of the practicability of the main scheme. It could also give a clue as to its cost and the length of time that would be needed to complete it. At the conclusion of the pilot there should be a reasonable interval allowed in which to assess the results. Too often this part of the exercise is apt to be hurried, particularly if the pilot survey tends to question the advisability of continuing with the main scheme.

RESULTS AND INTERPRETATION

It is the function of the market researcher to present his client with the basic facts upon which decisions may be made, but it is not his responsibility to make these decisions. Most independent research units are reluctant to interpret results or to draw conclusions from their findings, unless they are specifically commissioned to do so and are in possession of all the relevant marketing and commercial background information. The true function of the researcher is to present the facts in an orderly and lucid manner and to draw the attention of his client to any obvious discrepancies or inconsistencies. These may assume considerable importance and their true significance might be overlooked by the manufacturer unless they were pointed out.

If we take the hypothetical case of an investigation involving a new type of inorganic thermal insulating material, it might be shown as a result of sampling that whereas the claims of the material as a means of preventing condensation in cotton mills in Lancashire were fully substantiated, in woollen mills in Bradford and Leeds the results were inconclusive. The research team in the report would stress the importance of this inconsistency, although it would not be their responsibility to try and find an answer to the query.

The interpretation of the results of a market research exercise is the function of the manufacturer who commissions the work, and this poses many problems. First of all, whose responsibility is it to find the answer? Is it the sales manager, the marketing manager (if there is one), the advertising manager, or a member of the company's board of directors? The answer to this problem is, like most answers in business, a compromise. Those executive officers who are vitally concerned with the matter would be expected to hammer out an interpretation and then a recommendation for certain action to be taken. Both interpretation and recommendation would be passed to top management for consideration. It is, of course, most unlikely that those delegated to do this work would be so ill-advised as to ignore the men who actually carried out the survey, and at the committee stage the researchers are certain to be co-opted.

RESEARCH AND ADVERTISING

Whilst it is true to say that research in the consumer field has a direct and even obvious bearing on advertising policy, the same cannot be held to be as true in industry. Yet there are lessons to be learned from a piece of industrial research that must eventually benefit the entire policy of sales promotion.

Let us take, for example, a large engineering firm specializing in the manufacture of so-called 'packaged' conveyor systems. The object of the research was to determine the kind of conveyor system preferred in a dozen or so major firms, such as those specializing in the manufacture and packaging of foodstuffs, pharmaceuticals, chemicals, drink (including soft drinks), metals and ores, bricks and ceramics, plastics, rubber, radio and electronics and electrical goods. The findings of the research confirmed the policy of the company in developing its specialized conveyor system which was readily adaptable to the needs of all these industries. Amongst the conclusions reached in this exercise was the need to bring to the notice of the high executives in the leading industrial concerns the following facts:

(a) That the firm had assumed undoubted leadership in this field.
(b) That its system was the most advanced outside the U.S.A. and was of considerable importance to all engineers concerned with automation.
(c) That the so-called 'packaged' conveyor system was a novel idea which was still comparatively unknown in the United Kingdom and had considerable value as a sales promotion idea.

To the advertising manager worth his place in any company, these three disclosures could constitute a first-class brief for a series of prestige advertisements of genuine interest to all men who occupy positions of industrial authority. It would be patently untrue to say that industrial market research determines the pattern of advertising, but it can often give a valuable lead. For this reason the advertising manager should be kept fully informed of

27

all research programmes and given the opportunity to study the results.

Although the advertising manager is not generally consulted by the market researchers, it is usual for a copy of their report to be sent to him with the relevant recommendations underlined. Where surveys are of particular value is where they indicate new avenues of potential sales in which advertising could be usefully deployed. An example could be found here with a survey on corrugated paper for bulk packaging, which revealed a radical change in distribution, say a decision on the part of refrigerator manufacturers to sell direct to the public instead of through electricity and gas showrooms or other retail channels. This change would indicate new product areas for very substantial packs involving the extensive use of corrugated paper, and prove of considerable commercial value to the company. To the astute advertising manager this disclosure would be a green light for planning a series of advertisements designed to interest refrigerator manufacturers in new packaging techniques involving the use of corrugated paper.

3

MEDIA PLANNING AND RESEARCH

MEDIA PLANNING and research is a fairly high sounding phrase, but stripped of its non-essentials it is simply a matter of careful analysis, and of the application of knowledge, experience and common sense to the particular problem, in this instance, an assessment of the advertising value of trade and technical publications.

Industrial advertising and consumer advertising are two distinct forms of sales promotion, each one requiring its own particular and characteristic 'expertise'. Yet these two forms of advertising have a great deal in common. It is a mistaken idea to imagine that unless the industrial advertising is directed at Board level, it is largely wasted. In very many instances the initial chain of specification begins at a much lower level. Indeed, in the author's experience line management, and sometimes even the foreman or chargehand, is consulted in matters of this kind. The readers of the technical Press are all valuable contacts from the advertiser's point of view but, as in advertising to the mass market consumer, some are obviously better prospects than others. Although the types of skill that are needed to develop an advertising campaign in the popular weeklies catering for young women are peculiar to the consumer market, and differ radically from those needed in planning a series of advertisements in one of the chemical papers, there is an overall similarity in the method of approach and the means employed to break down the barriers of resistance.

The main difficulty facing the agency handling an industrial account, which involves the use of a very wide range of technical journals and annuals, is that comparatively little reliable information is available about the readership and circulation of these publications. With the national Press and the mass circulation magazines there is, of course, a wealth of information to guide the media planners. Not only are the advertisers in these publications, and also those who buy time on television networks, well served with data on circulation and readership, but they have available a great deal of useful statistical information on the financial, industrial and social background of the areas where the papers and magazines are read. Some of this information might appear to be of dubious value, but at least it is made available for the benefit of advertisers and its compilation involves the publishers in heavy expense for research.

The paucity of information about trade and technical Press has been discussed by advertising organizations on many occasions. Indeed, it was realization of the abysmal ignorance that exists on the readership of these publications that inspired the Research Committee and the Trade Relations Committee of the Institute of Practitioners in Advertising to initiate a survey of readership of electrical journals amongst members of the Institution of Electrical Engineers. It was thought that this kind of research would not only provide very useful audience data about an important slice of the technical Press, but also act as a sounding board for further media research on trade publications. The information provided by this survey, although it was somewhat restricted in scope, shows very clearly the kind of data that the media planner is anxious to secure for the advertiser. He not only wants to know how many people read the journals, but also the occupation and age of the reader, the type of organizations which employ him, his job and finally whether he bought the journals or whether his subscription was paid by his employers. The media planner would also like to know the extent of the reader's business purchasing authority; this is really of vital importance to the advertiser.

The media man in the agency, who presumably is watching over the interests of the advertiser, realizes that what really matters is not so much a high readership, but the influential small core of readership in the middle and upper echelons of management. When considering the quality of readership one needs to take into account the editorial contents of the journal, and in the media department of a progressive agency, a very careful assessment is made of the editorial standing of a particular journal. This assessment is based on the judgement and experience of the media planner who, in many instances, receives useful advice from outside sources, such as clients who are thoroughly familiar with the particular trade or profession covered by the journal.

Where trade and technical journals do not give details of circulation, the only possible yardstick to employ in judging their value as media for advertising is an evaluation of their editorial contents and also, to perhaps a lesser degree, their advertising contents. Continuity of readership applies particularly to controlled circulation journals and the validity of the lists upon which are based their readership figures. It has been said that in the U.S.A. some 30 per cent of men change their jobs every year and, unless a mailing list is constantly kept up to date, it must become unreliable. This figure of 30 per cent seems somewhat high for the United Kingdom, but with the trend towards larger commercial and industrial units, there is certainly a strong tendency towards greater movement of staff in most commercial and industrial concerns.

Publishers of controlled circulation journals admit that their readership fluctuates, but they point out that their advertisers appeal to the individual only because of his influence on the action of his company, and in the last analysis it is the company that represents the real target. This argument seems hardly valid as the company, although having an identity in law, in terms of advertising practice, has no identity at all. It only assumes an identity and a usefulness when it is linked with a name or a series of names of people holding positions of influence. The advertiser has a right to assume that his advertisements are being directed not so much to the individual, but to the position he holds in a particular company. If a journal is still being sent to Mr. Smith, who was previously the manager of the Supply Department, and is now the Chief Statistician, then it is wasted and an opportunity for promotion of a product or range of products is lost entirely.

Advertisers in the trade and technical Press do not always appreciate the fact that where journals are purchased by the management for their staff, then actual readership is arbitrarily fixed by an officer of the company. Journals are sent around the factories, offices and laboratories on a circulation list which is usually drawn up by a fairly junior member of the staff who may, in the first instance, be guided by general recommendations made by the secretary or managing director. The amount of attention given to these publications depends on several factors:

(1) The volume and importance of the paper work awaiting consideration and attention.
(2) The weight, that is the physical weight of the publication.
(3) Its rating in the eyes of the recipient.

The really busy and influential officers in any commercial or industrial organization, that is, men usually over 45, are finding it more and more difficult to find the time to read their own technical Press. As a defence measure they are becoming increasingly selective and, having chosen what they consider to be the most important publications in their field, scan their contents as quickly as possible. They are, as a general rule, worried by heavy publications running into hundreds of pages, and attracted to the less voluminous journals provided they have a good technical or commercial standard. In the writer's opinion, our trade and technical Press is being read less by the older men in industry and increasingly more by the younger ones. From the advertiser's viewpoint this fact, if it is true, presents something of a problem. He obviously wants to reach the middle and higher management and in order to do so he has to find out the identity of those journals that are finally selected for attention by the people who exercise purchasing authority.

There is no doubt that this question of pressure now being exerted by the well established and highly prosperous subscriber journals was undoubtedly one reason for the introduction of controlled circulation journals. Greater selectivity is undoubtedly being shown by the most knowledgeable and influential readers in industry, and media planners are most anxious to find out more about this process. Already they have an uneasy feeling that circulation and readership figures, although extremely valuable, can be misleading and that what is really required as a reliable guide to the advertising value of the journal is the depth of readership which it attains.

IMPORTANCE OF CIRCULATION IN ASSESSING THE VALUE OF A TRADE AND TECHNICAL JOURNAL

What would give the advertiser more confidence in the technical Press would be the declaration of certified sales and the publication of full details of readership broken down, not only under branches of industry, but also under actual positions held by readers in those industries. It is well known, of course, that media departments in the leading agencies have been trying for a long time to persuade trade and technical publishers to fall into line with their colleagues in the national and mass circulation magazine fields, but so far with limited success. Many publishers are haunted by the spectre of lost advertising revenue which may result from a declaration of low sales, and naturally they are unable to supply advertisers with reliable readership surveys without declaring circulation. They believe many advertising agents fail to appreciate the value of quality circulation. This bogey of small circulations is a real one, but there seems little point in trying to ignore its presence. Many highly successful and prosperous trade journals paid for by subscriptions, mostly obtained from industry, have a circulation of less than 2,500, and the bulk of the technical journals who provide A.B.C. returns have circulations of less than 5,000. On the other hand, controlled circulation publications seldom drop below the 10,000 mark.

With the more reputable controlled circulation journals there is a welcome move towards a greater selectivity of readership, and one excellent publication in the chemical field restricts its circulation to qualified readers. A qualified reader is 'an executive in a company of reasonable size where chemical, engineering or other processing operations are employed or chemicals manufactured. Also qualifying are technical purchasing officers and executives with authority in connection with installation and maintenance of plant used in these operations. In large organizations the technical librarian is eligible for a copy for internal circulation.'

It should be pointed out that it is not only a lack of guaranteed circulation figures that prevents a publisher from providing readers with research data, but the high cost of securing this information. It may not be entirely unrealistic to suppose that publishers could supply a great deal of valuable information on the depth of readership, if advertisers were willing to help in the financing of the necessary research.

DEPTH OF READERSHIP

The advertising value of any media must, in the ultimate, depend on the quality of readership, That is why it is so important to study the general pattern of readership in order to be able to assess the elusive quality factor. To the writer, this pattern appears to take the following form:

(1) The business or professional reader, who may be the owner of a small or medium sized manufacturing, commercial or professional establishment, and subscribes to possibly two of the leading journals in his particular field.

(2) The manager, foreman or chargehand, commercial assistant or senior clerk, etc., who is expected by his employer to read the trade and technical press so as to keep himself abreast of new developments, changes in price structure and movements of staff. Here again, it is assumed that he has no choice of media, this being prescribed by his employer.

(3) Foreman, line manager, departmental manager and director in a large company or establishment whose name is placed on a circulation list, either because he requests for this to be done, or because his immediate superior thinks he should read a particular journal. The larger the company or establishment the longer the circulation list, e.g. an executive in a large chemical company might reasonably be expected to read in any given month eight British weekly journals, four American weekly journals and four separate monthly journals.

(4) The student type who would be expected by his tutor to make himself acquainted with the trade, technical and professional Press, but would not be concerned so much with trade matters as editorial material of an educational nature. He might see the journals in his college or university or in public libraries.

Within this framework of readership there are two main types; those who read the editorial contents of a journal and also study the advertisements because they are anxious to find out what is happening in their wider business field and those who, because of increasing pressure from a number of internal and external sources, have neither the time nor the inclination to do more than scan the journals that appear in their in-tray. The readers are, of course, greatly in the majority, but the 'scanners' represent the most influential section of the readership and are mainly comprised of the higher executives in the larger companies and establishments. Scanning is, perhaps, a somewhat misleading description of the type of approach made by this section towards their own Press, but it can be defined as 'flipping through the pages, and dipping here and there wherever a name or a product, or a subject, happens to awaken a spark of interest'. The process of scanning may take five minutes or ten minutes, but seldom more. It should not, however, be dismissed as so superficial as to be valueless. Scanners with long years of experience are able to gather a great deal of information from even five minutes scrutiny of a journal. They have learned to be extremely selective and to read only those items of news which they know instinctively to be important.

The media planner in the agency has never yet acknowledged the presence of a scanner in his analysis of readership, although he has an uneasy feeling that he exists. No useful purpose is served by ignoring his presence, particularly as he is able to influence decisions on choice of suppliers, and it could be beneficial to the advertiser if the medium chosen to carry his particular advertisements was selected by the scanner for his 5–10 minutes scrutiny. The factors which weigh heavily with the executive in the large company in determining his selection of journal or journals 'to scan' are:

(1) Reputation of the publication, in other words, its general standing in the industry, trade or profession.
(2) The extent to which it is supported by his major competitors, both from an editorial and advertising viewpoint.
(3) The reliability of its editorial contents.
(4) The authoritativeness of its main editorial features.

Factors such as circulation, layout and general presentation, whilst important to the space buyer and the publicity manager, have no real significance to the executive. In self defence he chooses the most reputable and most reliable journals so as to learn what is happening around him, and also to appear to be reasonably well informed when conversing with his colleagues both inside and outside the company.

It is sometimes argued by agency men that because controlled circulation journals have an easy-to-read format, give emphasis to technical developments and feature regularly new plant, they stand a very much better chance than subscriber journals of being selected for reading by top management. Yet with the higher executives in many large and important concerns there is still some distrust of these new publications because of the tabloid nature of their editorial contents, and the way in which the editorial appears to be tied up with the advertising. To remove this suspicion, publishers of controlled circulation papers will have to make their editorials much more authoritative!

The media planner, in considering this difficult aspect of 'depth of readership' has, therefore, to determine what kind of reader he is aiming to attract. Is the advertiser likely to be satisfied with the middle strata of readers, or is the upper strata what is required? A great deal depends here on the type of goods being advertised, e.g. if a machinery manufacturer catering for the plastics industry were offering a bench type of small capacity injection moulding machine, costing about £150, he might feel justified in aiming his advertising at a very wide circle of potential trade buyers, but particularly the small manufacturer or the newcomer who wanted to do experimental work in plastics. On the other hand, if he were trying to interest the industry in a large injection machine costing £50,000, he could only reasonably expect to attract worthwhile attention from the highest echelons of management in the really large companies. For the small injection machine the media planner could justifiably recommend a journal of lesser standing, but slightly more popular appeal, than for the large machine involving a major item of capital expenditure. Here the advertiser would be well advised to use only those journals of the highest reputation and standing in the industry, in other words, the type of publication favoured by the 'scanner'.

A MEDIA POLICY

Media planning is not just another piece of advertising jargon; it has a real significance of direct importance to the advertiser. Unless the advertisements are placed in publications best calculated to attract attention in the markets known to exist for the product or service, then a great deal of money will certainly be wasted and the full impact of advertising lost. Successful media planning is based on a sound media policy. This should set out to define the market being attacked; territories where sales are expected; competitive position and competitive advertising activity; the number and status of readers to be reached in any given field; the frequency and weight of impact and the timing of the whole campaign. It is rare that a sound media policy for consumer advertising can be developed without utilizing some of the basic findings of market research.

With industrial advertising, market research does not appear to play any significant part, although it is difficult to see how media planning can be effectively carried out without knowing something about the pattern of sales, forward planning including profit forecasts over the next few years and the general background of commercial development. Agencies handling industrial accounts usually prepare a standard list of questions, the answers to which form the agency's 'media brief'. Some of these answers are provided by the client, but most of them are supplied by the account executive and members of the agency staff on the creative side. From the advertiser the media man will want to have a full description of the product or service to be advertised, its price and availability, distribution and audience to be reached through the Press. The account executive does not usually give his general opinion on the technical journals to be used, although he may reflect the views of his client.

With smaller agencies, specializing in technical accounts, the account executive may be expected to put forward recommendations on media depending, of course, on the type of account. As every media man knows to his cost, there are more 'Sacred Cows' in this branch of advertising than in any other, and a good deal of tact is often required in persuading clients to leave the selection of media to the experts. It does, of course, quite often happen that the advertiser knows a great deal more about his own particular trade journal than the agency; difficulties usually only arise when the advertiser widens his horizon and recommends publications outside his direct sphere of experience. The agency has, as a result of accumulated experience on many accounts, built up a great fund of knowledge on media and it is this knowledge that the advertiser should be anxious to tap. The focal point in terms of media is the media department in the agency – here the experience, gained through dealing with a wide range of technical products, is concentrated in the form of background data, previous campaigns, and one hopes, experience gained from past mistakes! The creative side of the agency, that is, the copy and the art sections, can contribute a great deal on presentation and their advice, based on experience, can help to fill in the gaps in the media brief.

MEDIA BRIEF

This brief, based on an imaginary product and advertiser, is one that might conceivably be prepared and form the basis of an advertising campaign.

PRODUCT

Synthetic rubber hose available in about 250 different sizes,

there are structures...

and BECKETT steel structures

Finished art work for industrial prestige advertisements designed by
Mario Armengol

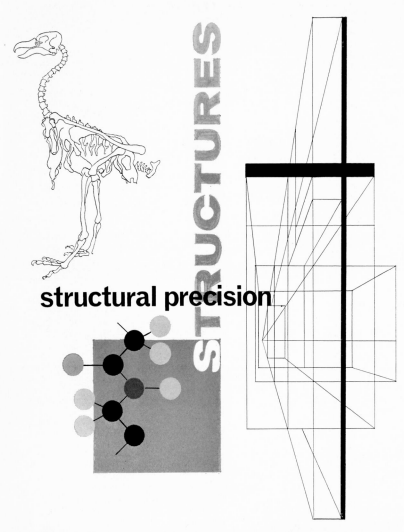

structural precision

STRUCTURES

structures in steel by BECKETT

Finished art work for industrial prestige advertisements designed by
Mario Armengol

grades and qualities. Non standard sizes and formulations are made to suit the specific requirements of the main user industries.

PRICE

Price structure of hose is complicated and would be difficult to explain in an advertisement.

QUALITY

In its own specialized field the company's product has a high reputation and its performance under the most strenuous conditions of use compares very favourably with the best of American, Continental and home produced hose. It would appear that the company is abreast of current technical developments in this field and has a modern and efficient plant. The works chemist is a young and imaginative Scot who is very well qualified. He carries out some research but concentrates on quality control.

APPLICATIONS

The main users are the chemical industry where the hose is extensively employed for the handling of corrosive fluids; in the soap and synthetic detergent manufacture for carrying soap lyes and strong alkalis; in refineries where special types of solvent resistant rubber are needed; in transport, i.e. ships, road tankers, aircraft; in the food industry where non-toxic grades are specified, also in breweries, distilleries, soft drink trade and dairies. Other industries where a market is being found for hose include the metal industry which uses hose for handling pickling and plating fluids; textile industry for handling bleaches and other corrosive fluids; leather industry; coal mining, etc.

DISTRIBUTION AND MARKETING

The hose is sold in several ways; mainly through accredited agents in the United Kingdom and overseas, also through machinery manufacturers and fabricators of specialized plant and equipment. It is also sold direct from the factory in Leeds. The real pattern of distribution is not clear and the company does not appear to know precisely where and how its products are being used.

(Account Executive's comment:
There's a real need here for research in depth to discover the actual users of hose. Such information could be valuable in developing an advertising policy. Some of the younger executives in the company are coming round to the idea that an independent market survey would be a worthwhile investment, but this is obviously going to take time to bring about!)

AMOUNT TO BE SPENT ON AN ADVERTISING CAMPAIGN

It has been decided by the company's Board of Directors that a sum of £25,000 could be spent in 1963 on an advertising campaign to include Press advertising, direct mail and literature.

(Account Executive:
This is purely arbitrary decision and has been reached without reference to the Agency. I have been unable to secure an assurance that we can expect a similar sum in 1964; everything appears to depend on the way in which sales move as a result of the campaign.)

MEDIA RECOMMENDED

There is a temptation here to spread the advertising over such a wide field of relevant trade and technical journals that no great impact could be made. Indeed, in discussion with the client, it would appear that this method of approach is favoured. In our view this is wrong. The advertising should be concentrated on the major outlets – i.e. the chemical and allied trades; petroleum and solvent refining; food industry; textile; metal industry and mining. By using six journals the main uses of hose could be fairly adequately covered. It is suggested, therefore, that the following proposition might be put to the client:

Chemical paper	Monthly; controlled circulation
	£53 per half page
	12 half pages
Petroleum journal	Fortnightly
	£60 per page
	12 pages
Food journal	Monthly
	£58 per page
	6 pages
Textile journal	Monthly; 7,500 circulation
	£45 per page
	6 pages
A machinery journal	Weekly; 11,299 circulation
	£43 15s. per page
	12 pages
Mining paper	Monthly
	£30 per page
	6 pages

The campaign might be planned so that direct mail is closely integrated with the advertising. Pulls of the advertisements could be mailed to the industries covered by these journals; mailing to take place at least twice a year in each industry. Alongside pulls, reply paid cards should be included so that recipients could send for literature applicable to their particular industry. Within a budget of £20,000 it should be possible to accommodate this kind of campaign.

FORM OF ADVERTISEMENT

It is suggested that the advertisements should be planned to tell a straightforward technical story designed to show the wide range of hose made by the company and also to give prominence to the fact that special sizes and grades can be produced to solve specific fluid handling problems. The campaign should be divided into two broad sections; the first advertisements could deal with the range of hose available and the second with testimonial type of advertisements which would set out to show how manufacturing problems have been solved by use of the company's synthetic rubber hose. Copy would have to be technical and acceptable to experts in the respective industrial fields; illustrations should be photographic and of the case book type.

COMMENTS ON PREPARED MEDIA BRIEF

After consideration of this brief it is safe to say that in order to plan an effective advertising campaign, the media planner could justifiably ask for a good deal more information, particularly on applications of the product. These need to be more specific and a rough idea given somewhere of the relative importance of the various industries in terms of potential. What would be extremely useful would be an indication of the percentage which each industry represents of the total market for this type of hose. This information might lead to an agency decision to concentrate on certain industries or to weight the media effort in terms of coverage, size and frequency of insertion in certain directions. Such information could be supplied by the client, or alternatively by the marketing department of the agency, but it could appear as part of the brief before the media man actually starts on his planning.

In the media brief, as prepared, there is a valid point made about potential rather than current users. As this brief is designed to help the media department to plan a campaign, unless an actual decision has been taken by the advertiser to attack potential users, then there is no useful purpose served in including this reference in the brief. Nevertheless, whatever marketing objective has been decided should be clearly defined under the 'Marketing' heading.

The media man would also like to know, either from the client or from some other source, who is responsible for specifying the hose, and who for purchasing? Does this vary from industry to industry and in what way? Do some industries consist of large commercial units only? If so, then how many people are in a position to influence the specification and purchase of the hose? Are they sufficient in number to justify the use of the technical Press, or should the advertising be limited to calls by representatives preceded and followed by direct mail shots? The kind of media

brief the media department would like to have prepared is out-
lined below.

Specimen Media Brief for an Industrial Campaign

Product

(1) Nature
(2) Selling price range in relation to competitors
(3) Technical ad-⎫ including whether the ⎫ from the
    vantages ⎬ product has to go through ⎬ client
(4) Technical limi-⎪ a middleman – e.g. pre- ⎪
    tations   ⎭ fabricator, etc.   ⎭

Distribution

(1) Present channels   ⎫ from the
(2) Proposed channels   ⎬ client/
                       account
                       executive/
                       marketing
                       department

Applications

(1) What jobs will it do   ⎫ from
(2) In what industries   ⎬ client/
                       market
                       research

Marketing

(1) Relative importance of industries concerned ⎫
    in terms of percentage of total market   ⎪ from
(2) New or potential markets – estimate of po- ⎬ client/
    tential by percentage of current total market ⎪ market
(3) Competitive activity – expenditure – media ⎪ research
    used, etc.   ⎭

Marketing Objective

(1) *To current potential users or both? ⎫ from
(2) First year's appropriation to be   ⎬ client/
    (*a*) a capital investment   ⎪ market
  *(*b*) to show a return immediately   ⎪ research
    (*c*) to show a return over a period of? ⎭

*Only one of the alternatives would appear in brief.

Specification/Purchase within Industries Concerned

(1) Who specifies

(2) Who purchases

(3) Who (in addition) influences 1 and 2

} client/ market research

Period of Advertising

(1) Length of period

(2) Any reasons for concentration or weighting of effort, e.g. seasonal buying, etc.

} client/ account executive/ market research

Creative

(1) Any special media requirement e.g. colour, bleed, insets, etc.

(2) Size required on creative ground

} account executive/ creative side

MEDIA RESEARCH AND CAMPAIGN PLANNING

In accounts mainly concerned with consumer goods selling in mass markets, the agency is sometimes commissioned to carry out campaign planning in collaboration with the client's marketing manager. Here the agency is taken fully into the confidence of the company and made aware of their profit margins, future plans, marketing schemes and production figures. This kind of collaboration seldom takes place with an industrial account where the tendency is for the company to keep the agency at arm's length. In many instances this reluctance to make full use of agency services and resources stems from lack of knowledge of the facilities that are available. Here the agency is to blame to some extent in not making the client aware of the full scope of agency work and the way in which a sales campaign can benefit from being integrated with an advertising programme – an opportunity is thereby being lost to develop the product and enlarge the market in the most advantageous manner. It is largely because of this lack of co-operation on industrial accounts that agencies find it so difficult to make the best tactical use of the advertising that has been chosen. Taking the example of the hypothetical rubber hose account, what is obviously lacking from this brief is any knowledge about new and potential markets; the entire campaign is centred on established outlets.

The tactical use of media is a subject to which only lip service is given, whereas it can be of considerable importance, embracing as it does direction and timing. Referring again to the widening of the market for rubber hose, it is necessary to find out who are the buyers: supply officers, purchasing officers, works manager, works chemist, works engineers, and so on. These are the key people whom the agency wants to reach and, to achieve this, something needs to be known about their buying procedure.

DRAWING UP A SCHEDULE

Once the media list has been agreed upon and the space actually booked, then a schedule should be drawn up. This is a large document which sets out the following information: name of publication, space booked, cost per insertion, number of insertions, total cost for the year, dates of insertions and, finally, the circulation of the journal. The schedule normally covers twelve calendar months and shows at a glance the entire advertising picture. The completed document is prepared by the agency and two or three copies sent to the client for retention. Copies of the advertising schedule may be of interest to sales representatives as indicating the advertising support being given to the product.

4

MARKETING ASPECTS OF LABELLING

IN THE consumer field labelling is now generally accepted as a vital marketing factor and a great deal of money is spent on the promotion of a trade mark or label. The Board of Trade's Malony Committee on Consumer Protection lays great stress on the importance of labelling, informative labelling – alongside the maintenance of standards which protect the buying public. Not only in the United Kingdom, but throughout the western world, there is a general awareness of the urgent need for improved standards of quality and more comprehensive and useful labelling to give better protection to the ultimate consumer.

In the industrial field there is not such obvious scope for labels, but there is a growing awareness that trade marks and labels can contribute substantially to the general acceptability of a product. In other words, the buyer, who is usually another manufacturer, will give a natural preference to commodities, no matter whether they are raw materials or processed goods, which carry the label or mark of a famous company or one which has been extensively advertised. Alternatively, a great deal of reliance is placed on commodities bearing the mark of some independent organization, such as the 'Kitemark' issued by the British Standards Institution, which indicates that the product carrying the mark conforms with the relevant British Standard.

There are two important aspects of industrial labelling which need to be considered:

(a) The straightforward informative labelling of goods leaving the manufacturer's works.
(b) The issue of identifying labels to link the customer's finished

46

commodities with the manufacturer's basic labels or trade mark.

No matter whether the manufacturer restricts the label to his own goods, or makes available labels to his customers who produce finished consumer goods made up wholly or partially from his products, the value of such identifications depends upon the general recognition, acceptance and reputation factor of his own trade mark, company name or brand name. This again stems back to the advertising support that is, and has been given to the promotion of the company or brand image. World famous companies, such as I.C.I. and Rolls-Royce, to mention just two internationally famous names, have built up over the years a fine reputation for high quality goods and, in addition, their names have been very widely advertised. Advertising has, in fact, merchandised the trade marks to such an extent that their acceptability both to the trade and the general public is of a high order. As a result of this, all commodities which are associated with these trade names gain in prestige and have therefore a higher market value. In other words, the company image, established by a sound trading policy, consolidated by favourable experience and promoted by generous advertising, can be passed on for the benefit of other manufacturers. For example, an aircraft manufacturer who installs Rolls-Royce engines in his aircraft profits from the high acceptance value of this world-famous company. In much the same way, the I.C.I. roundel, if associated with some other manufacturer's product greatly increases its merchantable value. A company or brand image is a marketable commodity which can be used in the sales promotion of other manufacturers' goods.

The vital factor to remember in any consideration of trade mark, company name or brand image, etc., is that their value, marketing value, is in direct ratio to their recognition factor. In other words, if a trade mark is not known, then it is virtually useless except as a means of identification. It has no marketing value.

One of the hidden bonuses of industrial advertising, which often goes unnoticed, is the establishment of a trade mark in the eyes of the professional buyer and the building up of a high recognition factor. Although the palpable results of a particular advertising campaign may seem disappointing, it should not be forgotten that if it carried the company's name and trade mark at all prominently, then it must have contributed something to the overall marketing of the firm's goods.

It is a fact that some industrial companies are not fully aware of the tremendous good-will value of their trade mark and the vast potentialities which such an asset offers, particularly as regards labelling. No opportunity of product promotion via labelling should be overlooked and this is something that the marketing departments should take up enthusiastically with representatives in the field. Labelling campaigns do not cost a great deal of money to promote and they can be tied in with the advertising easily and economically. All goods leaving the factory, whether in tankers or lorries, by rail or sea, should carry well designed, bold and distinctive labels giving prominence to the brand name of the product and the company's trade mark. In addition to this overall labelling of the company's manufacturers, every means should be taken to persuade customers to incorporate this trade mark or brand name in their own labelling. Double brand labelling is a highly effective method of marketing consumer goods.

THE NEED FOR MORE INFORMATIVE LABELLING

Labelling, as well as indicating quality, must also be informative, i.e. state clearly the origin and true character of the particular commodity. Where necessary labels should also give notice of hazards associated with the use of the product and any precaution which have to be adopted in use.

Generally speaking, industrial labelling is of little marketable value unless it complies with the following conditions:

(a) It gives information about quality standards.

(b) It provides an accurate trade description of the product.

(c) It states clearly the manufacturer's name and gives the brand name.

(d) It is given adequate advertising support.

There is no doubt that a brand image can do a great deal to sustain the popularity or appeal of a commodity. Advertising will give a product a 'uniqueness' which nothing else can afford and this means a great deal in the market place!

An American advertising specialist, Irving Zuckerman, aptly says: 'So many of us labour unyielding hours unsuccessfully attempting to sell products that are too much like the products that our competitors sell.' Labelling helps here to add distinctiveness to a product and advertising does a job of work in merchandising the labelling.

LABELS MUST BE WELL DESIGNED

Design is of vital importance in labelling and this is where the services of a first class designer should be called in so as to prescribe the best possible typographical formula. The old-fashioned idea of getting 'someone who can draw' to knock out a label design, is a fatal move and can only lead to a degree of mediocrity for which the manufacturer will suffer years ahead. The finest design that money can buy should be the aim of every manufacturer who is thinking of carrying out a labelling campaign. There should, however, be a house style which is reflected in the choice of type face, colour or design.

One very effective way to approach industrial label design is to produce a system of colour and pattern coding that makes possible the use of a large number of acceptable permutations. Such a system will enable a family likeness to be retained and also permit important economies to be effected when adding new products to the range. All that is necessary here is for the designer to develop the basic framework of the label in which is stipulated the shape, size, type, colour, etc. A safe formula includes a pleasing shape, size chosen in relation to the size of container, bright and emphatic colouring and clean, clear typography. Industrial labels usually fail in impact and appeal if the design is too fussy and irritating or too stark and funereal. When considering the choice of a designer for labels or trade marks, there is no better course to take than to make use of the Council of Industrial Design's Advisory

49

Service. The C.I.D.'s Record of Designers, which is at the disposal of manufacturers on payment of a nominal fee, can be of considerable value in helping to find the right kind of designer.

MERCHANDISING THE LABEL

The promotion of an industrial trade mark is not a 'gimmicky' idea borrowed from the consumer field, but a sober and realistic piece of marketing procedure. The trade mark symbolizes the reputation and acceptance of the company and in terms of hard cash is worth a great deal of money. It is, therefore, only common sense to utilize to the full the immense advertising and marketing potential of this vital asset. There is strong evidence to support the view that in the very large industrial companies there is a full awareness of the tremendous value of their trade marks and an insistence on their prominent use in all forms of marketing and advertising.

Labelling campaigns are just as relevant when applied to electric motors as electric shavers and pretty well the same arguments apply. A professional buyer is, after all, just an ordinary man who away from the office is subject to the same advertising pressures as anyone else, and although he may be a little more critical than most people, he is influenced by the same type of sales persuasion as the man in the street. When considering the merchandising of a label or a trade mark it is important to realize the opportunities which are open to the industrialist.

(1) All goods leaving the factory should carry well designed and distinctive labels giving prominence to the company's trade mark as well as the brand name of the product. There needs to be a balance of interest so that the trade mark is never completely subjugated by the brand name. For lesser known products a greater degree of prominence needs to be given to the company image, whilst for famous commodities the reverse might well be true. The marketing department, when considering the architecture of the label, should be sensitive to these reasonings.

50

(2) All promotional material leaving the company's premises should give emphasis to the labelling scheme.

(3) The field force should be made aware of the policy governing a labelling or trade mark scheme and provided with all the background information and promotional material, so that they are in a good position to discuss the subject with customers and potential customers.

(4) Every means should be taken to persuade customers of the commercial advantages of incorporating the company's trade mark or product brand name in their own labelling, in other words, the development of a double brand labelling scheme is a worthwhile marketing development for both seller and buyer.

All sales representatives in the field should be provided with a brochure designed to show the range of product labels in regular use by the company, and in addition the book should show visual suggestions for labels that might be affixed to the customers' own commodities. Such a brochure needs to be well designed, attractive and generally stimulating without looking lush or resembling some piece of consumer goods promotional material. In other words, to be effective and to create the right kind of impression with a manufacturer, the brochure has to be a soberly conceived marketing document. The emphasis throughout the book should be on the assistance which the seller can give to the buyer and the general sales promotion of his goods. Pulls of current advertisements should always be slipped into the brochure.

It is a fallacy to think that industrial labelling can only be exploited by the very large companies. Opportunities exist for small and medium size concerns to build up a company or brand image and to project this by means of modest advertising, direct mail and all the recognized forms of promotion. Obviously the less money a company spends on publicity the longer it will take to establish a trade name, but eventually the trade name or brand name will come to have a real significance. Provided the commodity is a good one and the company reputable in its business dealings, then the aggressive labelling of goods can contribute worthwhile quota to general sales promotion. Labelling is a link in the marketing chain which can help and strengthen it and it is just as applicable to industrial and to consumer goods.

THE LAW AND LABELLING

The Merchandise Marks Acts, 1887–1953, are of particular importance from the point of view of the manufacturer of consumer goods. The Acts prescribe penalties for the improper use of trade marks, certification marks or the Royal Warrant, and also for applying a false trade description to goods (see below). The Acts also prescribe that imported goods bearing the name or trade mark of a British manufacturer or trader must not be sold unless accompanied by an indication of origin and that, furthermore, certain imported goods must be accompanied by an indication of origin in any case. These goods are listed in various Orders in Council which have been made from time to time. For offences under this Act the penalties are very heavy but prosecutions need to be brought within three years of the commission of the offence, or within one year after the first discovery, whichever is the shorter. Chapter V in Leaper's *Law of Advertising* (2nd edition) deals exhaustively with the Merchandise Marks Acts.

When the Consumer Council is eventually set up as recommended by the Committee on Consumer Protection, it will have the following responsibilities:

(*a*) The preparation and publication of comparative test reports.
(*b*) The work of receiving and dealing with shoppers' individual complaints.
(*c*) Criminal or civil enforcement action.
(*d*) The promulgation or regulations possessing statutory force.

One of the recommendations made by the Committee is that the *Merchandise Marks Acts, 1887, 1891, 1894, 1911* and *1953*, should be consolidated and simplified and the consolidated act should be re-titled, e.g. 'The Trade Descriptions Act' or 'The Merchandise Descriptions Act'. It is further recommended by the

Committee that the definition of 'trade description' in Merchandise Marks legislation should be amended and extended in order to catch significant types of misrepresentation against which the consumer requires protection. Additional elements required in the definition are indications of size, newness (in the sense of being unused), date of manufacture, previous ownership or history, former or usual price, physical characteristics, testing claims, compliance with standards. The Committee also dealt with the possibility of controlling the industrial use of the word 'guarantee', and it seems likely that this is a matter which will be receiving a good deal of attention in the future.

THE VALUE OF INDUSTRIAL BRAND NAME RECOGNITION TESTS

Although very well known in the consumer field, brand name recognition tests are practically unknown in the non-consumer goods industries. Such tests can, if properly carried out, provide a useful yardstick with which to gauge the effectiveness of the company's overall publicity efforts, even in a carefully circumscribed field. The levels of correct identification of brand names are not only indicative of the success of the advertising, but the cumulative effects of the public relations and other promotional work. Once it is appreciated that brand names in the non-consumer goods industries have a real selling significance, then research is justified in order to obtain the index figure. Tests can usually be carried out every two years using small, but carefully selected samples in the industry being investigated and employing independent market research teams for the field work. Brand name recognition tests are usually carried out by the agency rather than by the manufacturer, and this is preferable as more impartial findings can be assured. In the usual consumer tests, the housewife is asked if she can say what a particular brand name stands for and the trade mark is shown alongside half a dozen or more allied brand names.

The recognition factor alone is not sufficient for the industrial goods manufacturer who really wants to know the trade standing of his brand name and its rating alongside competitive materials.

The questions that are put by the interviewer must, therefore, probe somewhat deeper than would be considered necessary in the consumer field. There is no doubt that professional market researchers should be recruited to carry out this kind of investigation in order to secure a reliable pattern of results that can be interpreted by the marketing and advertising sections of the company.

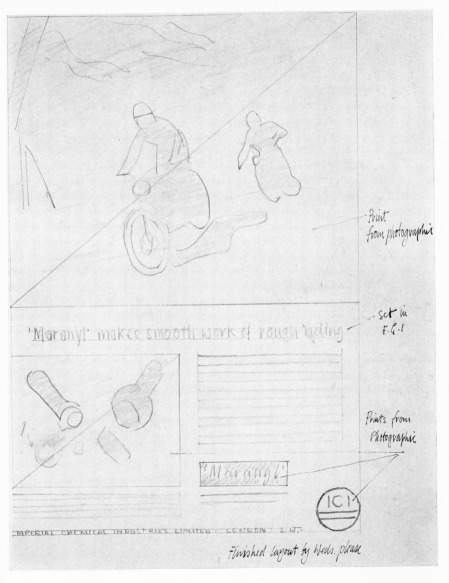

Four progressive stages in the preparation of an advertisement for
the technical Press (*see overleaf*)

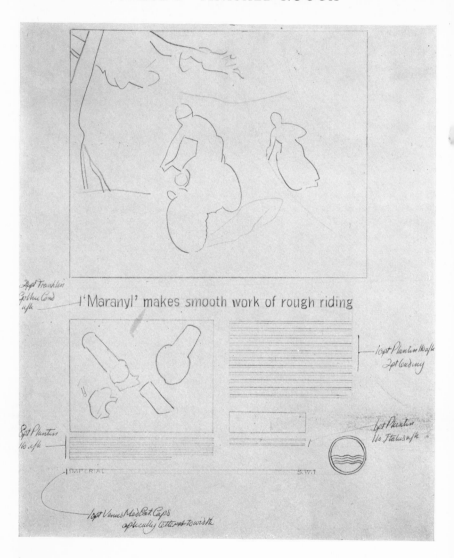

'Maranyl' makes smooth work of rough riding

COPY FOR ALL STAGES

'MARANYL' MAKES SMOOTH WORK OF ROUGH RIDING

The twist grips on these scrambler machines allow
very quick, smooth and accurate throttle control
without lubrication because their main components
are made from 'Maranyl' I.C.I. nylon. The use of
'Maranyl' also ensures that the grips are very tough
and extremely light in weight. More and more components for the motor and motorcycle trade are now
being quickly and accurately moulded from 'Maranyl'.
If you would like more information about the properties
and uses of 'Maranyl' nylon, any I.C.I. Sales Office
will be glad to help you.

'MARANYL'

'Maranyl' is the registered trade mark for the nylon
compounds manufactured by I.C.I.

IMPERIAL CHEMICAL INDUSTRIES LIMITED . LONDON . S.W.1.

CAPTION: Scrambler motor cycles fitted with "Sackville"
           twist grips with components moulded from 'Maranyl'
           by Moulded Plastics (Birmingham) Ltd., Reddicap
           Trading Estate, Sutton Coldfield, Warwickshire.
           (Below) Close-up of the twist grips which are
           made by Sackville Ltd., Mount Street, Birmingham 7.

(Stage 4 – see overleaf)

'Maranyl' makes smooth work of rough riding

Maranyl

'MARANYL' is the registered trade mark for
the nylon compounds manufactured by I.C.I.

IMPERIAL CHEMICAL INDUSTRIES LIMITED · LONDON · S.W.1

'Maranyl' makes smooth work of rough riding

The twist grips on these scrambler machines allow very quick, smooth and accurate throttle control without lubrication because their main components are made from 'Maranyl' I.C.I. nylon. The use of 'Maranyl' also ensures that the grips are very tough and extremely light in weight. More and more components for the motor and motorcycle trade are now being quickly and accurately moulded from 'Maranyl'. If you would like more information about the properties and uses of 'Maranyl' nylon, any I.C.I. Sales Office will be glad to help you.

'MARANYL' is the registered trade mark for the nylon compounds manufactured by I.C.I.

Scrambler motor cycles fitted with "Sackville" twist grips with components moulded from 'Maranyl' by Moulded Plastics (Birmingham) Ltd., Reddicap Trading Estate, Sutton Coldfield, Warwickshire. (*Below*) Close-up of the twist grips which are made by Sackville Ltd., Mount Street, Birmingham 7.

PN 179

IMPERIAL CHEMICAL INDUSTRIES LIMITED · LONDON · S.W.1

5

HOW DOES THE ADVERTISING DEPARTMENT FIT INTO THE MARKETING PICTURE?

IN THE consumer market the primary purpose of an advertisement is 'to sell the goods', but in the industrial field the advertisement is designed to interest and gain the goodwill of the potential customer. It would be foolishly optimistic to think that an advertisement for a printing machine costing £25,000 could possibly effect a sale, but if it appeared in the right media and at the right time, it could create interest by bringing the name of the company and the merits or claims of the machine to the notice of the printing industry. In other words, the industrial advertisement helps to prepare the ground for the salesman who can, once an introduction has been effected, arrange demonstrations and supply technical information.

Advertising is a function of marketing, which has been aptly described as an omnibus team covering the many business activities that take place between the actual production and the sale of manufactured goods. These activities can include planning, research, distribution, packaging, design, advertising, and, of course, selling. Marketing means, therefore, a great deal more than selling, which only represents the final link in a long chain of operations designed to make conditions favourable to a sale.

WHERE DOES ADVERTISING FIT IN ON THE MARKETING CHART?

In the consumer field it is a fairly common practice to involve the advertising department and the agency in early discussions on marketing. Indeed, with some companies the agency is often asked to design the pack, carry out the research and planning and even advise on the selling price. Unfortunately, the same close liaison rarely exists in that vast section of industry concerned with the manufacture of industrial goods, where the policy seems to be to keep both the internal advertising department and the agency at arm's length from the actual marketing sections of the organization. It is, of course, understandable that where the pattern of business is so different – after all, there is a vast difference between selling girdles and selling refractory bricks – it could rightly be presumed that the agency might not be able to contribute very much either on price structure or distribution, but it certainly could help on research and planning.

An experienced and reputable advertising agency should be able to draw on a wealth of experience derived from its many accounts for the benefit of the marketing sections of any company producing industrial goods. By not taking full advantage of this opportunity manufacturers are penalizing their sales force. It is true to say that the more technical the account, the more reliance the agency has to place on the client. This does not discount the fact that the agency, if invited, is able to make worthwhile contributions on the general strategy of selling, no matter what type of goods are being sold.

There has been for some years a strong feeling in certain sections of industry that the product is not close enough to the actual marketing, and that where the volume of business justifies, each product or each brand of a major product, should have its own individual marketing organization. This is, of course, a familiar pattern in those vast manufacturing concerns producing detergents, canned foods, biscuits, cake mixtures, etc., where brand managers are responsible not only for selling, but also for the promotion of sales by every possible means, including advertising. These executives are themselves responsible to a general marketing manager who dictates the overall policy.

By adopting this method it is possible to make certain that advertising is closely geared to selling, and, as a result, a much more aggressive attitude is taken in presenting the goods to the buying public.

In those branches of industry not concerned with the manufacture of consumer goods the brand manager idea has a very limited application, but what is receiving attention in the very large corporations and nationalized industries is the product manager.

Like the brand manager, he is responsible for the entire marketing arrangements for specific types of goods, e.g. in a large chemical works it is conceivable that product managers might be appointed to control the sales of 'Sulphuric Acid', 'Caustic Soda' or 'Chlorine', etc., depending, of course, on the volume of business. Although in this particular example, it is inconceivable that advertising would play a significant part in the general marketing scheme.

This very logical development has obvious advantages from the viewpoint of trying to rationalize the sales efforts, but alongside the brand manager conception it has certain weaknesses, particularly when applied to advertising. As mentioned previously, industrial advertising will not sell goods, but is essentially a reminder form of sales promotion supplementing the overall publicity afforded by the company's literature, exhibition, films, etc. The greatest good in advertising industrial goods is likely to be achieved by company advertising on a broad front rather than highly specialized campaigns on a narrow front. Generally speaking, however, the great bulk of industrial advertising is directed by the commercial director or managing director of the company and executed by the advertising manager working alongside the agency. In this more orthodox arrangement the advertising manager puts into effect the promotional schemes that have been agreed upon by the commercial departments, both home and export.

The modern trend in marketing practice would appear to indicate that the advertising manager, as such, is likely to disappear and to be replaced by a marketing manager specializing in advertising. This appears to be the pattern of business that is being accepted in the consumer market, and there are indications that it is attracting attention in other branches of industry.

Although the change may be regretted for many reasons, it is, perhaps, inevitable that marketing should be regarded as the vital function and advertising as the means of communicating the marketing message.

INTEGRATING THE ADVERTISING AND MARKETING POLICIES

Advertising is the shop window of the sales departments and it is for them to determine the size of the window, the type of goods to be shown and the degree of prominence to be given to each particular type. It is not, however, the responsibility of the sales department to say how these goods should be displayed, in other words, to dictate the method adopted by the professional window dresser, as this requires specialized knowledge and experience. Both sales and advertising sections of the organization need, therefore, to work closely together.

It would be quite absurd for the advertising department to make its own decisions on the selection of goods to be featured or the degree of prominence to be afforded each type, as no matter how well informed it may be, the advertising department cannot have available the wealth of information available to sales. Yet this kind of thing does occasionally happen. One finds that after laying down certain general principles, the sales department leaves it to the advertising side of the business to translate these into forms of promotion. The result is that a great deal of money is spent on 'woolly' campaigns about which no real enthusiasm exists and no one believes can make any worthwhile contribution to sales.

Advertising not only needs guidance and direction, but it also requires careful watching. It is, after all, a cog in the marketing machine and can only operate successfully if all the other parts of the machine are running smoothly. The dissatisfaction that so frequently exists with the advertising department usually stems from poor liaison with the marketing side, and lack of realization that both advertising and sales are part of the marketing team. The advertising manager, by reason of his day to day contact with the outside world, should be of considerable value in all marketing discussions and, unless he is brought into the inner councils of sales, then advertising is not being allowed to play its full and significant part in the promotion of a product.

What is required in industry today is a new appreciation of the ability of advertising, not only to promote sales, but to assist in the actual planning of campaigns and the forecasting of sales. The advertising manager needs, therefore, to be equipped with a great deal more than expertise, he should have a wide knowledge of the products he is trying to promote, be cognisant of the wider implications of company sales policy and know something about markets, both present and potential.

CAMPAIGN PLANNING

This is where the advertising department should be able to make a substantial contribution. If we take the hypothetical case of a manufacturer of non-ferrous metals in wrought forms, such as aluminium, brass, zinc and copper, who has developed new rare metal alloys based on titanium, zirconium, niobium and tantalum, there would be substantial advantages in integrating the advertising department with the sales department in the planning of actual sales campaigns.

These advantages could be set out as follows:

(1) Through the public relations section of the advertising department, it should be possible to secure very useful editorial coverage for these new alloys in the kinds of journals likely to have an influence on future markets.

(2) Advertising schemes could be worked out in support of the public relations so as to throw into relief the company's outstanding technical achievement in producing the alloys, and suggest their future applications in industry.

(3) The advertising department could organize conventions, open days, symposiums and other gatherings likely to bring together leading metallurgists and engineers and to provide opportunities for the company's technical experts to demonstrate the uses and advantages of the new alloys.

The tangible forms of advertising, such as reprints of articles in trade and technical and professional journals, pulls of advertisements and invitations to conventions, conferences, etc., provide excellent ammunition for the salesman who is breaking new ground. He is able to use such material as the basis for a mailing shot or to provide the material for a discussion with new customers. Advertising can, therefore, in such a highly technical field as rare metals, which may have specialized uses in nuclear engineering, space programmes and advanced branches of chemical engineering, help substantially to sharpen the sales tools.

It is, however, very disappointing and frustrating to find that the advertising department is so seldom drawn into the early discussions on marketing and is not, therefore, exploited fully to locate and develop new markets. In all campaign planning the first thought should be to involve the advertising department in every phase of selling. It can and should be able to make a substantial contribution.

Where the advertising department often fails, however, is in overlooking the vital necessity 'to merchandise the advertising'.

So often it happens that the representative in the field is not fully briefed about the advertising support being given to a product and without this knowledge he is unable to profit by the overall publicity. In the consumer field it would be quite unthinkable for the marketing manager or brand manager not to acquaint the salesmen and dealers with the type and extent of the advertising support being given to a product in the early stages of the sales promotion. The outside sales force is told about the advertising campaign, shown typical advertisements and schedules, and invited to comment upon them. He is made to feel that he has been taken very fully into the confidence of those responsible for formulating the general advertising policy. Unfortunately this procedure is not always followed in the general industrial field where the representatives are often ignorant of the advertising support that is being given to the product they are trying to sell.

MEASURING MARKET POTENTIALS

Sales forecasting is one of the most difficult and highly skilled forms of marketing clairvoyance, and yet it is upon the skill of the forecasters that the success of a sales campaign may depend. Forecasting depended at one time on experience in the particular trade, plus a certain amount of general marked intelligence and personal hunches. These hit-and-miss methods were quite acceptable in a rising market, where even gross errors were almost unnoticeable, but today the position is vastly different. The market is no longer buoyant and is highly sensitive to Government interference; moreover, the high cost of capital makes it no longer possible to absorb substantial errors in sales forecasting. Industry generally has become very nervous about forecasting and the institutional type of director has become increasingly conscious of the considerable bonus that is now offered for being right in forecasting, particularly middle-term and long-term forecasting. As a result of this general nervousness the modern forecaster now makes use of every possible weapon in the commercial armoury.

One of the most important of these is, of course, research in one form or another. Often it is not necessary to embark on an ambitious and costly scheme of market research, involving an expensive and elaborate sampling exercise as sufficient information can be obtained by using desk research methods supplemented by sampling surveys.

If we take as an example a manufacturer of machine tools who has developed an entirely new type of automatic lathe which he is anxious to sell on the Continent, the first step in any attempt to measure the market would be to evaluate the competition, i.e. the number of French, German, and Belgian firms operating in the territories who were offering comparable machines, also data about the performance of these machines, delivery periods, price, etc. The home manufacturer would also need to know something about each individual competitor's business, his size, reputation, capital and resources. This type of information could then be looked at alongside national statistics and trade trends so as to try and assess the volume of the metal working business – the various territories, and the probable rate of expansion. Slowly a picture would emerge which would indicate the size of the opportunity that might await this particular machine in a specific territory.

Advertising is a weapon that can be used to help evaluate the market and indeed this is commonly done in the U.S.A., where development products are featured in the trade and technical Press and designed to encourage inquiries. These are followed up and provide useful background material and often indicate valuable market trends. An extension of this type of research makes use of direct mail. Here the manufacturer sends out questionnaires to a sample of potential buyers with the hope of receiving intelligent answers indicative of customers preferences. In this way he is able to test the market and determine what opportunities exist for the new product, and how best it should be marketed.

In the consumer field, advertising research is fairly widely used to measure impact and penetration, but in the industrial field the smallness of the average advertising campaign hardly justifies the expense. It is, however, worth bearing in mind that a play-back of the advertising message can often give fairly valid clues to the effectiveness of the marketing approach. Advertising is still the most economical means of communication and not only can its effectiveness be measured by card tests and interviews, etc., but the customer reaction to advertising can give some highly significant and valuable leads to the expert marketer.

STUDYING COMPETITIVE ACTIVITY

Every manufacturer is constantly looking over his shoulder at what his rival is doing – his products – his research and his marketing methods. Intelligence about all these activities is fed into the commercial departments via salesmen's reports and these are taken into account in all subsequent planning and research. Advertising can help to fill in the gaps on particular aspects, such as:

(a) The effectiveness of the competitive public relations and advertising.
(b) The media chosen for competitive advertisements.
(c) The emphasis being given to specific products.

A careful analysis of competitive advertising should give a useful hint on their general marketing policy and indicate the type of markets in which they are concentrating and consider to have the best potential for growth. Information of this nature cannot fail to be of material assistance to planners in assessing the danger of competition in certain markets.

CHOOSING AN AGENCY FOR AN INDUSTRIAL ACCOUNT

WHEN CONSIDERING the choice of an agency it is advisable to look at the problem in relation to the actual advertising appropriation that is available. An agency in the top six would be unlikely to be interested in an account worth only £5,000 as the financial return, that is, commission and service fee, could not justify the work involved.

There is far more work involved in drawing up a series of half page advertisements in one of the trade journals than in preparing a quarter page in the *Radio Times* and yet the money involved may be equivalent, but the latter would certainly give the agency much more profit. Whilst it is generally recognized that the really large agencies, who derive the bulk of their income from consumer accounts, do not much care for industrial accounts, unless these come from world-famous companies having a high prestige value, there are a number of small agencies who specialize in this form of advertising. There are in London and the main provincial cities, small agencies who are able to provide manufacturers with a comprehensive promotional service, i.e. they are willing to assume full responsibility for whatever publicity is required. They draw up advertisements, prepare and publish trade literature, design and produce display cards, calendars, diaries, etc., in fact they take over the work of an internal advertising department and relieve the manufacturer of the cost of running it. For the small man in business who is only willing to spend a few hundred pounds or a few thousands, there is a great deal to be said in favour of such organizations.

It is interesting to note that some of the really big agencies have formed splinter groups who specialize in technical accounts and these can be thoroughly recommended. There is a point worth remembering in connection with small agencies, namely that not all of them are recognized by the Newspaper Proprietors Association, the Newspaper Society or the Periodical Trade Press and Weekly Newspaper Proprietors Association and so are not eligible to draw commission on advertisements placed with journals. Under the terms governing the sale of advertising space, commission is only paid to bona fide advertising agents, who incidentally, need not necessarily be members of the Institute of Practitioners in Advertising, but must be recognized by the governing bodies of the Press. If the small agency cannot benefit from the 10–15 per cent commission normally expected from space buying, then it has to make good this deficit by increasing its service charge. Generally speaking, therefore, it is in the advertiser's interest to use an agency that is fully recognized and can be classed as bona fide. Apart from all questions of fees, the fully qualified agency is a highly reputable organization of good standing in the profession in whom the manufacturer in search of advertising assistance can impose a high degree of trust.

ADVERTISING AN INDUSTRIAL PRODUCT – WHAT CAN IT ACHIEVE?

As mentioned earlier in this book, industrial advertising is not expected to sell a product outright. Its major purpose is to publicize the existence and merits of the product so that the representative's task of introducing it, when he pays a call, is made easier, or sufficient interest is stimulated by the advertisement to produce inquiries. These can then be followed up by the technical representative rather than the salesman. The period of time elapsing between an advertisement appearing in the trade journal and a call being made and an order finally placed may be quite considerable. It has to be remembered that a prospective purchaser has to be satisfied with the product before he contemplates buying it. He may, in fact, require to carry out extensive trials before he can establish whether the product is appropriate to his purpose. The technical advertisement has, therefore, to achieve several objectives:

(1) It has to communicate to the potential customer the right kind of commercial or technical intelligence in the right media at the right time.
(2) It has to reflect credit on the advertiser or his product and make a satisfactory impact so that the message is remembered.
(3) It has to satisfy the advertiser that an investment in advertising is worthwhile as a means of sales promotion.

HOW DOES INDUSTRIAL ADVERTISING DIFFER FROM CONSUMER ADVERTISING

Generally speaking, industrial advertising can be regarded as a means of communication between one type of manufacturer and another. It is presumed, therefore, that an industrial advertisement is aimed at readers who are receptive towards news of products, machines and services that are likely to help them in their business. The consumer advertisement, on the other hand, is a means of communication between the manufacturer or his agent and the ultimate buyer, and is designed to sell goods or services. In most consumer advertisements the price of the goods offered for sale is given prominence and so too are the main selling arguments. Both illustrations and copy are designed to have a high and immediate impact on the largest mass of readers, whereas the industrial advertisement makes a specialized appeal to a restricted audience.

There are millions of potential buyers for breakfast cereals, but only hundreds for aero engines. The motivating force for a great deal of consumer advertising stems from fairly elemental emotions, such as envy, fear, vanity, etc. For example, an advertisement to motorists for anti-freeze dramatizes the dire consequences of a frozen radiator and strikes an appropriate note of fear – an announcement of a new cosmetic preparation excites envy and also makes a strong appeal to the vanity of the fairer sex.

The difference between the two types of advertising is, perhaps, best illustrated by looking at the two distinct types of goods being promoted and recalling that whereas consumer goods are sold, the industrial products are bought!

Consumer advertising makes use of large circulation publications – the mass media, but industrial advertising, because of its specialized appeal, is generally restricted to the trade and technical Press.

There are, however, many examples that could be quoted where industrial advertising makes very successful use of the national Press although the cost of such campaigns is very heavy and the wastage considerable. Apart from advertising such products as steel tubing (Accles and Pollock) and power tools (Desoutter) the national Press does, of course, carry a large number of so called prestige or institutional advertisements for non-consumer goods manufacturers.

It should not be presumed that technical advertisements, because they are featuring industrial products, need to be dull, although a great many of them are incredibly dreary. There is a welcome trend in some quarters to break away from the deadly pattern of squared-up half tones and copy packed full of facts and figures. Readership research would appear to cast strong doubts on the view that an industrial buyer expects to find his technical facts in advertisements. It is believed that what he does look for, but seldom finds, is the advertisement that interests him and brings to his notice the name of a firm or a product.

HOW MUCH DOES AN ADVERTISING AGENCY COST THE MANUFACTURER?

Basically an advertising agency operates on a commission of 15 per cent which is paid by the media owner for placing the advertisement. If the commission paid by the paper, or indeed any other supplier, falls below 15 per cent, the agency charges the client the difference. Only for large accounts is this commission sufficient to pay for all the normal planning, creative and advertising services of an advertising agency, and service fees are therefore charged in addition to the normal remuneration so as to provide the agency with sufficient income. Where no commission is involved, such as in the production of art work and photography, additional fees are charged, the sum being based on a return on 15 per cent on the gross amount charged the client. In all dealings with agencies it is made clear that accounts are expected to be paid within 15 days after presentation of the invoice or statement, and if payment is delayed, then the agency has the right to postpone or cancel the residue of incompleted orders.

Although this method of paying for an advertising service is sometimes criticized it is, in the writer's opinion, preferable to a fee system which would have to be negotiated afresh every year. Such negotiations could well be quite complicated, and even protracted particularly where accounts were split between occasional advertising in the national dailies and heavy advertising in trade and technical. Added to the yearly ordeal of preparing a publicity budget, the idea of having to negotiate agency fees based on this budget would severely tax the nervous system of the most hard-boiled publicity manager.

Mention was made earlier about the service fees which may be charged by the agency where the annual expenditure by the client is insufficient to provide an adequate working return. How big does the account have to be to provide an adequate return? This depends to a large extent on the agency. A very large agency might well be unprepared to handle any account under £75,000, whilst another small concern which is specially organized to take on industrial accounts, might be quite happy with accounts of £5–10,000. It is, of course, quite obvious that an account of £15,000 would only yield a return of £2,250, which is certainly not a large enough sum to pay for a first class advertising service. A service fee of at least 10–15 per cent might be required to make the account worthwhile. Whilst advertising is certainly not cheap, it is at least some consolation to the client to realize that the media owner does help to subsidize his advertising, moreover, the commission paid by the paper to the agency could not be claimed by the client.

[margin note: 1962 figures]

SERVICES THE INDUSTRIAL ADVERTISER SHOULD EXPECT FROM AN AGENCY

A client is entitled to expect from an agency an expert advertising service in terms of media planning and buying, creative copy writing and artwork of a high order, technical competence and advertising research. These are the essentials in advertising practice. Ancillary services, such as market research, product research and consumer research, and also public relations, although extremely important, are not vital to the actual business of preparing advertisements. These are services that can be bought outside the agency and there are a number of reputable practitioners who specialize in them. There are sound arguments for letting the agency do the advertising and contracting out the market research to independent experts in this line. Research is really the advertiser's responsibility and not the agency's, although the latter should be kept fully informed of all the findings. Unless the agency is given access to research data it will prove difficult for its executives to understand the marketing policy.

Apart, however, from the type or variety of services offered by the agency, it should be obvious that it must be staffed with account executives of high calibre who are able to understand fully the advertiser's selling policy; to know a good deal about the products he is manufacturing; to appreciate his research and development plans and to be on good terms with all the senior executives in the client's business. Added to this the account executive should not only be aware of the limitations of advertising, but be honest enough to tell the advertiser about them when the occasion demands.

No reputable agency will take on a new account in the same line of business as an existing one, for example, it would refuse business from a paint manufacturer specializing in the retail market if it already handled the advertising of another paint firm.

On the other hand, the agency might take on the account of a company specializing in industrial finishes, even if it were responsible for the advertising of a household paint. In this borderline case the new account would only be taken with the full knowledge and approval of the two companies concerned.

ADVERTISER AND AGENCY RELATIONSHIP

An idea has a long way to go before it catches up with the actual advertisement upon which it is based. During its tortuous journey from the advertiser to the media owner it is liable to undergo many changes some of which are, of course, inevitable, whilst others are due to bad briefing, difficulties of communication or even incompatibility of people engaged in the business. Illustrating the whole complex business of industrial advertising is a study of the sequence of events leading up from the time when the advertiser decides to advertise to the moment when the advertisement appears in the Press.

Taking a purely hypothetical case, let us say the initiation and completion of an advertising campaign for steam traps, it is possible to lay bare the tenuous chain of communications that stretches from the managing director of the company to the media owner who puts the advertising pages of the paper or journal to bed. First of all, the desire to advertise! It is as well to examine this in some detail. In this instance it arose from two causes: the first was the urgent necessity to establish the name of the company as the leading manufacturer of steam traps and secondly to widen the scope of the existing markets and give support to the salesmen operating in the field. In addition, there were complex political and personal issues involved as the company had recently been absorbed by a large engineering group and the managing director was under pressure to take a more positive action in the promotion of the steam traps. The budget for the proposed advertising campaign was arrived at illogically on a purely actuarial basis and without reference to what it would buy in the way of advertising space.

At the briefing meeting, at which the technical and commercial interests of the company were represented, with the publicity manager and the agency's account executive, director and manager also present, the idea was put forward that the schedule should be divided into two parts – national and technical. It was pointed out by the managing director that a number of small as well as nationally known industrial concerns advertised in such magazines as *Punch* as well as the trade and technical Press, and that it might be a good scheme to try and put over the technical advantages of the steam trap on a broad as well as a narrow front. This

TO LIGHTING FITTING DESIGNERS

HERE ARE the optical properties of the I.C.I. range of opal grades of 'Perspex' acrylic sheet in convenient reference form. The diagrams show at a glance (for ⅛″ thick sheet) the transmission, reflection and diffusion characteristics of the materials enabling you to select the correct grade for your particular applications.

More than twelve years experience throughout the world has proved that the high efficiency of the opal, as well as the patterned and clear grades of 'Perspex' acrylic sheet, remains unchanged during prolonged use in adverse conditions.

In addition to the four opal grades illustrated, many other grades of tinted opal and patterned 'Perspex' are available.

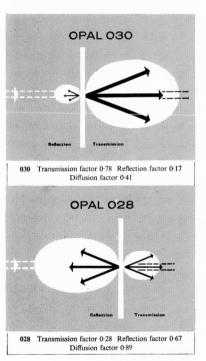

OPAL 030

Reflection   Transmission

030   Transmission factor 0·78 Reflection factor 0·17
Diffusion factor 0·41

OPAL 028

Reflection   Transmission

028   Transmission factor 0·28 Reflection factor 0·67
Diffusion factor 0·89

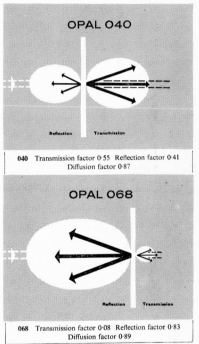

OPAL 040

Reflection   Transmission

040   Transmission factor 0·55 Reflection factor 0·41
Diffusion factor 0·87

OPAL 068

Reflection   Transmission

068   Transmission factor 0·08 Reflection factor 0·83
Diffusion factor 0·89

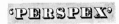

'Perspex' is the registered trade mark for
the acrylic sheet manufactured by I.C.I.

IMPERIAL CHEMICAL INDUSTRIES LIMITED · LONDON · S.W.1

Good technical advertisement telling a clear-cut technical
story

3-way proof that 'Propathene' makes a high fashion heel <u>tougher</u>

1 This pair of shoes has been worn for a week, without any top pieces on the heels, by a 12-stone woman. The shoe on the left shows the comparatively small amount of wear on the heel. On the right, a neat repair has been made with the minimum of trouble.

These illustrations demonstrate the remarkable strength of fashion heels made from 'Propathene', the new plastics material from I.C.I.

Besides providing outstanding strength, 'Propathene' makes heels 15-20 per cent lighter and keeps prices down by practically eliminating rejects.

These heels were made by Hollis Heels Ltd., Craven Hall, Hull, from 'Propathene'. Already, famous makers such as Lotus and the Mansfield Shoe Company are making wide use of them. You can cut production costs, too, while making high fashion shoes that are lighter and stronger, by using Hollis Heels in 'Propathene'.

'Propathene'

'Propathene' is the registered trade mark for the polypropylene manufactured by I.C I.

ICI

2 Three four-inch nails have been driven through these heels, without cracking or splitting the 'Propathene'.

3 The heels were clamped in a vice and eventually bent by hitting them with a 2 lb. hammer. Neither the 'Propathene', nor the metal insert was cracked.

PP5

IMPERIAL CHEMICAL INDUSTRIES LIMITED · LONDON · S.W.1

Advertisement designed to provide technical information – good impact value

suggestion was considered, but the agency felt unhappy with the figure of £25,000 and the executive director asked about future allocations; was this likely to be increased or decreased, or even discontinued after a year?

However, the advertiser had his way and consideration was next given to the form of the advertisement. The commercial men wanted hard hitting technical advantages to be put over in the advertisement and here they were supported by their technical colleagues. A long argument resulted from this, the agents winning in the end by persuading their clients that no one would read a catalogue of technical advantages and that the advertisement had to be designed both as regards words and picture so as to attract attention and sustain the interest not only of the hard boiled engineer, but also his employer who might not have the detailed technical knowledge of his staff, but who was quick to appreciate the commercial advantages attached to a good product. It was agreed that the advertisement would be built round an actual case history with full acknowledgements to the customer where the steam traps were fitted. The series for *Punch* would be given a more popular appeal than those going into the engineering papers. As only quarter pages were being taken in *Punch*, it was decided to use fairly tight line drawings and the minimum of copy, but to extend the copy in the trade and technical press.

The next link in the chain was the conference at the agency where the art director and chief copywriter were briefed. Here difficulties immediately arose. The art director favoured a semi-cartoon treatment, whereas the chief copy writer thought this to be quite unsuitable, particularly if the copy were intended to be purely factual. The inevitable compromise was reached and work was put in hand. In two weeks two layouts were prepared for submission to the client. One of these showed a Victorian gentleman resembling Mr. Gladstone, standing outside what looked like a Lancashire cotton mill and pointing to the chimney with his stick. The other layout showed an old man in a chair looking at the steam coming out of a kettle boiling on the fire. The copy in both cases stressed the efficiency and durability of the client's steam traps when used under strenuous factory conditions.

Needless to say, both these layouts were rejected out of hand by the advertiser and so the work started all over again. The art director at the agency was annoyed and the chief copy writer amused. The final accepted layout showed two men, one an engineer and the other his employer, examining a blue print of a new textile mill in which 'X' brand steam traps were to be installed.

Some advertising agents tend to look no further than the advertisement itself and to forget the public for which it is aimed, and the product which sustains it. In its chequered journey through the agency, both copy and layout tend to become more and more remote from both the product and the public and it is hardly surprising therefore, that so many advertisements-in-the-making have an oblique approach which dulls the edge of the advertisement and obscures the message.

On the other hand, the advertiser himself is sometimes not at all clear about the real purpose of the advertisement. He wants to please the board of directors and ultimately the shareholders; he is anxious to score off his competitors; he certainly would like to gain a little personal prestige for himself, and lastly he wants to promote the sales of his product. Born of such strange parents it seems a miracle that the advertisement, when it ultimately appears, shows no gross signs of abnormality! For every company there is somewhere, the right advertising waiting, but it does not follow that it will ever see the light of day. Whether it does or not depends on a number of factors and a number of people. There is certainly more chance of the really sparkling advertisement appearing if there exists a sound understanding between agency and advertiser, each party respecting the other for its specialized knowledge.

In this vexed question of advertiser/agency relationship, compatibility of people ranks high in importance as, if it is poor, then efficiency is lowered and the product ultimately suffers.

ADVERTISER'S CONTACT WITH THE AGENCY

The advertising manager is the person who is in day to day contact with the agency. It is his responsibility to plan advertising campaigns, both short range and long range; to instruct agencies; recommend media; work out advertising budgets; check expenditure against budgets and, in other words, to manage the advertising business. Authorities on advertising matters, and there are many of them about, always stress the fact that the job of the advertising manager is 'to manage' and not to be a copy writer, visualiser or artist, all of which he may be tempted to become. Whilst this advice is excellent in theory, it tends to fall down in practice, particularly in small publicity departments where the manager has to be something of a Jack-of-all-Trades in order to provide the organization with a real service. With an eye to the future, there is no doubt that the best advice one could give to any advertising manager would be to try and qualify as a marketing executive as quickly as possible, and to concentrate on 'planning' rather than 'doing'.

One of the day to day difficulties in running an advertising department is to clear the lines of communication, not only between the manager and the agency, but between the advertising department and all those sections of his organization concerned with market research, product planning, sales promotion, production and technical service and development. So far as the agency is concerned, the advertising manager should make sure that he is the official contact and should take quite positive measures to discourage the agency from consulting other members of the organization without his knowledge and permission. This may seem somewhat high handed, but it is of great importance in safeguarding future relationships with the agency. If the advertising manager is solely responsible for advertising, then it is part of his responsibility, and no one else's, to deal with the agency on all matters affecting the business of advertising. If he forgoes this responsibility, then his position *vis-à-vis* the agency and his superiors in his own company becomes impossible.

7

ORGANIZING AN INDUSTRIAL PUBLICITY DEPARTMENT

IT WAS stated in *The Times* some while ago that 'today's executive must be as versatile as a Cabinet Minister', and this applies very aptly to an advertising manager. Apart from any specialized knowledge which he might possess (he could, for instance, be a brilliant journalist or an experienced agency man) he needs to have a broad knowledge of the industry in which he is engaged. In addition, he should possess the rare gift of original thought and flexibility of mind. In industry, as distinct from the consumer trade, the advertising manager does not enjoy the same opportunities for promotion that are open to his colleagues on the marketing side. Advertising does, in fact, tend to become something of a backwater which is largely unaffected by the tides of modern business. This, of course, is fatal to the success of an advertising campaign which must be carried out as part of a general marketing policy.

RECRUITMENT OF STAFF

The advertising manager, if he is to be really effective, needs to show an awareness of the problems of marketing and be able to make his own contributions to the general sales promotion of the goods being manufactured. More and more one finds industrial publicity becoming remote from marketing, and this is to be deplored as it means that it is not making its full contribution to the business of selling. Because of the tendency to divorce advertising from selling, the advertising manager is sometimes regarded as the poor relation of the commercial departments and this is liable to be reflected in salary levels. By normal agency standards

74

the advertising manager in industry is underpaid. Moreover, the size of the advertising appropriation is not always taken fully into account when assessing salaries, and even in very large concerns with a budget approaching the half million, the advertising manager's salary seldom, if ever, approaches that of the account executive in the agency.

This tendency to scale down the manager's salary is reflected in the attitude which higher management adopts towards the rank and file employed in the department. As a result it is not always possible to recruit the best people in the field and one has to make-do with mediocre talent. The position is aggravated by the fact that vacancies in the department are sometimes filled by staff from other parts of the organization who are either surplus to establishment, unacceptable to the management in the job they hold, or indicate a desire 'to do' something in publicity. As a result, industrial publicity departments are liable to be made up of ex-filing clerks, commercial assistants and secretaries. It is not uncommon to find that as high as 50–60 per cent of the staff in the average industrial publicity department are unqualified. They operate on a low salary level, work enthusiastically and are loyal servants of the company, but unfortunately they are ill-equipped mentally to tackle a creative job like advertising.

The real reason why the standard of industrial publicity is so low stems from this cause – unqualified staff. Efficiency and originality can only be ensured if the company is prepared to pay the market price for these qualities and without capable staff the department can never hope to be more than a post office for the agency. It is far better to have a small but efficient team than a sprawling department made up of unqualified people who flounder about doing their ineffectual best.

If industry is to expand and prosper, it must be prepared to spend more money on recruiting the kind of staff who are capable of making positive contributions towards the promotion of industrial goods, using all the vehicles of communication known to the advertising man. As a condition of employment in an industrial publicity department, every advertising executive under 30 should, for instance, sit for the Joint Intermediate Examination of the Advertising Association, and every executive over 35 should hold the Diploma of the Association. The image of advertising in industry can only be improved by ensuring that the men and women who practice it are 'qualified practitioners', and not amateurs at the job. The M.A.A. is far more useful to the 'industrial' advertiser than a B.A.!

ALLOCATION OF RESPONSIBILITIES

There are many ways of organizing an industrial publicity department, and naturally, different managers have their own pet theories which they want to put into practice. Whatever plan is chosen, there must be a considerable degree of flexibility so as to permit re-deployment of staff to meet any emergency that is likely to arise. In other words, members of the staff must be capable of dealing with any facet of publicity – advertising, exhibitions, literature, etc., dependent on the pressure of work and the general pattern of the publicity budget. This throws into relief the vital necessity of employing qualified staff who have the background knowledge and experience to equip them for the job. From year to year the organization chart will vary according to the allocations made for the various publicity activities in the budget, e.g. a budget of £150,000 consisting of £80,000 for trade and technical advertising; £50,000 for literature, catalogues, price lists and training manuals, and £20,000 for trade exhibitions and displays, might need a department organized as follows:

With this type of organization the assistant manager would be expected to act as P.R.O. for the company. The salaries for such a department might run to £12,000. It would be capable of handling a much larger allocation, indeed up to £350,000 without adding to the staff. Beyond this figure some increase would no doubt be required. The important factor to remember is that re-allocation of responsibilities presents no serious problems if the staff is fully trained. Looking at this particular organization chart, it might be thought that on the literature side, the staff was too highly specialized and could not, for instance, readily assume responsibility for advertising. Such is not the case. Advertising is

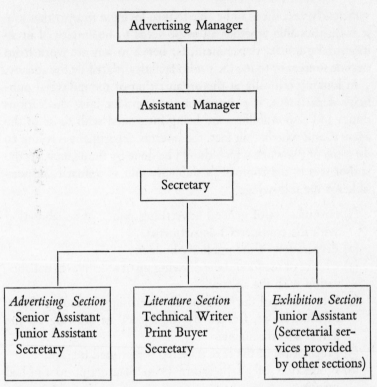

essentially a matter of copywriting and visualizing and a technical journalist should, at short notice, be able to contribute a great deal in this direction. The actual mechanics of advertisement production, such as checking schedules, voucher copies, etc., are largely a matter of routine which are soon learned by an intelligent junior, whom one assumes, is already well advanced in his studies for the advertising examinations and so familiar with much of the elementary background of advertising practice.

In the writer's opinion it is a mistake to retain one person too long in one job. There should be interchange of responsibilities at least once in two years. This prevents staleness, makes the job more interesting and also enables personnel to acquire more knowledge and experience. Where interchange of jobs becomes difficult, if not impossible, is where an artist is employed. Although highly skilled as an artist it is rare that one finds such a person

77

sufficiently versatile as to be able to turn his hand to any other job. It is questionable whether an artist needs to be employed in an industrial publicity department, far better to buy art work from outside sources or to use the studio facilities offered by the agency.

In looking critically at the organization of the industrial publicity department, it is important to consider how the various duties and responsibilities are being integrated with those of the agency, and whether, in fact, the internal department is trying to do some of the work which should be done by the agency. As the author sees it, the company's publicity unit is primarily responsible for the following:

(1) Formulation of general advertising policy in collaboration with the commercial departments.
(2) Preparation of the publicity budget.
(3) Choice of media and the drawing up of schedules in collaboration with the agency.
(4) Preparation of the brief for all advertising, including choice of illustrations, for use by the agency in drawing up the actual advertisements.
(5) Preparation of the text required for printed literature.
(6) Production of all literature from manuscript to finished printing.
(7) Briefing of designers for all exhibitions, collection of exhibits, preparation of captions, etc., and general progressing of construction and erection of the stand.
(8) Public relations in its entirety.
(9) Preparation of the first treatment of industrial films and liaison with professional or internal film units.
(10) Organization of direct mail.
(11) Provision of a good photographic library equipped to meet all the needs of the public relations side of the organization as well as the advertising, print and exhibition sections.

The advertising man inside the manufacturing company is not supposed to usurp the responsibilities of the agency which is paid to do all the creative work, but on the other hand, he is expected to make substantial contributions in the way of a first class brief, suggestions for illustrations and some constructive ideas on presentation. The inside advertising department and the agency should work together as a team. This means that when the agency contacts the client it should do so via the publicity department. This is most important, as if the publicity manager is by-passed and the agency is encouraged to contact the managing director or commercial director on matters of policy, then the manager's authority is undermined and his position becomes intolerable. It is not in the client's best interests to allow this kind of thing to happen as apart from making the advertising manager dissatisfied, it leads to confusion and often misdirection of effort.

THE CHAIN OF INFORMATION

The life-blood of advertising is information – information about the selling advantages and disadvantages of the products being manufactured, markets, trends, competitive activity, etc. There must be a constant flow of this kind of intelligence in order to keep the advertising department virile and progressive. For this reason, personnel in advertising should keep in constant touch with all departments in the company: production, technical service, research, commercial and personnel. The right contacts in all these departments should be encouraged to talk freely about developments. In addition, all reports from travellers and overseas customers should be scrutinized so as to glean from them the latest news on customers' developments and reactions. Good publicity can never be achieved in a vacuum – it needs space and air.

Outside sources of information should not be neglected and a great deal of valuable data can be secured from such papers as *The Financial Times*, *The Board of Trade Journal*, *The Economist* and *The Manager*. On a somewhat narrower front, the journals published by the various trade associations and professional bodies, and, of course, the technical Press all provide technical news of one kind or another. Key personnel in publicity should be regarded in the organization and also the agency as being extremely knowledgeable on all matters relative to the marketing of the company's goods. Dull advertising can usually be traced to dull people who look upon it merely as a job – and industrial advertising can be deadly dull if it is divorced from the exciting business of manufacture and selling.

IS THERE A CASE FOR CHANNELLING ALL PUBLICITY WORK THROUGH THE AGENCY?

Faced with dwindling profit margins, industry today is becoming alarmed about rising selling expenses, one of which is, of course, publicity. In an effort to reduce overheads to a minimum, some managements are now questioning the necessity of having their own internal advertising departments. It is being argued, particularly by the accountants, that all this work could be done more cheaply by the advertising agency, even though it charged a heavy premium. Overheads in a large company can increase the administrative expenses incurred in running a publicity department by as much as 100–200 per cent. Where services in industry can be provided at a competitive rate, then there is a case for using a sub-contractor. Already some engineering services are farmed out to free-lance draughtsmen and agencies specializing in this type of work and, of course, office cleaning and catering have for years been contracted out.

Whilst a first class advertising agency employs more highly qualified and also more highly paid staff than it is possible to engage in industry, it has to be remembered that the pick of the creative team tends to be deployed on consumer accounts. These offer the widest scope and provide the highest profit margin. Copywriters on technical accounts eventually become restive and have to be given refreshers in the form of periods of work on more interesting consumer accounts. This is easy to appreciate. A few months spent on writing copy for centrifugal mixers or cold storage rooms is enough to dull the edge of even a Henry Miller's creative ability! On complex technical accounts there is inevitably a wide movement of agency staff and the quality of work is liable to vary according to the extent to which talent is shifted within the agency. It is unfortunately true that in some small agencies specializing in industrial accounts, the copywriters are no more than 'catalogue-compilers' and are mentally ill-equipped to contribute anything in the way of creative thought. If industrial advertising is to make any progress it can only do so if the best brains are employed.

When the advertiser has his own publicity organization he is able to feed into the agency the right kind of information, often the right kind of ideas and also to reflect, as no outside source could possibly do, the policy of the company. In some ways the company publicity department is also able to make good some of the deficiencies of the agency, which, are liable to arise due to the complexity of most industrial accounts.

Whereas there would appear to be little difficulty in abolishing a consumer advertiser's publicity department and telescoping all its activities into the agency, to do the same kind of thing with an industrial company would present serious difficulties. To overcome these it would be necessary to set up a liaison office within the advertiser's company, and this might well assume proportions not dissimilar to those already existing in the publicity department. It is the complexity of the average industrial account that tends to discourge centralization, a course of action so popular with modern economists. In looking at this problem it has, of course, to be realized that when an agency handles the advertiser's business it demands a heavy premium and this might reduce the overall financial saving to an insignificant fraction.

It is worth pointing out that a few large industrial concerns are now tending to withdraw the creative work from the agency into the advertising department and to use the agency merely to book space. The reasons prompting this action can be summarized as follows:

(a) More concentrated effort can be made by the inside team than is possible by using agency resources.

(b) Time is saved by eliminating the interminable discussions which take place with agency personnel on copy, layouts, etc.

(c) Frustration due to changes in agency staff, most of whom become restive on industrial accounts, is avoided.

It is even reported that some manufacturers of non-consumer goods who have set up their own marketing departments, incorporating separate units dealing with publicity, no longer use advertising agencies. This means, of course, that they sacrifice the 15 per cent commission from periodicals, but against this loss it is claimed that they gain by not paying service and production charges.

There is no reason why a manufacturer should use an agency if he is prepared to take on the added and costly responsibility not only of production, but the actual mechanics of space buying and the checking of insertions, accountancy, etc. He has also to be prepared to sacrifice the valuable 'know-how' which a first class agency accumulates as a result of handling so many widely different accounts!

8

PLANNING THE PUBLICITY BUDGET

PRE-BUDGET DISCUSSIONS

A COUPLE OF months or so before the publicity budget is drafted there should be discussions with those members of the staff on the commercial side of the organization who are responsible for sales, both home and export. The object of these discussions should be to determine the general marketing policy for the coming year, and to learn something about the sales forecasts. This kind of reconnaissance is invaluable and is, in fact, the only way of building up the actual framework of the budget. What the publicity manager wants to find out at this stage is:

(*a*) Sales forecasts.
(*b*) Intelligence about the competition both at home and abroad.
(*c*) Where advertising, in one of its several forms, can prove most effective in the sales promotion of the commodities being handled.
(*d*) The amount of publicity in terms of £ s. d., that is likely to be needed for the promotion of specific products.
(*e*) The likelihood of new products being added to the selling range during the coming year and whether these will need any advertising.

In all these discussions it is advisable for the publicity manager to have in mind a mean average figure for his budget, i.e. a sum which he feels may be acceptable to higher management accountancy-wise, and to try and fit the actual working programme within the predetermined financial bracket.

THE RIGHT ALLOCATION OF EXPENDITURE – PERCENTAGE OF GROSS TURNOVER

The preparation of a publicity budget is an exacting and difficult task and many advertising managers view with considerable apprehension the long period of planning and forecasting which must precede the actual preparation of a working budget. Unfortunately there is no convenient yardstick to use when trying to work out a formula for the following year's publicity, individual companies varying so fundamentally in their views about the size of the advertising appropriation. Everything depends on the size of the company, the products it sells and its marketing policy. A large company manufacturing chemicals with a turnover of £25 million would probably consider 0·5 per cent a reasonably adequate appropriation for publicity of which some 40 per cent would probably be spent on advertising, mostly in the technical Press, and the remainder on the production of literature, exhibitions, films, photography and public relations work. On the other hand, a small engineering concern with a turnover of £100,000 would find even 1 per cent to be a little on the thin side, and in order to make any worthwhile impact, a figure of 3–4 per cent might well be necessary to finance a modest advertising programme, the preparation of some simple type of literature and perhaps an appearance at a trade exhibition. It is, of course, stressed that we are only dealing with industrial or technical accounts and not with companies who produce retail products demanding expensive consumer advertising. Here of course, the percentage spent might well exceed 15 per cent of turnover.

BUDGET EXPENDITURE MUST BE EFFECTIVE

It is not just a question of working out a figure that is acceptable to the commercial interests of the company as a reasonable proportion of the selling expenses, the budget must, if it is to be effective, allow for sufficient advertising to make the exercise worthwhile. It is easy to waste money on single insertions in trade journals and the spasmodic publication of trade leaflets, but publicity that is not continuous is generally wasteful and ineffective.

Although one instinctively dislikes the term 'expert', it is only the expert in advertising who will know, almost instinctively, whether any given sum is really adequate to do a set job of work. The campaign required for one particular industrial concern may, on the face of it, appear to be almost absurdly modest, but viewed against the marketing and general commercial policy of the firm it could be adequate. A company making one type of highly specialized engineering component would only require a fraction of the advertising appropriation necessary for a similar sized company which is making half a dozen or more different kinds of engineering components each of interest to a particular trade. Background knowledge of the marketing policy of the company is vital to the successful planning of a publicity budget.

To be effective, a publicity campaign must have a clearly defined objective. This may be to improve the prestige value of the company or the branded product; to interest a trade or trades in a range of commodities; to make known a new development or a new product; to ward off or discourage or to fight for survival against fierce competition. Where failure is certain and money is wasted is where the publicity manager has no clear directive from the commercial side of the organization and is unsure of the marketing position. This sense of insecurity is reflected in every facet of publicity that is carried out. There must be close integration of advertising with sales and this can only be assured if the management has complete confidence in its publicity manager. Publicity is part of the selling machinery and can be made to contribute a great deal to its overall effectiveness.

BREAKDOWN OF PUBLICITY EXPENDITURE

Having arrived at a reasonable and acceptable gross appropriation for publicity, then the next hurdle to jump is to decide on the most profitable breakdown of the figure. The right and proper percentage of an accepted publicity budget which should be spent on advertising may vary from 10–50 per cent, depending on the marketing policy of the company. Some very large and reputable concerns do not believe in Press advertising, except on rare occasions, such as special issues of say *The Times* or *The Guardian* which may be devoted to their particular industry. But such companies may spend large sums of money on the production of elaborate and costly technical brochures, participation in trade exhibitions and the sponsoring of films.

Unfortunately decisions on advertising policy by higher managements are not always based on sound commercial reasoning, but may be hopelessly biased due to prejudice against advertising. It is difficult to fight this kind of reaction, particularly where the decision rests with one man in the organization.

In planning the publicity budget for eventual submission to a Board of Directors or some executive committee, it is necessary to provide adequate background information so that every major item of proposed expenditure is supported by a simple and accurate explanation and commercial justification. For instance, under trade and technical advertising there should be references to choice of media, cost of insertions, cost of production. It is not necessary to write a long essay about these items of expenditure, in fact nothing infuriates busy directors more than verbosity in budgets, but concise and accurate explanations for proposed expenditure are expected and should be supplied.

JOINT CONSULTATION

The publicity manager cannot work in isolation and must consult his advertising agency at every stage of budget preparation. It is only the agency that is in the position to give up-to-date and accurate assessments of cost, not only of actual insertions but also production, to advise on the best media for any projected campaign, and to work out actual schedules.

HOW ACCURATELY SHOULD THE PUBLICITY BUDGET BE FORECAST?

Being a forecast of expenditure for twelve months ahead, the budget needs not only to be accurate, but its framework should be sufficiently elastic to allow for a reasonable rise in the cost of production. A 10 per cent increase in printing charges might easily mean over-expenditure and where advertising rates are increased this too could lead to an appreciable rise in expenditure. Very few companies permit a contingency figure to be included in budgets, although it could be argued that this is very desirable where advertising is concerned. The only acceptable method is to make reasonable allowance in forecasting expenditure so as to be able to absorb a 10–20 per cent increase in costs. Over-budgeting is naturally frowned upon by accountants as it gives a false figure of expenditure and tends to make nonsense of profit forecasts. On the other hand, overspending of publicity allocations tends to increase the incidence of coronary thrombosis and gastric ulcers among company directors and advertising managers. It can be said that too accurate a forecasting of expenditure, whilst theoretically very commendable, is, in practice, not recommended. If the costs of carrying out an advertising programme are slightly inflated at the planning stage this can be justified by the knowledge that all publicity costs are steadily rising and it would be foolish not to take this fact into account when budgeting.

SELLING THE PUBLICITY BUDGET TO MANAGEMENT

It is not sufficient for the budget to be meticulously prepared and in full harmony with the commercial interest of the company, it must be sold as a workable document to higher management. This may not, of course, be necessary in the case of a small firm where the boss is the commercial manager, the sales manager, and the managing director, all rolled into one, but for large concerns with different executive levels the situation is very different. Indeed, in some monolithic organizations a degree of lobbying is necessary to ensure that the budget can be given tacit approval before it goes up to the Board for official scrutiny. The publicity manager needs to be something of a psychologist in order to be able to understand and appreciate the reactions likely to be expected from certain proposals. The document needs to be slanted in such a way that at least the general conception will be received favourably. It should be short and yet adequate, meeting all the points likely to be raised by those persons whose job it is to make decisions. The reasons for the proposed campaigns should be given and these must be carefully thought out and well presented so that for every item of expenditure there is an adequate commercial case.

An awareness of the foibles of executives also helps in framing the budget in such a way that it is, at least sympathetically received.

EXAMPLES OF TRADE AND INDUSTRIAL PUBLICITY BUDGETS

A typical publicity budget for an engineering company specializing in making small machine tools and accessories with a gross turnover of £75,000 might look something like this:

PUBLICITY EXPENDITURE

Press Advertising		£1,000		
12 half pages in a machinery journal with production, approximately	£240 0 0			
12 half pages in a metal working journal	£420 0 0		£900	
6 half pages in a machining journal	£240 0 0			
4 half pages in an institute journal	£100		£100	
(Actual cost of space at series rates = £724 : Production = £276)				

Technical Literature		£750
Price List	£115 0 0	
Brochure	£385 0 0	
Leaflet for Direct Mail Campaign	£250 0 0	

Direct Mail	
Cost of Mailing	£150

Total Expenditure on Publicity	£1900

Looking at the selection of trade journals, the publicity manager chose these because in the first instance he was satisfied that they were good publications, and was also aware from salesmen's reports that they were widely read by the firm's present and potential customers. It might, of course, be argued that the two journals chosen cover pretty well the same ground, but this reasoning is rather superficial; the machinery journal is widely read by executives who buy engineering equipment and supplies, whilst the metal working publication is a favourite with directors, managers, and senior engineers. By staggering the advertisements, the advertising manager should be able to build up a schedule giving reasonably good coverage for a modest expenditure, the advertisements being planned to appear every other month in each journal. The institutional advertising is justified because the management of the company takes a prominent part in the affairs of the Institute.

Dealing very briefly with literature, the publication of a price list is obviously vital to the business of selling and so, too, is the publication of a well illustrated brochure. In the past, modest direct mail campaigns have proved worthwhile and the expenditure under this heading is a continuation of proven advertising policy.

This publicity budget is, of course, a very modest one, but the case presented would appear to be justified on commercial grounds. It might be argued that the rounded-off figures given for space and production charges are excessive, no allowance being made for 'repeats' of advertisements. This is true, but on the other hand, the slightly inflated costs given do allow for a reasonable amount of manoeuvring if printing charges, space rates or block charges are increased during the year, or if one or more advertisements require a certain amount of expensive art work. It would be foolish not to make reasonable provision for this kind of extra expenditure.

Another example could be quoted of budget planning, this time a plastics trade moulder specializing in industrial components for the motor, electronic and engineering industries, turnover £250,000. Here the problem is somewhat different, as sales are spread over at least three unallied industries which have little in common. The allocation might be justifiably 2 per cent of turnover, say £5,000.

A worthwhile advertising scheme could embrace the plastics trade journals, so as to invite trade moulding from the plastics industry itself and also take in the trade publications of direct interest to the main markets. To carry out a reasonably effective advertising programme it would be necessary to take space in at least half a dozen different journals. The ones recommended are:

Plastics journal	6 half pages black and white	£240
Plastics journal	6 half pages black and white	£273
Electronic journal	6 half pages black and white	£252
Engineering journal	6 half pages black and white and one colour	£276
Motor engineering paper	6 half pages black and white	£216

$$\text{Total allocation} = £1294$$
$$\text{Total space} = £1044$$
$$\text{Production} = £250$$

The cost of this is assessed at £1,294. In addition it is necessary to add £1,557 for price lists and technical brochures. Added to this should be an allocation of £2,200 for participation in trade fairs, support of the Trade Federation and for financing a modest programme of public relations.

BUDGETARY CONTROL OF EXPENDITURE

There must be control of publicity expenditure in order to make certain that the budget is not exceeded. This control should be devised so that it shows not only the current expenditure, but estimated expenditure. It should, in fact, be rather like a thermometer that is able to register not only the patient's temperature when it is put in his mouth, but his 'anticipated' temperature in a week's time. A control system, if it works efficiently, not only prevents over-expenditure, but also under-expenditure. Such a system depends for its operation on the following actions being taken:

(*a*) Close estimates of the costs of all goods and services are obtained from suppliers before firm orders are placed.

(*b*) Orders are placed on suppliers prior to any work being commissioned.

In a large publicity department it is sometimes difficult to discipline members of the staff so as to ensure that these steps are always taken, but without their full-hearted co-operation it will prove quite impossible to forecast accurately. Budget control depends on the efficiency and enthusiasm of those who administer it.

Whether it is a progress clerk in the publicity department itself, or a member of the accounts department, there should be someone whose responsibility it is to keep a record of all 'planned' expenditure and to advise the manager of the level of anticipated expenditure at fairly frequent intervals.

One of the difficulties experienced in this business of forecasting expenditure, is to find out in advance the agency commitments. This applies not so much to space charges, which can easily be seen from the schedules and actual advertisements checked by the checking and voucher department at the agency, but to production charges. These can assume quite considerable proportions.

SUPPLEMENTARY BUDGETS

Expenditure not included in the publicity budget has sometimes to be incurred, e.g. where promotion is needed for products which were in the experimental stage at the time the budget was prepared. To cover the cost of un-budgeted expenditure, it is usually necessary to obtain special sanction for the expenditure. Most managements require a supplementary budget to be put up to the Board to explain why the advertising is being undertaken and to give an estimate of the cost. This method is a tidy one and forestalls any argument that may arise in the case of over-expenditure at the end of the year.

9

CREATION OF THE TECHNICAL

ADVERTISEMENT – PART ONE

RANGE OF SERVICES PROVIDED BY AN ADVERTISING AGENCY

APART FROM buying space and the preparation of copy and layouts for advertisements, a really first class agency should be able to provide clients with a complete range of ancillary services. These may include marketing, including product testing and research, trade and consumer surveys, psychological and attitude surveys, media research, public relations, film production, including television commercials, exhibitions and displays, photography, direct mail and the arrangement of sales conferences. All these activities are designed to assist the client in promoting the sales of his products. In some large agencies research is given very high priority and some of them have subsidiaries solely concerned with market research.

Although the agency may have under its roof departments covering the main advertising activities, it should not be presumed that all the work is done on the premises. In the large agencies the roughs will be prepared in the studio but finished art work, if the standard aimed at is high and the account justifies the cost, will be sub-contracted out to free-lance artists and studios. Creative photography is also given out to specialists in the field. In other branches, such as films, exhibitions and even direct mail, use is frequently made of outside concerns.

CREATION OF THE ADVERTISEMENT

Whose responsibility is it to take facts and to translate them into ideas in the form of actual advertisements designed to enhance the reputation of a company or to create interest in a product or service? It might well be argued this is the copywriter's responsibility, and this would probably be the agency's ruling. In actual day to day work, however, it is a responsibility that is shared almost equally between advertiser and agency. Usually the client, in the form of the advertising manager, is not content merely to discuss general principles, he quite frequently has ideas of his own and it is often these that form the basis of the advertising campaign.

There is no magic formula for the production of effective advertisements; most of the really striking layouts and copy owe their origin to the pooling of ideas by advertiser and agency. Some of the most successful technical advertisements have been 'triggered-off' as a result of a chance remark or even a joke. It is fair to say that only someone thoroughly immersed in the business of advertising is able to be sufficiently selective to recognize the right kind of lead when it is given. For this reason, some 80 per cent of the ideas which find their way into print originate from the agencies and, indeed, creation of advertisements is their proper function. In the writer's opinion, this function of the agency should be recognized fully by the client who should quietly discourage his management to do the agency's job.

TECHNICAL COPYWRITING

Technical copywriters are usually men who have had experience in some specialized industrial subject, frequently engineering. Indeed, some of the most able copywriters in this field are ex-engineering draughtsmen who possessed the ability of being able to write and have the rare gift of creative thought.

No matter how gifted a technical copywriter may be, he needs a lot of briefing before he is able to write intelligently about a new industrial subject. Clear, concise copy with a high interest factor can only be produced if there is the closest liaison between the creative side of the agency and the client. It has to be remembered that the copywriter is often the key man on the account as he not only writes the copy but quite frequently thinks up the illustration, or at least suggests to the layout artist the most suitable form of presentation. The development of the illustration from a mere suggestion to something tangible is, of course, the responsibility of the layout artist. Bearing in mind the importance of the technical copywriter, it becomes immediately obvious that he not only needs to know the basic facts about a product but a good deal of the background information relating to its uses. It might even be advisable to let him talk to customers so as to find out the trade's reaction to the goods being advertised.

It is a cardinal sin in advertising to rely entirely upon the account executive to brief the copywriter instead of providing the latter with all reasonable facilities to understand the product by direct contact with those who make it, those who test it, and those who use it. Because only in this way can interesting and informative advertisements be prepared.

The function of the account executive is to recruit and blend all the various services which the agency offers to the client. This executive needs to be much more than a 'front man', indeed, to be really effective he must have a thorough knowledge of both the client's products and his organization. It would, however, be unwise to expect him to acquire and transmit the expert knowledge needed to give the copywriter adequate briefing on every aspect of the account. The only satisfactory way is to make possible direct contact between copywriter and client.

LAYOUT

In the agency the layout artist or 'visualizer' is responsible for transforming the idea of an advertisement into a recognizable form. Working in collaboration with the copywriter, who probably suggested the type of illustration to be used as this had to be referred to in the text, he works out a layout, incorporating the picture, the headline and the position of the copy. This pencilled-out framework of the advertisement, known as a 'rough' may be shown to the client but more often a more advanced treatment, the 'finished rough' is prepared for submission to the advertiser. Most agencies prepare all roughs and finished roughs within the building.

No two agencies employ the same system, but in the ones familiar to the author the real creative work is the responsibility of the layout artist, whilst the studio is largely uncreative. Actually all the client sees is the work of the layout artist or visualizer and rarely, if ever, does he see finished artwork which goes straight from the studio to the block-maker.

Finished art work is frequently sent out to free-lance artists or studios. The same applies to photography. Bread-and-butter work may be handled by the agency's own photographic unit, but the top grade picture is usually obtained from one of the acknow-ledged specialists in the field. Production charges are apt to take a high upward curve when work is sub-contracted out, but such a practice, although expensive, does achieve the best results. In agencies handling small industrial accounts, an effort is always made to try and do as much of the creative work in the agency as possible. Experience tends to show that where this happens, then the creative quality of work is liable to fluctuate according to the ebb and flow of talent throughout the studio.

MEDIA PLANNING

The fact is often overlooked that the value of even a first class advertisement can be wasted unless it appears in the right place at the right time. It can, of course, be equally wasteful to broadcast advertisements throughout the range of publications in the par-ticular industry. Each publication must be treated on its own merits and the correct assessment of these merits is a highly specialized and skilled job. Constructing a schedule giving proper weight to each publication is a task which calls for imagination as well as knowledge. For this reason, media planning is now often treated in some agencies as part of the creative function rather than as a service department.

ADVERTISING AN ESTABLISHED PRODUCT

The most difficult task confronting any advertising manager is to inject interest into advertisements for old and well established industrial products. The temptation here is to fall back on the well tried formula of showing the product in use in a customer's works – variations on the familiar testimonial type of advertisement so dear to the consumer trade.

This type of advertisement, unless revitalized by use of striking illustrations and interesting copy, can have rather a depressing effect on the reader and, in the mass of advertising such as one finds in so many trade journals, it stands the risk of passing unnoticed.

Where the subject matter itself is neither novel nor new, and where the aim of the advertiser is to keep the name of his company and the product in the forefront of the particular industry, then a good deal of creative thought has to be put into the advertising to lift it out of the common rut. The snag about all creative and thought stimulating advertising is that it is apt to be expensive because its design calls for the use of top-flight art or photographic illustrations and not many industrial accounts are prepared to pay the high price demanded.

Another cause of dullness in technical advertisements is that even the most brilliant copywriters when confined to industrial accounts, tend to become jaded and restricted when obliged to concentrate on what they consider to be uncreative advertising! It is, therefore, a wise precaution to put the copywriters on to new pastures occasionally so that they do not get stale.

So often a small appropriation buys only mediocrity – the advertisement that lacks distinction but can hardly be called 'bad'. The way out of this impasse is to spend one's budget on a short series of first-class advertisements and to repeat them where necessary rather than to use a different advertisement for every insertion. A really striking advertisement will stand constant repetition, but with a poor advertisement, once is too often!

ADVERTISING A NEW PRODUCT

An advertising approach to a new product needs a rather different approach to one that is designed to sustain interest in an established line.

The manufacturer who has developed a new plastic or invented a novel machine is in fact, using his advertising space to tell a news story. He is, therefore, fairly certain to find a ready-made audience. Business readers of the trade and technical Press, or indeed, the national Press, cannot afford to ignore industrial intelligence whether it is printed in the editorial or advertising sections of the paper. It is, however, very important that all the claims that are made in the advertisement be based on fact. If they cannot be substantiated then the manufacturer not only imperils his reputation but damns his future advertising. When it is stated in an advertisement that a new product has certain specific properties which enable it to be used in well defined industrial applications, then the reader expects these claims to be true and based on practical experience. If, however, the manufacturer sets out in the advertisement the advantages which his product offers over established materials, then such a statement is regarded more of an opinion than a fact.

In framing an advertisement for a new product the advertiser has to remember that what the reader wants to know are the following pieces of information:

(1) Brief description of the new product and its properties.
(2) Availability.
(3) Where to write for further information.

Of these, the last is the really vital piece of intelligence and all new product advertisements should be so designed that readers are encouraged to write to the firm for a descriptive leaflet. It is a mistake to try and tell the complete story in the advertisement and such a treatment defeats its own object, as every square inch of space has to be taken up in doing so, and the result is a very dull piece of copy. What is wanted is an advertisement that whets the reader's appetite for more information and encourages him to contact the manufacturers. For most types of industrial products the price factor need hardly be considered in the advertising although, of course, there are many exceptions to this.

CODE OF ADVERTISING PRACTICE

A code of practice has been drafted for the guidance of advertisers, distributors, advertising agents and, in fact, all those responsible for the preparation of an advertisement and its eventual publication. The code also refers to packaging, direct mail, display and, indeed, all forms of sales promotion. It has the full support not only of all the advertising organizations, but the Independent Television Companies Association, The London Poster Advertising Association, The Master Sign Makers Association and the newspaper associations and societies. Although the authorities who have drafted this code of practice are not in the position to take any legal action against offenders, they can bring pressure to bear on those agencies responsible for the preparation of the offensive advertisement and also, through their contacts with the newspaper associations, they are able to persuade media owners to refuse advertisements which tend to bring advertising into contempt or to reduce public confidence in it.

The code lays it down that advertisements should be presented in such a way that they do not weaken the acceptance of advertising as an essential service to industry and the public economy. A joint committee has been set up by the advertising profession to secure uniform interpretation and application of the code. This committee, known as the Code of Advertising Practice Committee (C.A.P. Committee), consists of two representatives from each of the sponsoring organizations (although for convenience the five Outdoor Advertising bodies are represented by two nominees from the Outdoor Advertising Council).

Although in the main this document relates to the advertising of consumer goods, particularly such products as patent medicines, foodstuffs, detergents, cosmetics, etc., it also applies to industrial advertising. It is unnecessary to consider in detail all the recommendations of the authorities who drafted the code, but all of them are put forward with the very commendable aim of preventing the appearance of advertisements that mislead about the product or service being advertised.

From the industrial advertising angle, special attention can be drawn to the use of scientific terms and statistics that are misleading or which have limited validity. Also to the use of testimonials that are not genuine or are calculated to mislead. The use of the word 'guarantee' is also hedged with danger and difficulty and should be avoided. If it is used, then the limits and terms of the guarantee should be stated clearly, or information given as to where full terms of the guarantee can be obtained. As regards the disparagement of other advertisers' products, this is a highly dangerous practice and is singled out for special mention in the code.

KNOCKING COPY

It is stated in the code of advertising practice that 'advertisements should not contain disparaging references to products or service of other advertisers. In particular, advertisements should not single out a specific product or service for unfavourable comparison.'

Not only individual firms, but trade associations, are apt to be very sensitive about unfavourable comparisons made in advertisements that can by any stretch of imagination be identified with the goods they make or the trades they represent.

There are various pitfalls that the unwary in advertising can fall into in preparing an advertisement, e.g. in drawing up what might seem to be a perfectly straightforward technical advertisement, the advertiser might seem justified in describing how his particular piece of equipment or product was chosen by a customer to replace one that had broken down in service. This kind of case history is a familiar one to all technical advertisers and would appear to be unexceptional. Yet such an advertisement could trigger-off the most violent protests from firms or associations that claimed to be able to identify their particular product with the one that failed in service. Truth in advertising, although highly commendable in theory, can sometimes be disastrous in practice.

It is the job of the agency to prevent all disparaging references from appearing in advertisements, but even with the utmost vigilance such references do sometimes occur. This is hardly surprising when one considers that practically every product that is made is regarded as the responsibility either of some company or trade association.

Such generic products as glass, pottery, lead, copper, leather, plastics, vitreous enamel goods, etc., have all watchdogs in the form of trade associations who are quick to smell out 'Knocking copy' and to bring pressure to bear on the offender to prevent it from appearing again. An advertisement which claimed that plastic bottles were more durable than glass bottles which broke if you dropped them, might well elicit a most energetic protest from the association representing glass bottle manufacturers, and such a protest would be justified. If there was such a thing as a free-for-all in technical advertising, then practically every product would stand in dire peril of being discredited.

In some overseas territories, particularly Germany, any suggestion of 'Knocking copy' is strictly forbidden and for this reason the use of superlatives is frowned upon. In the Laws Relating to Competition and Trade Marks which are in force in Western Germany, it is expressly stated that the claiming of exclusiveness is only permissible if it can be proved to be true. If a company maintains that its commodity is 'recognized as the best of its kind', this will create the impression that a seriously meant and objectively verifiable recommendation is concerned. If, on the other hand, it is said, without any concrete details, that the commodity is 'the best commodity there is', then such a statement will scarcely be taken seriously, since there is obviously no possibility of proving it. It is permissible in German advertising to say 'The best shoes in the world', but it is not permissible to say 'The best shoes in Frankfurt', because this can be verified!

FACTORS INFLUENCING MEDIA BUYING

The media for the general advertiser can be broken down under ten broad headings:

(1) National daily newspapers.
(2) National Sunday newspapers.
(3) Provincial daily and weekly newspapers.
(4) Magazines.
(5) Trade, technical and professional publications.
(6) Telephone directory and general directory advertising.
(7) Poster advertising.
(8) Transportation advertising.
(9) Television, radio and cinema.
(10) Overseas publications.

The industrial advertiser is, however, only interested in certain of these classes, notably the national daily Press for prestige or institutional advertisements, and perhaps a small percentage of magazine publications for the same reason. The great bulk of his advertising is, therefore, carried by the trade, technical and professional publications. Directories may find a limited use and overseas publications are of value to manufacturers who have an export business. In terms of cost it is, of course, fairly obvious that both national dailies and Sunday newspapers and the consumer publications generally with large circulations, are all very expensive when compared with the trade and technical journals.

A publication appealing only to one specific trade may only have a circulation of 5,000, whereas a paper printed for mass readership could run into several millions. The higher the circulation, the higher the price paid for advertising space. One factor in buying space, which may not be immediately obvious to the advertiser, is that where a media owner only allows 10 per cent commission, and the agency normally works on 15 per cent, then the extra 5 per cent is added to the client's bill.

The most expensive way to buy space is by 'dribs and drabs'. A series rate is always attractive and can represent quite a worthwhile saving to the advertiser. A one-page advertisement in one of the chemical trade journals might cost £41 10s., but twenty-six pages could be bought at the rate of £31 a page. When buying space it is, therefore, always advisable to gain the benefit of series rates in the minimum number of journals, rather than to spread the advertising over the maximum number of publications in a given field. It is possible to make quite substantial economies by wise planning in this way.

Having decided upon the space and the frequency, the next thing to consider is what form the advertisement is to take – black and white or colour, and its position in the journal. A premium is always charged for colour, where this is acceptable to the publication, for example, let us take a journal in the engineering field which normally charges £53 a page. If the advertisement is to be run in two colours and black, a premium of £24 is charged for the extra colours. As a rough guide, it can be taken that in trade and technical and professional journals two to four colours cost the advertiser about half as much again for space and, of course, extra for production.

Special positions are also costly, for example, advertisements facing first editorial page can cost 100 per cent extra, or even more. Advertisements facing last editorial page may be 50 per cent extra, and other special positions and specified display pages about 25 per cent extra. These are only rough guides and may vary considerably from journal to journal. Where the advertiser wants a guaranteed position in the journal, then he usually has to pay a premium of 20 per cent extra. Cover rates, which include front cover, usually in full colour, inside front cover, outside back cover and inside back cover, are all relatively expensive and quite frequently have to conform to the house style both as regards format and colour, e.g. in one famous engineering journal the inside back cover can only be run in black and one full colour ink to BS.3020:1959. In some journals carrying a great deal of advertising those pages in the back of the book are cheaper than those situated at the front, the rate might vary by as much as 10 per cent.

Is the special position really worth the money? There is some doubt in the writer's opinion about the value of special positions, although there is no disputing the fact that covers are well worth using. These are, of course, expensive. Incidentally, journals usually have a waiting list and manufacturers have to advertise in them a number of years before qualifying for this space.

All the above comments refer to the usual type of trade and technical journals sold by subscription, and not to controlled circulation papers. The latter are a good deal more expensive than the average journal, but on the other hand it has to be remembered that wastage in circulation and readership is cut to the minimum.

10

CREATION OF THE TECHNICAL ADVERTISEMENT – PART TWO

BEFORE DISCUSSIONS take place with the agency three major questions of policy need to be answered within the manufacturing organization:

(1) What is the objective of the proposed campaign?
(2) To whom is the advertising directed?
(3) When is the most appropriate time to advertise?

The objective needs to be clear and well understood by all the commercial interests of the company.

It is only possible to achieve this kind of understanding as a result of close co-operation between the marketing and the advertising section. All marketing decisions which involve advertising need to be arrived at through joint consultation. It is not always a question of choosing the right kind of advertising, but deciding if advertising itself is the most effective means of communication. In the promotion of technical products, advertising may, in fact, serve no useful purpose and this is where the advice of an experienced advertising manager can prove of service in helping to formulate the most effective marketing policy.

If we consider for a moment a typical case, it will be easy to follow the reasoning behind the decision to spend money on advertising: a cement manufacturing company, having recently absorbed two smaller concerns, is anxious to make known to the building and allied trades the fact that it has extended its range of depots and is now able to offer a nation-wide supply service. In a critical examination of the problem of communicating this news to customers, and thereby making better known the company's name and its products, the advertising manager would be justified in recommending Press advertising as an effective and economical means of broadcasting the information, supplemented by some direct mail. His decision would be influenced by the realization that:

(a) The company now had depots in 75 centres strategically located throughout the United Kingdom.
(b) Customers at present on the company's books exceeded 25,000.
(c) The recent mergers, although making possible a more efficient service to the trade, were bitterly resented in some quarters, particularly by customers of the smaller companies involved in the merger.
(d) Press advertising in the architectural and building papers, strengthened by a short series of prestige advertisements in the national daily Press would help to create the right impression, namely, that by pooling all the manufacturing and distributing resources of the companies involved in the merger it would be possible to give a better service to customers. Further, Press advertising would assist the salesmen in the field by softening-up the market and providing a suitable atmosphere for business discussions. Direct mail could also assist by making known the advantages of the new set-up to those firms most affected by the new organization.

If, however, we look at another, rather different case, it will be seen that the commercial objective cannot be achieved by Press advertising: The manufacturer of advanced instrumentation systems for use in petroleum refineries and very large chemical plants is anxious to advance the idea of greater automation in such industries and willing to spend a substantial sum on promotion. The temptation is, of course, to recommend extensive Press advertising in the petroleum and chemical papers and possibly some costly institutional coverage in the national daily Press, but examination of the problem reveals the following facts:

(a) The type of instrumentation made by the company is only

really applicable to the giant corporations and really large companies where the scale of production justifies the installation of elaborate and costly systems of automation.

(*b*) The number of customers and potential customers in the United Kingdom and Europe is very small.

(*c*) The company's own commercial intelligence is already aware of the opportunities which exist for future installations, those being dependent on sanction being given to new capital programmes.

After consideration of all these facts the experienced advertising manager would most probably not advocate spending money on Press advertising. His argument would be based on the view that as personal contacts with all the potential customers were already in existence, and that the possibility of breaking new ground was remote, then there was no commercial justification for advertising. On the other hand, the advertising manager might well recommend a fairly heavy expenditure on well-produced and elaborate brochures explaining the systems, also more comprehensive training manuals for operatives engaged in working the various processes. Whereas Press advertising of such a highly specialized and restricted product as 'instrumentation for automation in oil refineries, etc.' would merely tend to irritate the large companies, most of whom regarded instrumentation as highly confidential, the distribution of descriptive literature would serve a most useful purpose in making better known the name of the supplier's system among engineers and technologists.

It can, of course, be argued that part of the objective is to recognize the audience to which the advertising is to be directed. This is most important. In trade and technical advertising the men who can influence buying decisions are sometimes difficult to identify, but an attempt has to be made, first to track them down, then to reach them through the advertising pages of some appropriate journal. If, for instance, the manufacturer of industrial finishes wants to persuade buyers to specify his particular lacquers or paints, etc., then he must, as a preliminary to any promotional effort, find out the people in the user industries who make the buying recommendations – the men who specify. A little research here could not only help the manufacturer's own marketing machinery, but prove of assistance to the advertising department. Efforts on marketing a product can often be misdirected because no one has taken the trouble to find out the key men in the user industries who are responsible for specifying, and these key men are sometimes quite far down the executive line!

Turning to the time factor, which also plays a big part in the initial stages of preparing an advertisement, it is necessary to understand something about the general marketing background; to study the monthly sales figures and to try and understand the reason for seasonal dips in the sales curves. Discussions with the salesmen on the road are always profitable, and in this particular instance they can prove most fruitful. The men who are in day-to-day contact with customers, appreciate, but often cannot understand, the tides of business, why they ebb and flow! They can, however, often make some useful recommendations as to the actual timing of certain advertising campaigns which are directed towards specific trades, or sections of trades. The salesmen on the road know far better than anyone else the domestic conditions prevailing in certain industries and how these conditions affect the general attitude towards suppliers.

Sometimes a certain weight of advertising needs to be reserved for times just prior to a big trade fair or some international conference. The timing of trade advertising is most important. It would, for instance, be waste of money to launch a campaign at the start of a big industrial dispute affecting a particular industry, or to try and advertise agricultural machinery to farmers just when the Government had announced the withdrawal of the wheat subsidy.

When considering the actual timing of the advertising it is as well to bear in mind 'copy dates' and the interval which exists between the preparation of the advertisement and its publication. A large number of monthly journals have copy dates four to six weeks prior to publication, and production of the advertisement often has to stew 3 or 4 weeks prior to copy date. This makes planning in advance of vital importance.

THE MESSAGE

This is, of course, the real hub of the matter. Once the objective, the audience, and the timing have all been given careful thought, the next and most vital consideration is the kind of message to communicate. Whilst there are few rules to observe because it is impossible to prescribe a universal formula for all technical copywriters, there are certain broad directions which are worth following. The first of these points to clarity of thought and expression. It has to be remembered that the average reader of a trade advertisement is a busy man who is impatient to thumb through the journal and tick his name off the circulation list. His restless eye is apt to be wearied by small copy and compressed technical verbiage. What he is seeking, although perhaps unconsciously, is the advertisement that will make an immediate impact and hold his interest long enough for him to read the message. It has, of course, to be remembered that in looking through technical advertisements his mind is attuned to certain subjects or problems and he is apt to be sensitive to any published material bearing on these matters. A good advertisement will make the appropriate point sharply and clearly with the commercial message restricted to the minimum amount of copy. Briefness and clarity of expression are the two most important qualifications.

A few examples are worth quoting to illustrate what the author has in mind.

(Advertisement prepared for a trade journal to advertise to leather manufacturers a new type of tanning extract.)

The illustration, photographic, would show a stop watch superimposed over a pound note.

Copy:

CONVERTING HOURS INTO STERLING

These new tanning extracts, the results of five years' patient research, make possible substantial economies in time without sacrifice of quality. If you have a problem in production, where manufacturing costs have to be reduced to the lowest possible figure without fear of any complaints on quality, then these new extracts are worth a trial. Ask our representative to arrange a practical demonstration at our expense, or write to the address below for a technical brochure describing the advantages offered by this process.

(*Advertisement for rubber and plastic conveyor belting for use in chemical works planned for insertion in chemical journals.*)

Illustration, photographic, shows a smartly dressed youngish man, carrying briefcase, walking across the Transporter Bridge, Widnes, Lancashire.

Copy:

OUR MAN IN RUNCORN

Wherever there are problems to solve in the conveyance of difficult industrial materials, there you will find our man – an expert in his subject of mechanical handling. Yes! our man in Runcorn is at this moment helping to solve a tricky little problem set us by a leading chemical manufacturer who is trying to find a trouble-free method of handling sodium bisulphite.

(*Advertisement in the chemical Press for an engineering firm manufacturing gravity feed systems for use in the pharmaceutical industry.*)

Illustration, photograph showing an apple falling through space – cloud background.

Copy:

NEWTON HAD A WORD FOR IT

If our gravity feed system was not exactly invented by Newton, at least he carried out the first experiments – with an apple. We have progressed quite considerably since those early days in the orchard. Take, for instance, our new gravity salt feed now installed in Messrs. . . . soap works, Huddersfield, which has made possible a further advancement in automation. If you have a production problem where a gravity feed system may provide the answer, then you will be well advised to call us in for consultation.

In the opinion of the author this type of approach to technical advertising is preferable to the more orthodox approach, which entails use of a works picture showing the machine or the product in use with a wad of technical copy underneath it. It is, of course, rather more difficult to depart from the recognized pattern of trade advertising and to try and achieve some degree of originality; it is also more expensive.

TECHNICAL ADVERTISEMENTS VERSUS TECHNICAL LITERATURE

There is grave doubt about the truth of the assertion so often made that engineers, chemists and technologists want technical advertisements – facts, not fiction! Within the compass of a page, or even a double page spread, it is impossible to do justice to a full technical brief and in attempting to do so the advertiser sacrifices impact and appeal – the advertisement looks dull and by its dullness it diminishes its chance of being read. Technical subjects need elbow room to develop and the proper place to afford this room is with the pages of a catalogue or brochure. It is, therefore, a mistake to try and make an advertisement serve the purpose of a piece of literature.

If we take two examples it will be seen immediately what the author has in mind.

(Page advertisement in the plastics Press for a temperature control system to be installed on moulding presses, calenders, mixers, etc.)

Illustration, photographic, shows the control box, cut-out, against white background.

Copy:

NEW SYSTEM AUTOMATICALLY CONTROLS CRITICAL PLASTIC TEMPERATURES TO $\pm 0.5°$ F.

'X' system gives you automatic maintenance of correct temperatures and ensures a high degree of accuracy. This makes possible greater uniformity of production and the maintenance of quality. There are no hot spots with this system, which means that there is uniformity of quality in all fabricating work and electricity and water are conserved. This means greater economy in production. Even relatively unskilled operatives, can, after a short tuition period, operate the system which, incidentally, is so robust that even a considerable amount of abuse will not put it out of commission. The cleverly designed dial, which indicates both pre-set and actual temperatures, on the same large scales, permits a high degree of readability and accuracy. Works engineers will find no difficulty in connecting this new type of pyrometer to any existing fabricating machinery.

This copy sets out to tell the industry too much, and as a result the message becomes long, involved, and boring. It also defeats its own object, which is to create interest in the new system and to encourage inquiries. Moreover, such a dull advertisement would sink into oblivion against the background of the average trade advertising. In other words, an advertisement of this type could not be justified commercially.

The alternative would be to try to crystallize the salient technical advantages of the system and to set these out quite boldly, with the support of an illustration with a reasonably high impact value. One suggestion is to use as the illustration a close-up photograph of the dial against a fleecy blue sky and to choose a bold and highly-condensed heading, such as:

LOOK! No Hands!

The copy might well be on the following lines:

'X' Automatic Control Gives You These Production Bonuses
(1) Temperature control within $\pm 0 \cdot 5°$ F. – *completely automatic*.
(2) More even temperature throughout plate, mould or roll.
(3) Economy in use.
(4) Ease of installation and use.
Send for our illustrated brochure which gives you full technical details.

The advantages set out in the advertisement are merely appetizers and, although of course, incomplete, will at least catch the eye of the technologist or engineer who is looking through the advertising pages of the journal.

Admitted that the copy is grossly incomplete, but at least it is clear, brief and gives emphasis to the main selling points. The alternative is to use a long, involved and boring write-up which merely irritates the reader.

Manufacturers of machinery seem to be obsessed with the idea that the most elaborate illustrations should be used in their advertisements. Apart from the high proportion costs of preparing special detailed drawings, it is maintained that these do not always add interest to an advertisement, which is to appear in journals full of similar illustrations. If, on the other hand, advertisers in this class turned their back on all technical drawings and illustrated their advertisements in some oblique manner, then there might be some momentary advantage gained in using an illustration taken from a blue print in the engineering drawing office.

No matter whether the product to be advertised is an injection moulding machine, a pyrometer, a dust-collecting system, etc., it is not always essential to show the actual commodity, in fact, it is often a virtue not to do so. Any legitimate advertising device can be used that will attract attention and encourage the reader to pause long enough to read the copy.

TESTIMONIAL TYPE OF ADVERTISING?

The most familiar and often the most abused form of technical advertising is not dissimilar to the old-fashioned testimonial so beloved by certain sections of the drug trade. The pattern usually followed makes use of a photograph showing the process, machine or product in a customer's works with copy setting out why the advertiser's commodity was chosen. At its best – that is, where the customer's name is known and respected internationally – then this type of advertising may be justified, but otherwise it is likely to be undistinguished. The trouble is that the advertising department is usually under considerable pressure to feature some particular customer's name as part of an insidious process of 'softening up' the customer, and it is difficult to fight against this kind of argument.

The outstanding disadvantage is that it tends to handicap the advertiser because he not only has to please himself, but also his customer. The result is a compromise of mediocre appeal.

Whilst it is, of course, apparent that every customer likes to have his name mentioned as frequently as possible, there is little justification for his wish being gratified at the expense of the advertiser. If, however, the latter is irrevocably committed, then a formula should be devised that will give the advertisement a reasonably high impact value. The best way to illustrate this is by means of an actual example. Let us take the case of the manufacturer of nickel-cadmium batteries who wants to feature in his advertising the most prominent industrial users. The temptation here would be to show power tools without dependence on electric outlets in use in aircraft factories, motor car and engineering works, etc. Instead of illustrating the advertisement with photographs of factory interiors in the accepted and ordinary way, it would be preferable to adopt some kind of novel approach, for example, the illustration could consist of a line drawing of an overhead power line stretching over the countryside with the following heading superimposed:

NO POWER LINES NEEDED FOR THESE ELECTRIC TOOLS

Copy:
In aircraft factories, motor works and engineering establishments the tendency today is to dispense with dangerous and unsightly cables feeding current to power tools, and instead, to use nickel cadmium batteries. These revolutionary batteries provide a compact source of power without dependence on outside sources. World famous manufacturing companies are already making use of these batteries and so are independent of the vagaries of national electricity supplies.

CHECKING THE COPY

It is the responsibility of the advertising agency to check the advertisement for literals and presentation, but not for technical accuracy of the copy. The client is expected to ensure that all the claims made in the advertisement are true, relevant and suitable. Every reputable agency will, of course, query with the client any statement which it considers to be suspect. It sometimes happens, particularly in consumer advertising, that the agency initiates the copy and treatment and persuades the client to agree to a particular course of action. In spite of this, however, the ultimate responsibility for the claims made in the advertisement as relating to a specific product rests with the client.

In industrial advertising the three most important points to look for when checking are:

(1) Technical accuracy of copy.
(2) Correctness of captions and acknowledgements.
(3) Permission to reproduce testimonials or case histories supplied by customers.

Dealing with the first point, it is advisable for all technical queries to be referred back to the relevant authorities in the company; these may be engineers, chemists, technologists, etc., depending upon the type of copy. Whoever checks the copy must be the most appropriate authority and hold a position of responsibility in the company. He should be required to initial the advertisement pull. Abbreviations are quite frequently a source of trouble. Unless they are correct they can, of course, make nonsense of an advertisement. Technical words, particularly chemical terms, also present difficulties to the uninitiated, e.g. in an advertisement for a chemical balance the copy could read as follows: '... periodic chemical and micro-balances ...' instead of 'a periodic ...' On the face of it, the loss of an initial 'a' might not be immediately apparent, and yet its loss would render negative this particular advertisement. Its publication would cast some doubt on the technical ability and reputation of the company responsible for its appearance.

The reader of a technical advertisement expects the information that is contained in it to be accurate. If, for instance, he reads that the injection pressure of a certain type of injection moulding machine is 795 Kg/cm², he automatically compares its price and characteristics with other similar machines on the market. The fact that the pressure stated was incorrect and should have been 995 means that the advertisement did the advertiser positive harm and was, in fact, a bad commercial investment.

In the author's experience, more trouble arises from inaccurate or incomplete captions and acknowledgements than anything else. Customers whose names or products are mentioned in an industrial advertisement are extremely sensitive about the accuracy of all the references which are made. All such references should be referred back to them for checking and initialling.

Where testimonials or case histories are to be published then permission must, of course, be obtained from the companies in question. In law, the copyright of a letter belongs to the writer and not to the recipient, and the mere sending of a letter does not in any way imply that permission is given to publish it. This must be sought from the writer before publication. What may be referred to as the mechanical side of advertising, that is the actual production of the advertisement and its publication in the right kind of journal at the right time, is the responsibility of the agency. If, for instance, an advertisement appears in the wrong journal, or is printed twice in the same journal, then the agency will be expected to make restitution by paying for the right insertion or the extra unwanted page.

11

ADVERTISING IN OVERSEAS TERRITORIES

IT IS all too evident that British manufacturers approach the subject of marketing in overseas territories from the viewpoint of selling their goods to foreigners. This attitude of mind is reflected in so many advertisements now appearing in overseas journals which are prepared in the United Kingdom without any local knowledge. Among many British business men there is a strong feeling that advertising abroad is a necessary evil that has to be done in order to support the local sales effort, whereas it should be looked upon as an investment, often long term, which is likely to widen the scope of the market.

Not only is our foreign advertising inadequate, but it is not spread evenly over the export field; a comparatively few firms being responsible for a very high percentage of the overall publicity. This is not surprising as the bulk of Britain's export trade is in the hands of a relatively small number of companies. In 1958 some 30 per cent of our exports of manufactured goods was the responsibility of only 40 firms.

THE ADVERTISING MESSAGE – DIFFERENT MARKETS – DIFFERENT ADVERTISING MESSAGES

The vital need to increase our exports to the E.E.C. countries and the fact that many British firms have opened up manufacturing plants in Europe, are factors which are now influencing a change of heart in overseas publicity. It is at last being realized that British salesmen cannot expect to match German, Italian and French salesmen in their own domestic markets unless they are given adequate publicity support – advertising – literature – exhibitions – and films, all in the language of the country. Makeshift publicity can no longer be tolerated unless the present low percentage of sales is going to be allowed to drop even further.

In most of the European countries the total advertising expenditure is not as high as it is in the United Kingdom. Annual *per capita* expenditure figures are as follows:*

Switzerland	£10·2
Great Britain	8·4
Sweden	7·9
West Germany	4·2
France	3·0
Belgium	3·0
Italy	1·2

It will, therefore, be appreciated that with the exception of Switzerland the readers of daily and weekly papers, consumer magazines and trade and technical journals are not yet under the same advertising pressure as they are in this country. It is true to say that in general any technical journal published outside the U.S.A. has a much more enthusiastic readership than is commonly found in Great Britain. Trade and technical publications issued abroad are all very well read and so also are the British journals that circulate in overseas territories.

In the under-developed countries the European pattern is not, of course, relevant and an entirely different approach has to be made to solve the problem of communication. There are no real technical journals in these countries and little use is made of the general Press for industrial advertising. In the Communist countries, particularly the U.S.S.R., there are hundreds of trade journals published, but comparatively few carry any advertising. Although it is pointed out quite rightly that the Russians are voracious readers and that every engineer, factory manager, co-operative store buyer, etc., reads his appropriate trade journal, it is doubtful if any of these people have very much influence on buying decisions made by one or other of the Central Buying

*International Advertising Expenditures prepared by the I.A.A.

Organizations. However, as a long term investment it is probably a good thing to advertise in carefully selected trade and technical media if only as an indication of sympathetic support.

Before reaching any conclusion about the value of advertising in any foreign publication, it is advisable to consider the recommendations not only of the United Kingdom agency representing the potential advertiser, but also those made by his representatives in the territory. If these recommendations differ widely from those put forward by the agency, and this may happen, then somehow these conflicting views have to be reconciled. Although it might be argued that the men actually on the spot know more about media than an agency in London, this is not always so as representatives abroad are more concerned with selling goods than buying media. Their knowledge about media is usually superficial and fragmentary and they are mainly guided in their judgement by the course taken by their competitors in the field.

It is rare, indeed, that an advertisement which is acceptable to a United Kingdom Industrial audience is suitable for a foreign one. The message itself may be unexceptional, but its presentation might give it an odd look alongside advertisements prepared specifically for a foreign paper. This is why it is so important to study each territory in terms of media and to become familiar with the way in which overseas companies in a similar line of business are 'putting across' their sales stories. It might be argued that this kind of research is really the responsibility of the agency and, indeed, any reputable United Kingdom agency would normally be expected to advise the advertiser on the selection of media. However, the advertiser himself should also do some homework and try to understand about the media where his advertisements could appear. The knowledge he gains by doing this will help him in several ways. It will act as a check on agency results and enable him to talk intelligently to account executives on overseas schedules, and also help him to gauge the intelligence and business acumen of his overseas representatives. More important still, an understanding and appreciation of overseas advertising as applied specifically to the advertiser's own business, will facilitate the promotion of creative ideas that are orientated to the territory.

Advertising abroad is somewhat hazardous as, unless it is well directed, it can be wasteful in both time and money. Prefacing every campaign there should be a period of study to find out the kind of advertisement most suited to the particular trade and territory. This is essential.

UNITED KINGDOM OR FOREIGN AGENCY

It is a fact that apart from the United States of America, there is no country in the world that is so well equipped with advertising agents as Great Britain. A growing number of these organizations operate on a global basis and either have wholly owned companies operating in overseas territories, or work through associate agencies abroad. These international agencies have already established themselves with new agencies in the major markets or have come to working arrangements with established advertising agencies in these territories. It would seem that these hybrid agencies are able to offer the best kind of service because they are not only able to utilize the expertise and services of the home agency, but have the benefit of local knowledge which only the 'man-on-the-spot' can hope to acquire. By operating through such an agency the British manufacturer can secure these very worthwhile advantages:

(1) He will be able to advertise in overseas markets with the minimum of staff, it being unnecessary to recruit extra personnel to deal with all the administrative work in connection with the dispatching of material abroad, collection of voucher copies, checking of vouchers and accounts, etc. All this will be done by his own agency in the United Kingdom.

(2) The advertiser will be able to pay for overseas advertising in sterling, the foreign papers being merely added to his existing schedule. He is thereby saved the trouble of working out foreign currencies and arranging payment.

(3) Centralization of advertising control in the United Kingdom through executives he knows helps the advertiser in conducting his business quickly and efficiently. It also saves him

money which might be spent in making foreign trips to discuss policy with overseas agencies.

(4) The United Kingdom agency understands his client, his product and his marketing policy, but the local agency knows its market and its media. The best advertising approach might well result from close co-operation between the local agency and the United Kingdom agency with the client providing the essential background to the whole policy.

(5) A first-class international agency is not only able to handle overseas advertising for the client, but can provide market research facilities which may prove invaluable if the advertiser has not first-hand knowledge of the country. On general distribution problems and sales organization the agency is often well qualified to assist.

These benefits, which the home manufacturer can secure by using international agencies with competent organizations in the main overseas markets are considerable and there is no doubt that this is the pattern of advertising for the future. There are, however, still a large number of agencies operating in the United Kingdom who are not properly organized to give a first-class service overseas. They may claim to be able to do so, but careful inquiry usually reveals that in fact they are merely sub-contracting the work out to foreign agencies, some of very doubtful ability. This arrangement is unsatisfactory and, indeed, it would even pay the British advertiser to deal directly with a foreign agency himself. Advantages can only be claimed if the United Kingdom agency is properly organized, either through overseas companies, branch offices, subsidiaries or associate agencies to have complete control over the account in all its phases.

REASON FOR ADVERTISING

This has to be well thought out and the objectives clearly defined before any campaign is planned. The agency will want to know if the manufacturer is intending to enter the market, or to step up the existing market. A desire to do overseas advertising merely to promote sales is a completely inadequate brief and a great deal needs to be known about general marketing plans before a suitable scheme can be evolved. Consultation with the overseas agents or selling company is a necessary preface to any advertising and it is as well to involve the agency in any discussions.

COST

Generally speaking overseas advertising is more expensive than comparable advertising carried out in the United Kingdom, as apart from the higher space rates which may be charged by some overseas publications, the United Kingdom agency requires a higher commission to handle the account. It is a comforting thought, however, that some of the larger international agencies are prepared to work on quite small appropriations and there usually is no minimum sum involved as there often is with United Kingdom accounts.

The commission charged by the international agency varies according to whether the advertisement is prepared wholly in the United Kingdom, or by one of their subsidiary companies in the particular overseas territory. This commission tends to vary from $17\frac{1}{2}$ per cent to 20 per cent on gross media billing but these figures are only relevant in 1962 and are merely given as a general guide.

In fairness to the agency, it has to be pointed out that working in some overseas territories presents many problems, as space rates are often uncertain, commission tends to be a matter of negotiation and taxes are levied on many transactions. In Italy, for instance, television contractors do not grant commissions, radio gives 2 per cent, posters and cinemas give 5 per cent, most newspapers from 3 to 5 per cent and even top magazines and periodicals from 5 to 10 per cent. (Recently it has been reported that certain press media give as much as 15 per cent.) Rates generally are very unstable and commissions, when they are paid, are available to almost anyone who buys space.

121

CHOOSING THE MEDIA

Broadly speaking, there are two kinds of journals open to the British advertiser wishing to promote the sales of his goods or services overseas. There are journals published in this country for circulation overseas, and there are the great bulk of publications produced in the country of origin. Dealing briefly with the home produced articles, these are highly specialized British magazines, printed entirely in the foreign language or available in foreign editions, such as *Industria Britanica* in Portuguese and Spanish editions and *British Industry and Engineering* produced specifically for Russia. There are also a number of journals and highly specialized magazines which do a valuable selling job abroad, such as *International Construction* and *New Commonwealth*, *Machinery*, *Electrical Industries – Export*, *The Ambassador* and, of course, *The Board of Trade Journal*. Admirable as they are in their way, there is no real substitute for the home produced journal and the British advertiser planning to make any worthwhile impact overseas must support the media in the territory where sales are expected to take place.

On the choice of media in specific markets the advertiser must, of course, be guided by his representatives on the spot and the advertising agency handling the account. Although there are British accredited representatives for most worthwhile foreign publications, the majority of these are usually unable to provide the potential advertiser with anything more than basic rates. There is, however, an exception with the established American journals whose representatives are always eager to supply the British manufacturer with a mass of data on circulation, readership and markets. In choice of media it is stressed that a good United Kingdom agency is in a better position than anyone else to present an independent and reliable recommendation as to media in any territory in the world.

It is a fact that in Europe, which is the market of primary importance to the British advertiser, the trade and technical Press is much more selective than in the United Kingdom. Instead of four of five journals covering one field in any given territory, say,

Germany or France, there are probably only one or two. This, of course, is an advantage in one way as it makes the task of drawing up an advertising schedule somewhat easier. On the other hand, it gives the advertiser less room for manoeuvre than he would normally hope to have in the United Kingdom.

In the Communist countries reliable information about publication dates is still rather difficult to obtain. At one time it was a matter of luck whether an advertisement which was scheduled to appear in, say, one of the Russian chemical publications, would actually be published within three to four months of the date promised. New arrangements with United Kingdom publishers have resulted in a marked improvement. It should, of course, be realized that relatively few Russian journals carry any advertising, although this can often be arranged as the result of negotiation with the appropriate Soviet government department.

In the Far East the potential is immense, a market of 1,200,000,000 people, but living standards are very low and trading conditions in some countries, notably China, are extremely difficult. Apart from Japan, which is, of course, highly industrialized, most of the Eastern countries issue only a few journals suitable for carrying general advertisements, and most of these publications are newspapers with fairly small circulations, e.g. in Burma, which has a population of 19,300,000, the highest circulation for any newspaper is 25,000 for *Kyemon* (The Mirror), whilst in Ceylon, population 8,050,000, the *Ceylon Trade Journal* has a circulation of 900. In China, with its immense population of 650,000,000, the *People's Daily*, which is the most successful newspaper published and one that enjoys full Government support, can only reach 800,000. If one takes into consideration the very high percentage of illiteracy, these low circulation figures are not perhaps, surprising, but the fact remains that all the publications produced in the Far East have a very limited circulation and readership. It is extremely doubtful whether industrial or specialized advertising is of any value in these media, although the local representative, who may be a general factor or merchant handling hundreds of products, might benefit from a modest campaign.

In addition to the papers produced locally there are, of course, several reputable and independent journals which are printed in English and published in the United Kingdom and enjoy limited circulation in English-speaking business circles in the East.

Buying space in overseas publications is a highly specialized business and it should be left to the experts in the field who have the benefit of local knowledge. There is, of course, nothing easier than to buy space in the numerous overseas journals which have offices in Fleet Street, but to do so indiscriminately is to waste money.

ADVERTISEMENTS ALONE ARE INSUFFICIENT – SUPPORTING PROMOTIONAL MATTER ESSENTIAL

Advertising in overseas publications, although useful in its way, is ineffective unless it is supported and followed up with other promotional material, such as literature and direct mail. In every trade advertisement published in a foreign paper, there should be an open invitation to readers to write to the agent or overseas company for appropriate trade literature. This must be printed in the language of the country where the advertising is carried out, and be available in quantity. It is too often assumed that English literature is adequate as a follow-up, but this is faulty thinking. In spite of the fact that a large number of people do speak English abroad, the actual percentage is still very small. In Germany, for instance, only 8 per cent of the population are conversant with our tongue.

In addition to the availability of trade literature printed in the appropriate language, there is also a need to carry out mailing campaigns using, of course, specially prepared leaflets. Indeed, the whole success of the advertising campaign depends upon its close integration with other complementary methods of sales promotion. Timing is also of great importance; the mailing shot should go out at the same time as the advertising is appearing.

In some parts of the East and undeveloped countries where the Press does not offer any worthwhile opportunity for communication, other means have to be found, such as cinema advertising using slides, or even loud speaker vans which, in effect, broadcast commercials in the shopping and business areas of large towns and rural areas. Blotters carrying advertisements, diaries and calendars, are useful as vehicles for carrying the advertising message. In the Caribbean territories, commercial radio is often utilized as a means of advertising and for certain types of goods, it can be quite an effective form of publicity.

SOME SNAGS IN CARRYING OUT OVERSEAS ADVERTISING

In framing advertisements to appear in overseas journals it is important to consider very carefully what claims can be made without the possibility of serious repercussions. As mentioned previously, in Germany, for instance, the superlative can mask an insidious reference to certain competitors. Whether this is in fact the case depends on the individual advertisement, but it is not necessary to refer to or name the actual competitor. The superlative wording may have a comparative effect, for instance, in the use of such a claim as 'Gadsburg's silica bricks are the best'. This is regarded in German Common Law as a comparative statement, since a certain competitor, who is un-named is obviously meant. The British advertiser who was so foolish as to make such a claim, might find himself involved in a costly law suit in which he might find great difficulty in substantiating his claim to the satisfaction of a German court! There are, however, other territories where the most outrageous claims can be made with impunity. It is all a question of knowing the media and the territory involved.

12

PUBLIC RELATIONS

It is as well to start off this chapter with a clear definition of public relations as so much confusion exists about the true functions of a public relations officer. As the author sees it, public relations can best be described as the effect produced by the sum total of an organization's contacts with every section of the public, whether external or internal. It is also the outward manifestation of its administrative philosophy. In other words, the function of a public relations officer is to create a healthy climate for his company so that all its operations will derive some benefit from it. The shareholders who own the firm, the customers who buy from it and the employees who work for it, all of them are highly susceptible to the conditions of this climate.

Although public relations has nothing to do with actual selling, its functions can certainly affect the reception given to the company's salesmen by customers and potential customers. If good-will towards the company has been created by inspired public relations work, then this will certainly help the representative in his initial contacts and facilitate friendly discussions. Public relations will never sell goods, but it can create the right atmosphere for selling. All the public relations officer's efforts are directed towards the reflection of the 'Company Image', but the creation of that image is the responsibility of the directors who are in actual control of the company and who formulate its policy. In other words, public relations is made or marred in the Board Room. It is impossible to obtain public recognition and respect for the company if it is being run inefficiently or is at loggerheads with its employees.

To be successful in creating the right atmosphere the public relations officer must have full confidence in the company he is representing.

It is unfortunate, but true, that today the whole business of public relations is regarded with suspicion, if not open hostility, by certain sections of the Press and general public. This is a great pity because public relations activities can make a valuable contribution to modern industry by establishing a two-way channel of information between the top management of a company and those on whom it depends for its sales, supplies, labour and capital. Unless the channel is kept open and working smoothly, there must arise misunderstandings which could have a serious effect on the firm's trading position. Shareholders can quickly lose confidence in a company if they are not kept informed about major re-shuffles and merger negotiations. Similarly, labour can become extremely restive unless rumours about shut-downs, loss of orders, automation and take-over bids are dealt with quickly and truthfully. The public relations officer in modern industry is probably criticized more for his attempts to control, filter or censor industrial or other news than for his attempts to use the editorial columns of a newspaper or magazine for the publication of a sales promotion story that by rights should be paid for at advertising rates. It should, however, be realized that although the Press is somewhat critical of the function of the public relations officer, editors have come to accept him as a necessary link in the chain of industrial communications. The best practitioners are treated with respect and the public relations office in the really large companies is regarded as a most reliable source of information about the firm's activities. It is fair to say that public relations, as a profession, is now recognized and accepted; it has its own Institute of Public Relations and its own accepted code of practice. The uneasiness which persists relates to the methods of some public relations officers, particularly those independent ones who undertake public relations activities for an organization on a fee basis.

It is not always fully appreciated that the public relations officer is not only concerned with press matters, although these are a vital part of his duties, but with communications in the widest sense of the word. Through the medium of the Press, radio and television, films and printed literature, visits to factories and laboratories and conventions or symposiums, etc., the public relations officer can present the company's case to the world.

OBJECTIVES FOR PUBLIC RELATIONS WORK

If public relations is to be really effective it needs to have certain clearly defined objectives, in other words, there must be a public relations policy formulated and agreed by top management. No useful purpose is served by the Board suddenly deciding that it must have some public relations work done without having a very clear idea of what the directors are seeking to do, or if in fact, it is public relations that they are looking for and not merely editorial publicity or advertising. If public relations is, in fact, a function of top management, then management has the responsibility of determining how it is to develop this profitably.

It has been contended by more than one authority that it is only in the giant corporations and national organizations that a public relations job is waiting to be done, and that in the majority of the large, medium and small concerns, the company, if it works efficiently, produces a good product, sells it at a fair price and enjoys reasonable labour relations, does not need any public relations. The corporate image of the organization has already been created by the company's own trading record and reputation. This argument goes rather too far and the author believes that in many companies the public relations officer can contribute substantially towards a better relationship between the company and the public and the company and its employees. To be effective, however, the public relations officer must have an objective; a plan of campaign. For example, in a company concerned with the manufacture of automation equipment, a worthwhile objective would be to try and dispel the notion that everything worthwhile in automation comes from America.

To a public relations officer equipped with a real story of his own company's outstanding achievements in this field, such an objective might present relatively few difficulties. On the other hand, if he were expected to cover up for his company's technical deficiencies and lack of inventive genius, then all his efforts would be unavailing; the public relations campaign would be a failure. Truth is far more dangerous an ingredient of public relations than advertising!

WHAT PART DOES ADVERTISING PLAY IN PUBLIC RELATIONS?

Although the public relations officer likes to think that his work, so far as the Press is concerned, is alien to advertising, this is not so. In a number of large concerns, and particularly the giant corporations and nationalized industries, so-called institutional advertising has come to be regarded as one of the main planks of public relations. Here the advertising has no obvious commercial objective but is designed to secure public recognition and respect for the company's name or trade mark. Such advertising, which is very expensive, depending as it does on the use of massive spaces in the national Press, is often the forerunner of fairly heavy product advertising.

This type of advertising does a great deal more than build up confidence in the organization; it helps to achieve good relations with shareholders and the financial world generally, impresses potential customers and perhaps dismays competitors and also assists in displacing any element of distrust which may exist in the minds of employees. The planning of institutional advertising is the responsibility of the public relations officer. Here he is using paid advertising space to tell what is really an editorial story. This may attempt to set out the outstanding achievements of the company; its excellent relationship with employees or its high reputation and standing in the world. Excellent opportunities are provided for prestige or institutional advertising by a discovery which offers great benefits to humanity, for example, a new type of insecticide which makes possible the cultivation of vast areas of the world that would otherwise be unproductive. This is the type of material that forms the basis of a good prestige advertisement that is calculated to win public approval and enhance the reputation of the company, both externally and internally. The latter can be of far reaching importance.

ORGANIZING A PUBLIC RELATIONS SECTION

In a large industrial company with a publicity budget approaching £500,000, the public relations section of the publicity department could consist of five people – the public relations officer himself, his press officer, an assistant and two typists. This would make a well balanced unit. In many commercial concerns with smaller budgets, the public relations officer and the press officer are usually one and the same, but this is not an ideal arrangement as the public relations officer becomes so immersed in press work that all other aspects of public relations go by default. It is, of course, agreed that the Press is one of the most important vehicles for public relations activities but, nevertheless, it should not develop to the exclusion of other fields of public relations work.

There is something to be said for the recommendation that the public relations officer himself need not have any publicity experience, and that a journalistic or advertising background may be more of a liability than an asset. What is needed, it is claimed by some authorities on the subject, is that the public relations officer should be a senior executive of the company with great experience in all branches of management and with an understanding and appreciation of the need for opening up the lines of communication. Provided the public relations officer has available the various skills there is, of course, no real necessity for him to be either a journalist or an advertising man, but it certainly does help if he has the ability to put his creative thoughts on paper in a convincing manner!

CHANNELS OF COMMUNICATION

First and foremost, the public relations officer must be able to make immediate contact with his 'boss' and share his confidence. Unless this is ensured, then the whole public relations venture is undermined. There is little purpose in setting up a public relations organization, no matter whether this is inside the company or outside, unless efficient channels of communication have been set up between the public relations officer and the commercial and technical departments, so that a steady flow of information is assured. It is a sad fact that in some large concerns the public relations sections are not only starved of information, but insidious efforts are sometimes made to prevent them from gaining access to 'stories'. This is largely due to distrust and suspicion on the part of the technical departments.

It pays handsome dividends all round if executives in all branches of the company are encouraged to become public relations minded and to discuss with the press officer or public relations officer, whatever he is called, how best to publicize some new development. Top management must not only set up channels of communication between the public relations officer and the commercial or technical departments, but see that these are clear and able to function properly. The public relations officer himself can help a great deal by becoming thoroughly immersed in the technicalities of the business, so that he knows intimately the products, the policy and the personnel. Even if he cannot discuss the company's business with all the authority of a technical director, he should be able to talk about it with sufficient knowledge to inspire confidence.

PRESS LIAISON

The public relations officer in industry needs to maintain the closest possible liaison with all sections of the Press – newspapers, magazines and trade and technical journals. He should belong to the right clubs and take every opportunity of meeting those editors and writers who specialize in news about his particular industry – for example, the editors of the trade papers, city editors and correspondents who feed the city columns of the dailies and the science and industrial correspondents. These are the people whom he should know on Christian-name terms and be accepted by them as a source of sound information.

Under the general heading of press liaison comes press conferences, general Press releases, exclusive stories to selected newspapers, magazines and trade or technical journals, and facility visits to factories, laboratories and offices. In all this work he is dependent on his own management for information, most of which is required promptly to meet actual deadlines.

Now that Europe is becoming almost part of the home sales territory, the public relations officer is finding it essential to possess a good working knowledge of the foreign Press, including the technical Press overseas. It is significant that in Scandinavia particularly, the specialized publications, including the trade and technical Press, are assuming increasing importance. There are, for instance, 400 journals published in Sweden alone and these have a total advertising turnover of about £5,000,000 a year. Germany is another country which has a most comprehensive technical Press. There are, for instance, eighteen quite important chemical publications appearing in Western Germany.

PUBLIC RELATIONS ORGANIZATION – INSIDE AND OUTSIDE THE COMPANY

There are valid arguments put forward in favour of both types of organization. On balance, however, it would appear that the public relations organization inside the company is of greater value than one outside. The reasons for making this assertion can be summarized as follows:

(1) He is part of a team and should have a more intimate knowledge both of the organization and the products or services being sold.

(2) His activities are more closely integrated with the policy-making sections of the organization and as a result his reputation is somewhat higher in Fleet Street.

(3) He is less likely to run out of information than a public relations officer who is working with an independent organization, as he has readily available all the commercial and technical resources of the company.

Against these advantages, marginal or otherwise, must be weighed the fact that the independent public relations officer, particularly if he handles a number of accounts, may profit from the wide experience gained and in dealing with several companies rather than just one, have available more channels of communication.

A well-planned and well-conducted press conference will set out to do three things – to provide a news story in a form known to be acceptable to the types of publications invited to the function; to give members of the Press the opportunity to ask questions and to supplement the information provided in the hand-out by a top level talk. Journalists are sometimes suspicious of films shown at Press conferences as a means of providing information. Even the best of these are impersonal and present a biased picture of any new development. Newspapermen generally prefer to be told the facts by the boss of the firm, and most important of all, to be afforded the opportunity of a private and informed talk with him or his lieutenants so that they can present the news in a non-stereotyped form.

A press conference needs to be strategically sited and the date and time chosen in relation to publication dates and the weight and importance of competing news. It is, for example, no use trying to obtain good coverage for an industrial news story in the middle of a common market conference, a moon rocket probe, a major earthquake or change of sex by noted woman athlete. Whilst London is, perhaps, the ideal location for many press conferences, particularly those dealing with finance and commerce, specialized subjects are best dealt with in specialized localities. A major development in cotton would, for instance, best be handled in Manchester; shipping in Liverpool; farming in Norfolk and canning in Lincolnshire. The Press would naturally expect these venues to be chosen, and rather put-out if the pattern were not followed. As regards time, the most suitable is between 11–12 noon. This allows for some coverage in the evening papers, if the story is topical, and also gives the daily papers sufficient time to treat the subject matter adequately. Time is rarely so critical to the trade and technical Press.

In planning the Press conference, it is important to compile a fairly exhaustive list of journals likely to be interested and then to send personal invitations to the editors and industrial correspondents, together with a very brief (single paragraph) synopsis of what it is all about. It always creates a good impression with the Press if invitations are made out to individuals and not just to *The Editor* or *The Industrial Correspondent*. A good public relations officer will know instinctively who are the right people to invite to any Press function. As regards the timing of the invitations, this is always a somewhat tricky matter. If sent out too long in advance the date may be forgotten but, on the other hand, if insufficient notice is given, then it may well be crowded out of the busy editor's diary. About two weeks is just about the right kind of notice, and it is a wise move to follow up the actual invitation by ringing the individuals 48 hours before the conference, just to find out for certain who is coming along. A conference that is attended by only a handful of people is a very bad advertisement for the public relations officer and a great disappointment to the company financing and running the event. Far better to have people crowding in the aisles than an empty church!

Turning to the actual event itself – the hall or room where the conference is being arranged should be well sign-posted. There should be a reception table with an intelligent (but not necessarily pretty, although this sometimes helps) girl in attendance, and every visitor asked to sign his name and give the name of the paper he represents in the visitors' book. The object of this is to check up on the attendance and to send round copies of the release to those papers and journals that were not represented. A copy of the press hand-out should be given to every journalist on his arrival and, where relevant, his attention drawn to the photographs made available. These should be whole plate glossy prints accurately captioned. Refreshments are always provided, but it is advisable not to give too much emphasis to the hospitality side of the function. The chief consideration is always the story.

Whoever is to speak on behalf of the company should be well briefed and, in his address, give all the salient facts as concisely as possible. He should not talk for longer than 20 minutes and be prepared to answer questions for another 10 minutes.

The public relations officer must arrange for journalists to enjoy a few minutes private conversation with either the chairman or managing director in order to secure their own exclusive quote, this is most important. Editors dislike and will not readily publish a prefabricated story when they know that all their rivals in the business have been handed out the same material. It is always a good practice for company executives present at a press conference to wear distinguishing badges in their button-holes so that journalists know whom to approach for information. And, of course, there must be sufficient high calibre company representatives present to be able to deal adequately, not only with all types of queries, but also to discuss with authority and knowledge the wider implications of the company's business.

When preparing the actual Press release it is important to ensure that all the facts are presented in a logical and straightforward manner without padding and with the minimum of technical jargon. The vital piece of information should be included in the first one or two sentences. The Press does not require a preamble or explanatory paragraph – the qualification can come later, but first of all the news. It may be that two versions of a release are needed – a simple summary of the story for those papers, such as the dailies and weeklies who merely want to publish the bald facts, and a full account for the technical or trade papers. If the story has any news value at all it will be reported, and if it has not, then it will not create even a ripple on the journalistic waters. It is useful at this stage to give typical examples of a well prepared Press release issued by I.C.I. for general release.

FIRST I.C.I. SEVERNSIDE PLANTS IN PRODUCTION
New Chemical Complex in South-West

The first plants to be completed on I.C.I.'s new Severnside site, near Bristol, have come into full production. They will make 35,000 tons per year of ethylene oxide, ethylene glycol and associated products.

Ethylene oxide is used in the manufacture of ethylene glycol and detergents. Ethylene glycol is best known as the basis for motor anti-freeze, and it is also one of the two raw materials for the manufacture of 'Terylene'.

Plans for these plants – which comprise the Ableton Works of I.C.I.'s Heavy Organic Chemicals Division – were announced in

February 1960. It was then stated that about £5 million would be spent on initial site development at Severnside and on the construction of the first plants. Later in 1960 I.C.I.'s Billingham Division announced its intention to spend upwards of £10 million at Severnside on an ammonia plant with a capacity of 100,000 tons a year, together with plants to make fertilizers. Construction of these is well advanced and they will come into operation during 1963.

On 19 July, 1962, the Billingham Division announced that it was to build a plant to produce liquid carbon dioxide at Severnside. This will also be completed during 1963. Liquid carbon dioxide is used in atomic energy installations as a heat-transfer medium, in foundries and in the chemical, brewing and soft drink industries.

78-mile pipeline

The raw material for the ethylene oxide and ethylene glycol plants – ethylene – is supplied through a 78-mile pipeline from the Fawley oil refinery of the Esso Petroleum Company Ltd. Ethylene is converted into ethylene oxide by a process of the Scientific Design Company Inc. Some of the ethylene oxide is then converted into ethylene glycol, in an I.C.I.-designed plant, which yields diethylene glycol and triethylene glycol as useful co-products.

A fleet of special road tankers has been constructed to transport ethylene oxide from Severnside to the Wilton Works in Yorkshire, where I.C.I. makes the detergent 'Lissapol', and to convey it to other U.K. customers.

The glycol to be used for 'Terylene' production will be moved from Severnside to Wilton by rail; a number of rail tank wagons specially constructed to an I.C.I. design have been provided by British Railways (Western Region) exclusively for this traffic.

PHOTOGRAPHY AS AN AID TO PUBLIC RELATIONS

There is always an unsatisfied demand for good news-worthy photographs, and the Press is often willing to publish a picture where it might be reluctant to give space to a paragraph. With this thought in mind, the public relations officer working in industry makes good use of the camera, both for industrial pictures

and what might be termed 'application pictures'. People throughout the world are curious about 'how things are made' and this
applies equally well to the chemical engineer as to the greengrocer
round the corner. Good, clear and sharp press pictures, with a full
explanatory caption, can create just the right impression in a
whole host of journals, ranging from *The Financial Times*, which
is very factory conscious, to the *Muck Shifter*, which is always
eager to publish good photographs of new earth-moving equipment. Some industrial public relations departments feed the Press
with a regular stream of pictures, each one designed to appeal to
a specific journal. This is a sure way of keeping the name of the
company or the product in the public eye. There is always more
chance of securing publication for a picture than an article, particularly where the article has an advertising bias.

A 'picture service' should form a vital part of all public relations
activities. Such a service should include photographs of prominent
personalities in the industry. Many trade and technical journals,
as well as the financial or city papers, now welcome pictures of
executives, particularly if they are well captioned. Promotions
and high-level changes in the staff of large industrial concerns are
all acceptable and can be labelled as good public relations material.
Although directors and members of the staff at managerial level
may initially show some modest reluctance to this type of personal publicity, they can usually be persuaded to agree. The public
relations officer will be well advised never to accept a 'No' as a
final answer – there are very few people, including chairmen and
managing directors, who are adverse to a little personal publicity
in the right papers. The public relations man will always be at a
great disadvantage if he treats staff unfairly in the matter of publicity or fails to persuade top management of the vital necessity of
'personal publicity'.

FILMS

The 'editorial' use of films is an aspect of public relations work
which is sometimes lost sight of by publicity departments, but it
can often be exploited to good purpose. Good industrial films
make excellent copy and their showing offers a further occasion

for members of the Press to meet company representatives. It sometimes happens that technical films, or sections of them, can be given a wider audience through the medium of television or the public cinema. Both the British Broadcasting Corporation and the Independent television companies occasionally use industrial film material if it is of general interest, or if the subject matter is highly dramatic or original in conception. Some producers of magazine material for the public cinema also make use of privately sponsored films, particularly if these are taken on 35 mm. stock, and it is always a wise plan to invite such people along to a showing.

PARLIAMENTARY CONTACTS

Although the public relations officer engaged in industry does not usually have regular contact with Members of Parliament, it is sometimes necessary to take into account the question of liaison with them when issues of national importance are involved. In any contact with Members of Parliament it is, of course, essential that they are not given the impression of being 'lobbied'. On the other hand, Members who are connected in some way with specific industries do welcome the opportunity of visiting new plants and of being told about new developments before they form the subject of headlines in the national daily Press. By keeping Members well informed, it is sometimes possible to create a favourable atmosphere in the House when questions are asked or industrial issues raised in debate. Sometimes even 'dry as dust' matters, such as atmospheric pollution in a particular industry, or some special industrial hazard, may trigger-off a great deal of misinformed and damaging comment in Parliament and it is, therefore, a wise precaution to provide full information to those Members specially interested as soon as all the facts are available.

ASSESSING THE COMMERCIAL VALUE OF PUBLIC RELATIONS WORK

This is always extremely difficult, but the occasion frequently arises when some member of the Board or the executive questions the 'profitability' of public relations work and asks if this kind of activity is really necessary. Naturally when trade is booming such queries are unlikely to arise, but the inevitable fall in profits will certainly prompt misgivings in some commercial quarters about expenditure on public relations. To forestall criticism, or rather to answer criticism, necessitates some planning. In the writer's opinion there are three ways in which the work of the public relations officer can be brought to the attention of the management:

(1) A monthly report, giving details of the success achieved in gaining publicity for the company's products, personnel, policy and prestige.
(2) Circulation of photostats of the pick of the Press cuttings to the commercial managers and members of the Board.
(3) Arrangement, say two or three times a year, of facility visits to the factories by editors of trade and technical journals and the industrial correspondents of both home and foreign papers. This kind of occasion serves two purposes; it makes the management aware of the activities of the company's public relations officer and gives the sales and technical staff, as well as the directors, an opportunity of meeting the Press and gaining at first hand their views on the company's activities. In this way, the management is able to assess the value of its own public relations and to arrive at some opinion of the efficiency of its practitioners.

Occasional talks to staff and works committees and other local bodies within the company on the ramifications of public relations work and the policy governing contact with the Press, radio and television; this kind of internal publicity can do the public relations section a great deal of good as it encourages people within the company to become public relations conscious and tends to create the impression that public relations serves a commercially useful function and is a vital part of the selling effort. Far too many public relations officers work like beavers in making outside contacts and promoting useful publicity, but fail to 'sell' themselves to their own companies and are relatively unknown in the various commercial, technical and production departments. Many excellent stories are lost because they originate a long way down the line, in the factories, maintenance department or workstudy section, where no one has ever heard of public relations. New channels of communications must constantly be cut and kept open if new ideas are to be fed into the public relations section.

CONTACT WITH STOCKHOLDERS

In the United States, many of the really large companies make a practice of keeping in regular touch with stockholders and this is known to pay handsome dividends in the form of improved relationship and increased confidence in the management. The Cohen Committee of 1945, and recently the Jenkins Committee have insisted on a better flow of information between the managements and owners of public companies. It is a justifiable criticism of British industry that few public companies make any serious attempt to put their shareholders fully into the industrial picture, and a great opportunity is lost to the public relations officer to build up a sound company–stockholder relationship. There are many ways in which contact can be maintained with shareholders, apart from annual or half-yearly company reports. Popular editions of these are always welcomed by both employees and outside investors, and so also are printed brochures giving information about new technical developments or interesting commercial intelligence. There is also a great deal to be said for organizing visits of shareholders to the factories and laboratories so that they can see for themselves the kind of firm in which they have invested.

13

PUBLISHING AN EXTERNAL
COMPANY MAGAZINE

THE REAL purpose of an external magazine is to enhance the prestige of the company, to interest customers and potential customers, to create good-will and pre-dispose or condition the recipient in favour of the firm issuing the publication. In many instances a well produced house magazine is a very useful link between those who make and those who buy, particularly in the overseas territories where the opportunities for members of the company to meet customers, as distinct from agents, are somewhat rare. On the other hand, some excellent company magazines are devoid entirely of any propaganda and rely for their public relations effect on the high standing of the editorial contents. An excellent example of this is *Endeavour*, a scientific publication produced by I.C.I. In the field of international science this quarterly magazine receives the fullest marks. The only reference in it to I.C.I. is an acknowledgement of the fact that this company is responsible for publication.

TYPES OF MAGAZINES

Industrial company magazines fall into several categories, the most important being the following:

(1) Public relations or soft-selling magazines.
(2) Technical or technological.
(3) Sales promotion or hard selling publications.
(4) Dealer magazines.

The first is usually a highly sophisticated and glossy production with the commercial message cunningly disguised. It is designed to appeal to the executive type of reader and the contents vary widely from modern art to bird watching and alchemy to Strindberg. The hard core of the magazine which really justifies its publication may be a somewhat 'frothy' article on some aspect of the company's business.

Technical or technological magazines are assuming growing importance as media of public relations. The term technologist is used here to cover scientists, technologists, and others in higher technical grades, engaged on either research work or production supervision, or management. In the Common Market countries, and, of course, in the U.S.A., there are a number of excellent technical publications issued by the larger companies. The primary purpose of most of these magazines is to build up an image of the company as a forward looking and progressive manufacturer in any particular field, i.e. one equipped with first class research and technical service facilities and operating a modern plant on the most enlightened lines. With this type of publication it is common to find great emphasis placed on achievements in the field of technology as well as description of new plant and extended applications of the company's products or services by its customers. Capital is usually made of any humanitarian aspects of the company's business, such as might result from the wider application of the company's products or services in underdeveloped countries, but seldom does one find articles on thought promoting or perhaps disquieting subjects such as works study or 'ergonomics'! Occasionally, of course, one finds a technological magazine issued by a company to promote scientific knowledge, such as *Endeavour*, but this type of publication is somewhat of a rarity!

The sales promotion or hard selling publications are planned on down-to-earth commercial lines. They are, in fact, an extension of the company's sales literature and set out to attract attention and to stimulate interest by lively presentation and easy to read editorial contents. Within their panoramic remit their publishers are able to describe their products, services, etc., in an uninhibited manner, and to highlight any new developments. These magazines are also useful for internal publicity purposes and generally enjoy a considerable circulation inside the organization among the junior staff and works foremen. In these hands they do an excellent job of work by inspiring confidence in the aggressive sales policy of the firm.

Dealer magazines are more applicable to the consumer rather than the industrial field, but they may be indispensable to certain types of industrial concerns, such as manufacturers of agricultural machinery, woodworking machinery, power tools, etc., all of whom sell through dealers. With these publications the emphasis is on sales promotion and both presentation and editorial contents are designed to instil confidence in the manufacturer and his products. The articles are usually loaded with persuasive arguments likely to assist the dealer in effecting a sale.

PRESENTATION

This is a most important consideration. In general it can be said that soft-selling publications are always fairly lavish in their presentation, making generous use of colour, heavy art paper and advanced layouts. As the object of this particular type of magazine is to impress the reader, all the cunning devices of the young typographical designer are fully exploited so as to make quite certain that the publication creates the maximum impact. Public relations publications of this nature are highly sophisticated pieces of literature and cost a great deal of money to produce. On the other hand, technological magazines are modelled generally on the technical Press and are fairly sober publications. Unlike the average trade journals, however, where colour is generally restricted to the advertising sections, the technological magazines make fairly generous use of colour where it can be justified editorially. Hard selling publications and dealer magazines tend to have a typical advertising agency look about them. They are, of course, designed to attract and to impress and have a smart and often somewhat brittle look about them. Liberties are often taken with the typography of these magazines which can only be regretted.

It is apparent from these comments that presentation varies a great deal with every type of magazine and there is no readily prescribed formula for the successful publication in any one class. Everything depends upon the policy, the editorial contents and the readership.

READERSHIP

There is very often a big question mark set against circulation or readership, as it quite often happens that publications are produced without anyone in the organization having a very clear idea of their destination once they have been printed. With dealer magazines this difficulty does not arise, as the audience is ready made. Unhappily the solution is rather more elusive in the case of the other types of journals. For each type of publication there must be a well defined circulation, carefully and accurately planned and controlled. Once the publication has been launched, readership surveys should be carried out to determine who actually reads the magazine, their status in the company and their opinion of its contents. This kind of check can be of great value to the public relations section of the company as it will help to determine if the publication is worthwhile. Looking at the readership of the technological type of magazine, a breakdown might look something like this:

Customers	40 per cent
Leading industrial concerns	20 per cent
Universities	15 per cent
Technical colleges	15 per cent
Libraries	5 per cent
Scientific and Technical Press	4 per cent
Major Competitors	1 per cent

The customers would, of course, include overseas agents and Government bodies (particularly those in Communist countries).

With the public relations or soft selling publications it is much more difficult to define the audience. Logically the pattern of readership should show a wide circulation to potential customers as well as those already on the books and exclude Universities, Technical Colleges and competitors, etc., although copies should always be sent to the Trade Federation and the Press. An analysis might look something like the following:

Customers	45 per cent
Leading industrial concerns	45 per cent
Trade Federations, Institutes Embassies, etc.	5 per cent
The Press	5 per cent

The circulation of a public relations magazine would not be dissimilar to the hard selling or direct sales promotion publication where the entire emphasis would be placed on present and future customers. Sometimes it is advocated that company magazines be sent to shareholders, but this practice can create problems, particularly when the stockholders are unconvinced that the magazines are worthwhile and contribute anything towards the company's profits! On balance it is not recommended that shareholders should be on the circulation list. There is, however, a great deal to be said in favour of sending to shareholders an illustrated and popularized version of the company's annual report!

PRODUCTION

The editorial contents of a company magazine are usually written within the organization, although on occasion outside contributors may be called in to write special articles. If we take the magazine *Endeavour*, which is a highly specialized publication, almost 99 per cent of the contents are written by eminent scientific authorities outside I.C.I., the odd 1 per cent being the responsibility of the editorial staff. Layout is generally contracted out to an independent designer or studio, or this may be passed over to the advertising agency which is highly competent to deal with either soft-selling or hard-selling publications. Generally speaking, the author would advise against the public relations department being responsible for layout as a greater sense of freshness and originality is achieved by allowing this work to be done outside.

There exists with certain companies a mistaken impression that unless their magazine has a very lush appearance it has a low readership rating and small impact. This is nonsense. Indeed, the reverse could well be true. If a technological publication is too glossy, then it tends to look somewhat spurious and is liable to be regarded as a rather blatant piece of sales propaganda. Whilst not losing sight of the aesthetic side of the production, the real value of a company magazine lies in its contents, its appeal to the reader, the amount of information it conveys and the kind of company image it creates. The use of heavy art paper, lavish spread of colour and a pretentious layout, all tend to undermine confidence and defeat the object. The writer is of the opinion that colour should be used discreetly and only when it serves a useful purpose, i.e. if the subject matter is concerned with colour from a technical angle. This view is diametrically opposed to that held by many managements who look upon colour as an essential ingredient of every prestige publication, a kind of status symbol! If the competition in the form of rival house magazines issued by other companies at home and abroad makes extensive use of colour, then considerable pressure is often exerted by the commercial departments to 'keep up with the Joneses'; an expensive and usually quite unnecessary procedure. Some of the best and most effective publications published by industrial concerns are quite modest in their presentation. The steady erosion of profits and the urgent need to reduce selling expenses should make most managements realize that lush publications, costing many thousands of pounds a year, create no more goodwill, and often less, than those produced at a fraction of the cost.

CHOICE OF EDITOR

Without doubt, the most suitable person to edit a house magazine is a man or woman with previous editorial experience who has a natural flair for descriptive writing and a good eye for layout. He could be on the public relations side of a large company, or the assistant advertising manager of a medium-sized concern. A journalist is certainly desirable for a job of this kind. Whoever is appointed, the man or woman should be given ready access to everyone on the staff, from the boss to the stoker, and be allowed all reasonable facilities to visit factories, laboratories, warehouses and offices. It is little use buying a dog and then fitting a muzzle to stop him from barking, and this too frequently happens in industry today. Not only must the editor be given freedom of access to personnel and departments, but reasonable freedom of choice in the features which go to make up each issue. Naturally, there are policy rulings which have to be studied, but the general editorial pattern should be left to the discretion of the person delegated to produce the magazine.

From a personality standpoint, the editor of a house magazine should be easy of manner, approachable, sympathetic, a good listener and not over-awed by authority.

VETTING THE COPY

On many house magazines one sees the names of three or more persons constituting the editorial panel, which in theory advises the editor on contents and acts as a final court of appeal when matters are in dispute. This is an excellent idea as long as the panel actually does function, but so often it exists only on paper and fulfils no useful purpose.

The editor, no matter how competent, should have advisers drawn from the commercial and technical interests of the company, who are capable of recommending features of topical interest, leaving the editor to make the final choice. The idea of an editorial panel is an excellent one if it is made to work, and this is certainly possible if top management is really convinced that a company magazine makes a worthwhile contribution to company prestige or fulfils a genuine commercial purpose. Ideally the panel should be made up of three or four younger executives nominated by the managing director and given the responsibillty of keeping the company's magazine a virile and at times even a provocative publication. These advisers should be asked to serve on the panel for six months at a time. It is stressed that their function is purely advisory and they have no power to dictate policy or to try and brow-beat the editor. As long as he has the confidence of the

Board, he alone is responsible for choosing the contents and for presentation.

FOREIGN VERSIONS

Such great emphasis has now to be placed on Britain's export business, that every house magazine should be available in the languages of the chief export markets. This can, of course, be done in two ways; by publishing complete foreign editions in say three or four of the main languages, or by tipping in foreign translations printed on very thin paper or tissue which act as overlays on the pages printed in English. Another method is to publish summaries of the chief articles in the most important foreign languages and to print these at the end of the magazine. No matter which method is adopted, foreign versions are essential if the publication is to have any appreciable impact in an overseas market. It does very little good to send a magazine printed entirely in English to customers in Germany, Russia or Italy.

COST

It is impossible to generalize about the cost of producing a company magazine, each one differing so widely in presentation. Every publication should, however, be subjected to strict budgetary control and a close check kept on expenditure. What has to be restrained is the tendency shown by every ambitious editor to improve the appearance and appeal of the magazine by use of a more extravagant layout, more expensive photography and art work and the more lavish use of colour.

14

TRADE AND TECHNICAL LITERATURE

DEFINITION OF TERMS AND THE PURPOSE OF TRADE LITERATURE
TRADE LITERATURE has been aptly defined as printed material which supplies the reader with information enabling him to select, specify and use a product or service. In every trade and profession there is a growing appetite for technical information and, of course, in some trades and professions this is vital to the efficient running of a department or business. If one takes the case of an architect or surveyor, he needs the information contained in the technical literature so that he can prepare drawings, specifications and bills of quantities. In other words, technical literature is required so that the user can actually put the product or service into practical use. Abroad, this type of material is even more important as it usually represents the only link between the home manufacturer and the foreign buyer. If it is inaccurate and badly produced then not only does it do incalculable harm to the British manufacturer, but reacts violently against British prestige overseas.

Trade literature, and this includes both sales promotional material and actual technical information, should not be produced haphazardly, but form part of a carefully integrated marketing policy. So often it happens that expensive brochures are printed without anyone in the commercial departments having a very clear idea of what to do with them when they are made available. The urge to go into print should be restrained until the policy is made clear, and this can only be achieved by some pretty clear thinking on the part of the commercial interests of the company.

TYPES OF PUBLICATIONS

The average British manufacturer is concerned with three main types of printed promotional material – sales, technical and prestige. The first named is designed to promote direct inquiries and is usually initiated by the commercial departments who require it to support selling campaigns in the field or to supply material for direct mail. Technical literature may cover almost a complete library: brochures dealing specifically with the properties and uses of products, technical advantages of services, instruction manuals, colour guides and charts and pattern cards, etc. Prestige publications are generally expensive glossy brochures aimed either at enhancing a reputation or the building up of a company image. All of these publications need special treatment and many of them have to be planned well in advance. The number, style and general treatment of technical literature is, of course, influenced to a marked extent by the amount of money allocated to this work in the budget, the type of readership at which it is aimed and the marketing policy governing the whole exercise.

Looking somewhat closer at the range of publications produced by British manufacturers, these vary a great deal in size, quality and nature of contents, manner of presentation and the numbers made available. The architecture of every publication, if it is to be successful, needs to be based on the sound foundations of a well planned marketing policy.

UNIFORMITY OF SIZE

It is generally accepted throughout British industry that whenever possible, technical and instructional literature which is intended to be kept for reference and for filing, and distributed largely overseas, should be produced in one of the International 'A' sizes. (International Organization for Standardization. I.S.O.) There is also a strong case to be made out for standardization of the size of all literature intended for home consumption and in some trades, such as the building trade, there is a marked resistance to the acceptance of what may be termed 'bastard' shapes and sizes. It is obvious to every user of trade literature that when dealing with a variety of sizes of pamphlets and catalogues it becomes

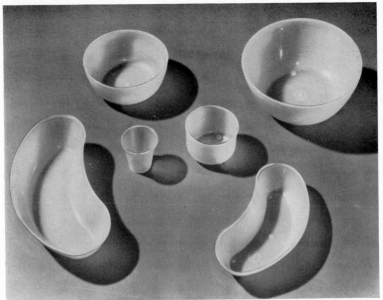

Hospital ware moulded from 'Propathene' by Industrial Mouldings (Warwick) Ltd., Emscote Road, Warwick.

INTRODUCING 'PROPATHENE'–A NEW I.C.I. MATERIAL FOR HOSPITAL WARE

'Propathene' is a new plastics material made by Imperial Chemical Industries Ltd. from propylene, a hydrocarbon gas in the same family as ethylene from which 'Alkathene' is produced. Articles made from 'Propathene' are light in weight, quiet in use, rigid, able to withstand frequent sterilization by normal autoclaving methods and highly resistant to attack by chemicals.

FIRST HOSPITAL EQUIPMENT IN 'PROPATHENE'

Our picture shows a range of kidney dishes, dressing bowls and medicine glasses made from 'Propathene' and now available to all hospitals. These articles are rigid and will not crack or chip during normal washing, storage or transport. They will retain their glossy, stain-resistant surfaces and present a clean and attractive appearance after months of hard use. Their quietness helps to eliminate undesirable "clatter" in wards. They are also extremely light in weight—six 'Propathene' kidney dishes weigh only the same as one stainless steel dish of the same size.

NON-STAINING . . . . STERILIZABLE

Two more qualities of 'Propathene' are extremely important in this field—its chemical resistance and its acceptance of standard sterilizing procedures.
'Propathene' is resistant to nearly all the inorganic materials encountered in the hospital and highly resistant to organic media including alcohols and natural oils. 'Propathene' articles will not readily become crazed or stained under the conditions of daily hospital use.
'Propathene' will withstand repeated autoclave sterilization cycles at temperatures up to 145° C (290° F), retaining sufficient rigidity at this high temperature to permit handling without distortion.

INTEGRALLY-HINGED CONTAINERS

Another use of 'Propathene' which is of considerable interest to those concerned with hospital supplies is for containers with captive, integrally-hinged lids. Large containers with integral-hinge lids can be made in one moulding from 'Propathene'. The lid hinge of one such container has been flexed over half a million times in an I.C.I. laboratory without sign of fracture. Containers using this principle, with consequent freedom from metal parts, are of obvious interest.

FURTHER APPLICATIONS FOR A UNIQUE MATERIAL

Water carafes, bedpans, components for medical appliances and instruments—even complicated equipment like defibrillators in which 'Propathene' electrode handles provide electrical resistance and resistance to sterilization—exceptionally clear barrier film—these are some of the uses to which 'Propathene' has already been put in the hospital supplies field. 'Propathene' is available in a wide range of attractive colours and in grades designed for specific end uses. It has not however yet been possible to eliminate electrostatic charge build-up and 'Propathene' articles are not recommended for use in operating theatres when anaesthetic atmospheres are present.
To know more about 'Propathene' and the hospital supplies equipment made from this unique material, please write to I.C.I. at the address below.

 'Propathene' *is the registered trade mark for the polypropylene manufactured by*

PPII

IMPERIAL CHEMICAL INDUSTRIES LIMITED · LONDON · S.W.1

Poor advertisement – too much copy – general cluttered-up appearance

I.C.I. plastics materials with a big future in building chosen for the House of the Year

'PERSPEX' The handles on the front door of the Woman's Journal House of the Year will have caught your eye. They're made from 'Perspex' acrylic sheet, an I.C.I. plastics material which is also used for the lighting fittings on the porch and in the main living room. Corrugated 'Perspex' has been used to form an original and decorative windbreak for the small sun patio. 'Perspex' has been used for very many years for interior and exterior lighting fittings and in Corrugated sheets for roof lighting.

'CORVIC' Another innovation in this house is the PVC soil and rainwater system which is built into the structure of the house and is made from 'Corvic' I.C.I. vinyl polymer. Pipes and fittings are light in weight, easy to fit. These will not corrode, and require no maintenance.

Another use of 'Corvic' vinyl polymer is in 'Vynide' made by I.C.I. (Hyde) Ltd., used for covering the inner folding door.

1. A section of piping in the 'Terrain' soil and rainwater systems used throughout the house. 'Terrain' is produced by A.B. Plastics Ltd., from 'Corvic' vinyl polymer, and distributed by Burn Bros. (London) Ltd., St. Mary Cray, Kent.

2. Front entrance, showing door handles made from 'Perspex' acrylic sheet by Taylor Industries Ltd., Rowlands Gill, Co. Durham, specially designed by George Wimpey & Co. Ltd. The lighting fitting in the porch was designed by George Wimpey & Co. Ltd., Architects Dept., using 'Perspex'.

3. Superfold door made by The Bolton Gate Company, Waterloo Street, Bolton, covered with 'Vynide' made by I.C.I. (Hyde) Ltd., and based on 'Corvic'.

4. Two of the four ceiling lighting fittings in the main living room designed by George Wimpey & Co. Ltd., using 'Perspex'.

5. Windbreak on the back patio made from Corrugated 'Perspex'.

6. Close-up of front door handles made from 'Perspex'.

'Perspex', 'Corvic' and 'Vynide' are registered trade marks, the property of I.C.I.

PG5

IMPERIAL CHEMICAL INDUSTRIES LIMITED · LONDON · S.W.1

Advertisement with indifferent appeal – too many illustrations and too much copy – general effect confusing

difficult to file them easily. The 'A' sizes, which are covered in the British Standard for Trade and Technical Literature, BS.1311, amended 1958, includes 4 sizes, and of these 2 are International Standard Paper Sizes. ($11\frac{3}{4}$ in. $\times$ $8\frac{1}{4}$ in. which is the A4 size, and $8\frac{1}{4}$ in. $\times$ $5\frac{7}{8}$ in. the A5) which are accepted and used abroad in 26 countries. In order to conform with economical paper sizes these figures would become $11\frac{7}{10}$ in. $\times$ $8\frac{3}{10}$ in. and $8\frac{3}{10}$ in. $\times$ $5\frac{3}{10}$ in. In some trades, both at home and abroad, a marked preference is shown for a particular 'A' size, for example, A4 is advocated for all trade literature to be distributed to the building trade. It is recommended that this is pre-punched for filing (80 mm. or $3\frac{1}{8}$ in. hole centres). The idea behind this standardization of size is that all technical information from whatever source would fall neatly into the office filing system and so facilitate easy reference. Subdivisions of these sizes are permissible under the conditions laid down by the I.S.O.

Although one can see the obvious advantages of standardization in running an office, particularly an architect's, the proportions of 'A' sizes are not altogether too happy from a layout angle. For sales literature the 'A' sizes are rarely suitable, and if the publicity manager is aiming at originality of approach it is doubtful whether standardization on these lines is desirable. Although one can appreciate the practical advantages of standardization of size, it is becoming increasingly apparent that there is an insidious move in many quarters towards an extension of this to embrace typography and layout. In the writer's opinion this is a decidedly retrograde step as it may lead to regimentation of design and the production of literature that lacks both freshness and originality of approach.

SHOULD THE AGENCY BE RESPONSIBLE FOR PRINT PRODUCTION?

Whilst most advertising agencies are able and willing to provide their clients with an efficient design and print service and, indeed, do so on quite a large scale, such a service is likely to be more expensive than if the clients placed their work direct with the printer. After all, all advertising agencies run their business on the commission they receive from suppliers, including printers but excluding studios and photographers, as commission for the agency bringing them the work and this commission, usually 15 per cent, has to be passed on to the client. The theory is that printers are supposed to charge the agency 10–15 per cent less than they would charge the client, but usually the reverse happens. This means, of course, that the print bill is immediately 15 per cent higher than it would normally be if the client handled the work himself. To avoid this kind of thing happening, agencies are now insisting on printers quoting realistic prices, i.e. not to give any commission to the agency, which then charges the client a handling charge. Added to the inevitable high cost of the agency handling print there is the general fiustration of having to arrange publication at long range with all the interminable discussions and delays. If the client has facilities for doing all the work that an agency normally does in connection with print jobs, the amount he has to charge in overheads, salaries, etc., for this work may be less than the amount charged by the agency. With some of the large corporations it is, however, questionable whether it is not more profitable for the agency to do this work, in spite of the handling charge!

IMPORTANCE OF GOOD DESIGN IN PRINT AS A SELLING FACTOR

It has been said that design is 'intelligence made visible' and this is as good a definition as one is likely to find. In the United Kingdom the printing industry, which is abreast of the world in technical development, lags behind in design. Although lip service is paid to the importance of this, it is a fact that only a handful of the really large printers employ fully qualified designers with an intimate knowledge of typography.

Those that do employ such specialists frankly admit that their design studios work at a loss. In fact they are only sustained so as to provide a service for a few big accounts. The real patrons of design in modern British industry are the mammoth manufacturing companies, such as I.C.I., Distillers, United Steel, A.E.I., etc., who do their best to encourage the production of well designed trade literature. It would be untrue to say that even in these monolithic concerns there is any great enthusiasm about design, but there is at least tacit approval of the principles of good design and a realization that it is a good thing to foster.

In Germany, Italy and Scandinavia the printed word is generally presented in a fresh and stimulating manner that attracts and sustains attention, whereas too often British print has a stale, tired and pinched look. It is still not realized in this country that it is only good design that can lift print out of the ordinary and make it look distinctive. In these days of fierce competition in overseas markets, the acceptability of the print that goes alongside the product or service plays a significant part in creating a favourable sales reaction. There is some evidence accumulating that British business-men abroad are slowly beginning to appreciate the importance of design as a selling factor and maybe this will, in time, have its effect on manufacturers at home.

To say that British manufacturers are antagonistic to good design would be untrue; they are simply indifferent. In fact, in most instances the thought never occurs to a business-man that print needs designing. He usually assumes that it is the printer's responsibility to see that 'the thing looks all right'. Indifference is more difficult to fight than active dislike but, as stated earlier, there are signs that pressure from overseas agents and representatives may eventually force British manufacturers to try and keep up with competitors in Sweden, Düsseldorf and Rome. We may therefore reach the interesting stage where an attempt is made to go one better than foreign rivals and to recruit the services of a new Farina in print!

CONTROL OF DESIGN IN PRINT

Having put in a strong plea for recognition of the importance of design in print, particularly print that is being aimed at securing new business, it is necessary to think rather carefully about the ways in which design can be used by the manufacturer to the best possible advantage. It is not only essential to employ a designer to design a brochure, but to use the right kind of man and to brief and control him in the right kind of way. There is a whole army of so-called 'creative designers' specializing in print production, but entire divisions of this army are of very questionable ability. Any designer who is worth employing should be a fully qualified typographical designer with as good a knowledge of printing as of designing, and preferably be a member of the Society of Industrial Artists. The Council of Industrial Design also has a register of designers specializing in graphic and typographical work.

Before recruiting the services of a designer the client should see specimens of his work that are applicable to his particular industry, for example, a designer specializing in mail order catalogues for women's underwear would hardly be suitable for designing a brochure on refractory bricks! It is largely a matter of 'horses for courses' and the selection of a suitable designer needs a good deal of care and thought. He is the architect not only of the format and general artistic presentation, but he should be able to specify the kind, size and distribution of type on every page. That is why a mere superficial knowledge of type is not sufficient; a booklet can look extremely distinctive without a single illustration merely by designing the print on the page.

Whilst it is stupid to engage an expert and then to ignore his advice, it is a fact that even the best designers need some kind of control, which may be quite flexible and yet positive. A free hand is all very well, but it has to be assumed that the client who is paying the bill has some idea of what he wants, or at least he is aware of the general style and presentation of print issued by his competitors at home and abroad and, probably more important still, the receptiveness of the market in which he is operating. It is not the function of the manufacturer to dictate to the designer on choice of type, colours, size of page and general presentation, but if he wants a sales leaflet or brochure that is going to be effective for a specific purpose and in a prescribed market, then the designer must be briefed on the following general lines:

(1) He must be told the underlying commercial purpose of the publication; the audience for which it is intended; the mar-

ket where it is to do a selling job; the number of copies and the languages in which it is to be printed.

(2) In general terms, the kind of publication which is required and how such a piece of literature fits into the general pattern of promotional material issued (*a*) by the company (*b*) by its competitors at home and abroad.

(3) The amount of money budgeted for the publication, which has to consist of x pages and x number of illustrations in line, monochrome and colour.

(4) The client will also want to know what kind of a fee the designer is likely to charge. This kind of signposting will be invaluable to the print designer who should, after studying the background information supplied, be able to gain a fairly clear picture of the kind of publication required.

It will be necessary at this briefing session with the designer for the client to find out how the work is to be done and, most important from the costing angle, how 'rough' should be the 'roughs'. Publicity departments in large and even medium-sized industrial concerns are experienced in dealing with independent designers and studios, and are well able to visualize what the finished leaflet or brochure will look like from roughs or pencil sketches. Smaller companies with only skeleton publicity sections may find this kind of visualization difficult, in which case more finished visuals will have to be prepared, but the cost will be higher. In print design, it is as well for the designer to be in fairly close touch with the printer who is ultimately going to be responsible for producing the work. Printer and designer must be encouraged to work as a team so as to achieve the best results.

On the question of fee there is, of course, a scale of fees suggested by the Society of Industrial Artists, and for nationally known designers this is fair enough. For lesser known practitioners a lower scale might reasonably be expected. To give some idea of the kind of fee likely to be charged, 20 to 30 guineas should buy the design for a simple, but imaginatively planned four page sales leaflet, and 35 to 45 guineas would be sufficient for an eight page brochure. These are very rough guides based on experience, but fees are a matter of negotiation between client and designer. The more complex the job the higher the fee.

When dealing with design studios run by printing houses for the benefit of customers the position is rather different. First of all, the best of these studios tend to be of a higher calibre than independent designers and more experienced in the graphic and typographical arts. They have the added benefit of knowing their composing room and being able to integrate their design into the printing capacity of their employers. Designers working for print houses also have a greater awareness of timetables, and as they are under two direct but different kinds of pressure, one exerted by the customer and the other by the printer, who is their boss, work is turned out more quickly than it would be possible to secure from an independent designer or studio.

When dealing with first-class printers who are associated with good design in print, and there are about a dozen or so in the United Kingdom, the print buyer need have no qualms about the standards of design. These will be high. Moreover, he will be in an advantageous position regarding fees, which are usually less than those charged by outside agencies. Design fees are really of secondary interest to the printer, whose main concern is the printing order itself. Some printers charge only a nominal fee, based largely on the time actually taken by their artist on the design work and reckoned at so much an hour. This does not cover the overheads and these are regarded as part of the selling expenses, just as advertising is charged. Design work for clients is therefore regarded as a service which may be the means of securing very lucrative business. There is a danger here, of course, particularly with those printers with plenty of capacity but very little work, that they may offer clients speculative designs free of cost in the hope of securing orders. This practice, which is encouraged by some of the smaller agencies, tends to debase design, lower the standards and deprive young, independent designers of a livelihood.

FASHION IN PRINT

Discounting fashion trends in type, which are hardly worth

considering as they are so ephemeral, it is a recognized fact that some type faces appear to suit some kinds of subject matter better than others. This has nothing to do with readability or the general acceptance of the page. Experience tends to show that the serif type face is more acceptable for layouts calling for a mass of heavy type matter or for the printing of instruction manuals than the sans-serif faces. On the other hand, for effect in many advertisements and well illustrated catalogues the sans-serif type makes a greater impact and is probably better fitted for this purpose. These are, of course, generalities but even so they are worth considering.

It is not really surprising that the sans-serif faces are better suited to smaller pieces of copy, and particularly display copy, than the older serif type as the modern grotesque or sans-serif type face was designed originally by Johnston for use in London Underground posters in 1916 and Gill with his individual sans-serif face for the Monotype Corporation in 1928. If used for continuous reading, the sans-serif type can become somewhat irritating because of its uniformity and lack of relief. The serifs are not just ornaments, but do help to make the type more readable by forming links between one letter and another, particularly when unrelieved in solid masses of continuous type. Beatrice Warde speaks with great feeling on this subject and explains that the serif letters unobtrusively mark the line on which lower-case characters are ranged and are more efficient as a book type than the sans-serif.

Among the many founts of excellent book type available to the print buyer the Times New Roman is a general favourite. It was designed originally for maximum legibility in a newspaper and is still most highly esteemed wherever there is a call for a mass of type matter unrelieved by illustrations. Since its introduction in 1931 this type face has been very widely used, particularly in general technical literature including book production.

When considering the choice of type it is, of course, most important to attempt to match the type to the subject matter. For example, it would be ridiculous to set an engineering catalogue with its mass of technical data in a delicate type face like Futura Light, which would suit a cleverly designed brochure put out by a pharmaceutical house to advertise a new hypnotic. Futura Light is now becoming popular for certain types of promotional material of an intimate nature e.g., pharmaceuticals. On the other hand, the engineering catalogue would look well in Rockwell or Plantin, both of which are very readable faces and popular with publishers of trade and technical journals. One very important aspect of choosing a type face is not only its suitability for the subject matter, but also for the size of type specified by the typographical designer. Some type faces do not show up to advantage in the small sizes, such as 6–8 pt. and are at their best in 10–11 pt, For example, Bodoni, Caslon, Garamond and even Baskerville. look somewhat stifled and suffer in readability when set in 6–8 pt., whereas Monotype Plantin and Fournier are perfectly satisfactory.

Every authority on typography, when discussing this highly controversial subject of choosing a type face, stresses the great importance of allying the type to the subject matter – the printed page must always look right! If a type face utterly alien to the subject matter is chosen it tends to destroy the confidence of the reader and so defeats the primary purpose of the publication. Some 'off beat' designers do, however, set out to create an impact by shocking the reader and one of the common devices is to use unusual, even erotic type faces for rather mundane subjects, e.g. Victorian Gothic for an essay on essential oils or Perpetua for a piece of copy on structural steel work. This is just a stunt and is not worth serious consideration. The important fact to remember, however, is that in striving to effect a well balanced printed page orthodoxy in typography must not be confused with dullness. There is a great deal to be said for experiments in type, provided they are designed to create the right kind of effect and are not merely novelties without any real typographical justification. When considering the re-vamping of trade and technical literature to meet the demand of European agents there are sound commercial reasons for thinking of new type faces with a strong continental flavour, such as Univers designed by the Swiss typographer, Adrian Frutiger. In its Monotype adaptation it opens up some interesting possibilities wherever the 'Sans' or 'Grot' is appropriate.

HOUSE STYLES – HOW TO CREATE ONE?

House styles have been built up over the years by many famous industrial concerns, such as I.C.I. and A.E.I., The Container Corporation, U.S.A., Pirelli and Olivetti, to mention just a few, and these have come to mean something very tangible in both home and overseas markets. The company image, now so often referred to in streamlined business courses, is a very valuable asset which contributes quite appreciably to the general acceptance of products or services offered for sale.

This purely synthetic personality has been built up by the reiteration of a symbol or name on every piece of paper, package and vehicle coming out of the works or offices. It is not suggested that the symbols or company names which identify highly successful industrial concerns are necessarily good examples of design, indeed many are quite nondescript, but they can be cleverly and effectively exploited by contemporary designers in many different ways so as to sustain, and, indeed, develop the 'image'.

The writer is not so much concerned with House styles already existing, but rather with the creation of new ones. There are two ways of tackling this problem. First through the advertising agency, whose ultimate responsibility it is to promote the client's interests graphically, and secondly by making use of the services of an independent designer or studio who should be given the opportunity to review the visual impact of the company or, where this does not exist, to create such an impact.

Clear, fresh and contemporary design as applied to advertising matter, publications, business stationery, external and internal forms, address labels, packages, schemes for paintwork for all vehicles, staff, overalls, etc., can achieve a great deal in giving the concern a personality which it never had before. This development is certain to be beneficial; moreover, the company, by these comparatively inexpensive innovations, some of which can be timed to take place over a period of months, can acquire a reputation of being very progressive and forward looking.

In markets at home and abroad, where selling is becoming

increasingly aggressive, the cultivation of a distinctive house style offers the manufacturer the opportunity to carry his advertising message forward on every visual form of matter: letter, leaflet, package and vehicle. This is good business. Creation of a symbol or style is difficult, but once a good designer is made aware of the problem he should be able to suggest a graphic solution. Simplicity is the keynote of success; incisive symbols and meticulous typography together make possible the best possible means of company identification. Difficulties only arise when too many people are consulted and where efforts are made to try and reach compromise decisions: good design is the decision of one man and not a committee. It is quite impossible to arrive at a really distinctive design by committee procedure. Marketing research exercises occasionally throw into relief the sales significance of a well designed symbol and, indeed, there is evidence that this can sometimes prove of greater value in winning new business and retaining old accounts than complex advertising schemes involving heavy expenditure on space and production.

WHO WRITES THE COPY FOR TRADE LITERATURE?

In many small industrial concerns who do not boast a publicity department, it is not uncommon to find the commercial manager or managing director taking over the full responsibility of technical literature alongside the agency. The copy departments in most agencies do undertake a great deal of writing for their clients; they prepare sales literature, catalogues, mailing shots, and, in fact, prepare all the printed promotional material required for both the home and overseas markets. The cost of doing this work is naturally charged to the client, but where the advertising account is of reasonable size, then only a nominal charge is made, this being worked out on a time basis. There is no doubt that this method of preparing the actual copy for sales leaflets and catalogues is a good one where no facilities exist at the source for the work to be done.

It becomes a little more difficult, however, when highly technical brochures and instruction charts, manuals, etc., have to be prepared, as these require highly specialized knowledge. Here the agency may be prepared to work alongside the expert in the company, but usually the copywriter prefers to use a brief supplied by the client. There is, therefore, no reason why the agency should not produce every type of promotional material and, with a good copywriter with a background of technical accounts, this is certainly feasible. One advantage of working with the agency is that the copy department can, in the early stages, consult the art department and between them evolve a form of presentation most suitable for the subject matter and the market where the literature is to circulate.

It is emphasized that, whereas the agency can usually prepare all the copy needed for sales literature, the client is well advised to try and write it for himself. The 'Do It Yourself' method will result in a more informative and direct approach to writing and achieve results more quickly and at less cost than when using an agency. No problem arises with large manufacturing concerns who have their own publicity departments where literature production is part of the day-to-day work of the print section, the section head, who might be considered as the equivalent of a chief copywriter in an agency, being responsible for writing, compilation, research, etc.

No matter who undertakes the actual work of preparing matter for the printer, accuracy and speed are the vital requirements. Literature must be reliable, that is essential, but it must also be available at the right time and the right place. Large sums of money are wasted on literature projects that do not meet publication deadlines. There should not only be adequate literature to support the sales campaign, but leaflets and other promotional matter must be topical, out of date material can do the company a great deal of harm. For this reason, if for no other, it is recommended that the manufacturer should actually write his own sales and technical literature, even if he delegates design and production to the agency. Where the journalistic resources within the company are very limited, then it is sometimes possible to recruit the spare time services of a technical journalist to prepare material for trade publications. This is an economical way of producing literature that has a professional look about it and is well worth exploring!

RESPONSIBILITY FOR POLICY

Whilst the ultimate responsibility for policy rests with the chairman or managing director, who in turn is answerable to the shareholders, delegation of responsibility passes down the echelons of management to various executives. The sales manager is responsible for the commercial policy of the concern and the development or technical manager for the quality and function of the product and all the technical aspects of production. Finally it is the responsibility of the advertising or publicity manager, who acts as the mouthpiece of the company, to present these various interests in visual form in advertisements and literature in such a way as to promote sales and to increase the prestige and general acceptability of the company. The successful implementation of company policy therefore depends on the extent of the co-operation, understanding and mutual trust that exists between those sections of the organization that sell, those that make and those that advertise.

The actual presentation, that is, the way in which an advertising message is laid out or a leaflet set out, is the sole responsibility of the publicity manager and he should be answerable only to the managing director or chairman. Whilst publicity is an integral part of the sales organization, it is also geared closely to the technical or production side, therefore, its efficacy as a sales force is a measure of the collaboration that exists and the efficiency of lines of communications within the company. The acceptance of responsibility for statements and claims made in advertising is one that presents great difficulty. Sales managers are usually rather reluctant to identify themselves positively with an advertising message unless, of course, it proves to be a phenomenal success, which is rather unlikely! On the other hand, many technical people instinctively mistrust and often actively dislike advertising and all such vulgar forms of sales promotion. The advertising manager therefore occupies the unenviable position of being out on a limb; he is seldom if ever proved right and more often than not he is shown up to be a person who exaggerates or at least makes grossly inaccurate claims calculated to infuriate his technical colleagues and mislead the customers.

Naturally it is the avowed aim of every advertising manager to try and underwrite the responsibility for advertising statements, but in this he is usually unsuccessful!

FOREIGN TRANSLATIONS

In the markets of the world there is an increasing demand for foreign translations of both sales and technical literature, but unfortunately there is still a woeful lack of awareness among British exporters of the importance of having available an adequate supply of advertising material in the language of the country where a sales campaign is being planned.

This is a constantly recurring criticism from foreign representatives trying to gain new business for Britain.

It is still assumed by many home manufacturers that the expense of providing foreign translations is only justified if there is an established market, or if powerful competitors in the field are setting the pace by making available foreign editions of their own sales literature.

For new and undeveloped markets, leaflets and catalogues, etc., printed in English are usually considered adequate, and only when trade is established are these gradually replaced by advertising matter printed in the language of the country. This is a policy which many British manufacturers follow, but it seems to be illogical and shows a complete disregard of the whole psychology of selling in new markets.

To be effective, foreign translations must be technically accurate. That is the first requirement, but it is not the only one. The style must be reasonably good and the printed matter should, in fact, be read without it being realized that it is a translation at all. Major criticisms of foreign editions usually arise if the translator has no knowledge of the subject and does not understand fully what he is translating. It is, therefore, desirable that for industrial material the translator should be a specialist, e.g. only a man with some chemical background should be given the task of translating a document on 'New Industrial Amines' or 'Radio-active Isotopes'. Similarly, a translator with a knowledge of engineering should be asked to translate material with a direct bias towards the subject such as corrosion, metal fatigue or the operation of a new machine tool.

All translations of highly technical matter, no matter how competent the translator may be, should be checked by another authority. This can, of course, be done at the proof stage, although it saves both time and money for author's corrections if the checking is done before printing actually commences.

There are two courses open to the British manufacturer who wants to provide foreign translations of his sales literature. He can secure these from his agents in the territories concerned or make use of outside translators in the United Kingdom through the Institute of Linguists.

This body is a highly reputable concern which has among its members translators with specialized knowledge of many technical subjects. In addition, there are a number of agencies in London and the main provincial cities who are able to translate straightforward copy, but for technical matter it is advisable to use the services of the Institute.

The standard rates payable for translation work vary according to the language, for example, £2 17s. 6d. to £7 7s. per 1,000 words may be charged for translating from English into German, and £10 17s. 6d. to £15 15s. per 1,000 words from English into Turkish or Persian. It always costs less to translate from a foreign language into English than English into another language. For highly-technical copy where the speed of translation is necessarily slowed down, a surcharge amounting to 50 per cent or more, may be made. It should be appreciated that the figures quoted are minimum basic rates, liable to alteration, and they are only provided as a rough guide to the cost of translation work. One disadvantage of sending copy abroad for translation is that it is usually a long and tedious process, particularly if proofs have to be sent off as well. Where rigid time-tables have to be kept, for example, in supplying literature for an overseas exhibition, then it is generally impossible to make use of translators outside the country.

Some foreign markets, particularly the U.S.S.R., present special problems. They have their own governmental translation services which they make available to foreign companies doing business with State Departments, and they vouch for the technical accuracy of all translation work carried out. There is, for instance, in Moscow the very efficient State Scientific Society which can be thoroughly recommended. The difficulty here is the time factor and if the British manufacturer is in a hurry, then use of the official State translating services can hardly be recommended. He is therefore forced into the position of having to use translators resident in the United Kingdom, and these can generally be found. Their work is, of course, liable to be criticized, as the Soviet point out, probably with complete justification, that Russian emigrés are out of touch with the new idiom.

When planning the production of foreign editions it is a wise move to employ printers who specialize in foreign languages. Some printing houses do a great deal of work in the better known European languages and others in Russian and the Mid-European and Eastern languages. It pays to go direct to these firms rather than to use ordinary jobbing printers who have to send out to trade houses for foreign settings. Foreign language printers have their own highly trained readers who can check proofs and often detect errors which might escape the general printer. There is also a sound economic advantage for using foreign language printers insomuch as they are generally able to offer more attractive quotations for this work, and certainly turn out printing more quickly than when dealing with non-specialized concerns.

CHOICE OF PRINTER AND PRINTING PROCESS

It is rare that one finds anyone in the publicity department of an industrial concern who has a really intimate knowledge of typography and the printing processes, indeed, this is a highly desirable but not an essential qualification for a print buyer. Certainly the person responsible for buying print would find it a great advantage to be able to determine how many pages the copy will come to in any given space, taking into account all the niceties of printing, such as point size, width of the setting, number of lines, etc., but this is really asking too much. All that one can reasonably hope for is to find someone with a working knowledge of the business who understands at least the difference between a serif and a sans-serif face, and can recognize the most commonly used founts.

The same general recommendations apply to the printing process itself. The main features of the standard processes should, at least, be understood and here it is possible to obtain sufficient working knowledge by visiting printing works and reading books about printing. What is really important from the print buying angle is to know the trade – who are the best printers for certain types of work; who are unreliable and who can be trusted to meet promised delivery dates. This kind of 'know-how' is difficult to acquire and a useful fund of knowledge can only be built up as the result of experience. Probably the ideal man to buy print to the best advantage would be an ex-estimating clerk from a large firm of jobbing printers; such a person might well prove invaluable to a manufacturer spending say £50,000 a year on print. No single printing process is perfect, each one has its limitations and in the apprentice stages of print buying one becomes extremely sceptical about the rival claims of competing printers. The only way to judge a printer is on quality, delivery and price and if these are satisfactory then this is the firm to handle the printing business. It is a mistake to flit from one printer to another in the hope of securing some 'will-o-the-wisp' advantage. A printing house which knows a client, understands his problems and is familiar with the subject matter of the copy being set, can give far better service than a printer who is being used for the first time.

This does not mean that its a good thing to use only one printer. The recommended practice when handling a reasonable print budget of say £10–25,000 is to employ at least three printers. One should be a medium sized to large letterpress or offset litho printer who specializes in high quality brochures and catalogue

Umbrella for an Emperor

Fifteen hundred years ago the Emperor Maximianus Herculius caused a lavish hunting lodge to be built for him in a Sicilian valley. And there he remains to this day, immortalized with gods and goddesses, dancing maidens and all the beasts of the hunt in a spectacular carpet of mosaic. Overhead, to ward off the weather and temper the harsh Sicilian sun, is a 75,000-square-foot translucent canopy of a truly 20th-century material—'Perspex', the acrylic plastic discovered and developed by I.C.I. of England.

Tough, weather-resistant and easily shaped, 'Perspex' appears in one form or another in nearly every country in the world. It provides windshields for Dutch scooter riders and cockpit canopies for French air pilots. It gently diffuses the lighting on German roads, in Swedish petrol stations, Canadian hospitals and Italian trams. Australians mould it into brilliantly coloured lightweight baths and sinks, and it features in many of the world's famous shopping streets in the form of advertising signs. Yet it is only one of a wide range of plastics—the widest in the world—that I.C.I. exports from Britain every year to the value of £18 million.

Careers
in I.C.I.
for
Engineers

Design for the cover of a technical brochure – good impact value

work and is well equipped to print in colour. The second should be a smaller jobbing printer, also capable of producing first-class colour work who could act as a check, price-wise on No. 1, and also make available an alternative source of print supply. The number three might well be a small offset printer organized to handle the more simple and relatively inexpensive advertising matter, such as price lists, direct mail literature and instructive leaflets. In reserve there might be a further printer, specializing in high quality offset work, who could be used where very long runs of fairly high quality print were required, say for a large exhibition or for some special overseas selling campaign. It is becoming increasingly obvious that offset-litho is enjoying increasing popularity for single or multi-colour sales literature and a very high standard is now being achieved by a number of British printers. One interesting development is the web-fed offset-litho printing process which is capable of a very high output of top quality colour work, and offers great possibilities where exceptionally long runs are being planned.

Some print sections buy their blocks direct from process engraving houses and send them to the selected printers for printing. It is doubtful if any economy is achieved by this move as the publicity department of an industrial concern cannot obtain the normal trade discount from the blockmaker, as this may only be paid to printers, and the printer himself charges his client a fee for handling. The only advantage, and this is a bit problematical, is that the print buyer is able to use whatever blockmaker he chooses, whereas if the printer were responsible for the blocks, then the choice might well be left to him. There is, of course, the fringe benefit of having a check on block charges and where colour is extensively employed, it may be possible to achieve some economies by going direct to process engravers.

ESTIMATES FOR PRINT

Whilst it is appreciated that reasonably close estimates for all print work are expected and, indeed, demanded by the accounts department, it is sometimes very difficult to ensure a high degree of accuracy in the forecasting. The reasons for this lamentable state of affairs are many and varied. Probably the most common reason is that the publication is usually required very urgently, and in order to meet a deadline the printer has to put the work in hand immediately. He may not, at the initial stage have all the illustrations, indeed, the layout provided might be somewhat ill-defined and later changed to incorporate new art work or new half tones. Only when printing can proceed at a leisurely pace, can really accurate estimates be given. This is, of course, regrettable, but it is certainly understandable and as long as print is wanted in a hurry the accountants must be prepared to accept, if not to like, discrepancies amounting to 10–15 per cent between the estimate and the invoice.

It is rare, indeed, that comparative quotations can be secured for the print required in industry, although it is recognized that this is highly desirable and is, of course, standard practice in Government Departments. In the highly competitive world in which we live, at least in the Western hemisphere, there is always great sense of urgency in most of the advertising matter distributed by industry – prices are changed, new products are introduced – new developments take place and these facts have to be made known to an ever widening technical public.

15

ORGANIZING TRADE EXHIBITIONS

EXHIBITIONS ARE the only form of media at which the products of the manufacturer are physically shown, handled and demonstrated, and trade shows provide a convenient opportunity for buyers to compare and evaluate a wide variety of goods, materials, techniques and machinery – all under one roof. The most successful exhibitions are usually associated with some kind of trade conference or convention where papers of a technical nature are read and discussed. This general principle applies equally well to overseas as well as home exhibitions, and the former are certain to assume greater importance in the future.

Without doubt there exists in Britain today the highest exhibition standard in the world, but the big problem facing manufacturers is cost. Everywhere this is increasing – space rates are going up, and so too is the cost of design and stand construction, and all the ancillary services that are associated with actual participation in a trade show. There is now rapidly approaching the moment of truth, when the manufacturer has to sacrifice prestige for hard selling. The lush and expensive prestige-cum-trade stands of the last five years are not likely to be repeated, and the trend is towards the prefabricated unit type of stand construction favoured by so many American and Continental manufacturers. This method of simple shell construction has a good deal to commend it. First of all, it is simple and inexpensive to build, and it may be used either as a single unit for a small exhibition or trade convention, or a number of units can be put together to cover a large stand area. An exhibition contractor's premises in New York, or any other large city in the U.S.A., is mainly taken up with the storage of these unit type stands and only a relatively small space is provided for actual construction work. American stand contractors are mostly hiring and storing agencies rather than actual stand builders.

Another very interesting trend in exhibitions is the move away from the nationally organized shows to smaller and more intimate exhibitions held in hotels and offices, and sponsored by the manufacturer himself and not a professional promoter. This arrangement offers the outstanding advantage of enabling the manufacturer to have complete control over invitations, hours of opening, entertainment and even presentation. There is no need to 'pull punches' at an exhibition put on in an hotel, whereas it might be deemed necessary to do so in Olympia or Earls Court when the stand is alongside one's competitors. Although lacking national publicity, these smaller shows give a better commercial return than some of the more pretentious and vastly more expensive ones held in recognized exhibition halls. This development is the logical result of a general disillusionment about the commercial value of professionally organized national exhibitions which, over the last five years, have given a diminishing return in the way of inquiries and orders. Added to this sobering fact is the knowledge that there are far too many trade exhibitions, many of which overlap, both as regards products and dates. Organizers are now realizing the truth of this and, as a result, some yearly exhibitions are being converted into biennials or triennials. It is a direct result of this disillusionment that efforts are now being made to rationalize the exhibition calendar to ensure that exhibitions appealing to the same trade audience are timed so that they do not clash in the same year.

When examining the value of an exhibition from the viewpoint of the manufacturer who has not previously taken part in it, there are various factors to consider. First of all, the credentials of the organizers. A great deal of money can be wasted by taking part in exhibitions which are either not well supported by the trade associations or poorly publicized and presented by the organizers or both! There are, unfortunately, a number of exhibitions, organized both in the United Kingdom and overseas, which are doomed to failure before they actually take place. The second factor of importance is the cost of space and conditions laid down by the organizers. In assessing the commercial value of participation in any trade show it is highly desirable to find out before actually applying for space how much it is going to cost, and what the conditions are if, for some reason, it becomes necessary to withdraw from the exhibition. These seem quite elementary precautions, but experience tends to show that they are not always taken.

The location of the exhibition hall and, of course, the actual position of the site being offered, need careful thought. Some halls, even in London, are not easily accessible and have a diminishing appeal to trade buyers. Some sites, because they are badly located near exit doors, or even public lavatories, or away from the main streams of traffic, are largely shunned by visitors. There is also the question of timing to think about, and this could be quite important. Not only can the opening of an exhibition clash with some great national event which completely eclipses it in interest and appeal, but it may overlay some other trade or company function which makes it difficult to provide the necessary staff to run it successfully.

BUYING SEASONS

Timing for an exhibition is most important as there are well recognized buying seasons, e.g. farmers naturally congregate in London at the time of the Dairy Show and the Smithfield Show, when the harvest cheques have been paid into the bank! However, as there is no flexibility of movement allowed so far as nationally organized exhibitions are concerned – you either take it or leave it – the idea of having a plastics exhibition in June for instance, is by no means a happy one, but it so happens that this is the only time accommodation at Olympia is available. There is, however, plenty of room for manoeuvre when the exhibition is privately sponsored and organized. Here it is necessary to take careful note of the established trade practices and customs, and to try and catch customers when they are in the locality for some special occasion, say the Motor Show or the Building Exhibition, etc. This 'catch crop' idea is generally a sound one, although it does happen occasionally that for some quite inexplicable reason visitors to Earls Court or Olympia cannot be coaxed to visit a small exhibition held in a London hotel, even though gin is running like water! A great deal depends here upon the weather – if this is reasonable, then travelling does not present any difficulties and attendances are usually quite satisfactory. On the other hand, if snow is falling fast and the thermometer is well below zero, then the audience is usually very thin.

WHO ORGANIZES TRADE EXHIBITIONS?

Generally speaking, there are four main types of organizers of trade exhibitions:

(1) Professional exhibition organizers.
(2) Trade publishers usually operating through subsidiary companies, which may be specially formed to promote and organize exhibitions.
(3) Trade or professional associations.
(4) Governmental departments.

Some of the most successful exhibitions are organized by independent exhibition organizers in collaboration with professional bodies, and many examples could be quoted. Trade publications or publishing houses are also becoming prominent in the exhibition field and stage some of the most notable and successful trade shows; indeed, there is no denying the fact that exhibitions organized by trade publishing houses are providing a most useful service. An unwelcome trend, however, is the formation of consortiums made up of publishers-cum-exhibition organizers-cum-exhibition contractors. Because these organizations tend to be monopolistic they are able to deny manufacturers complete freedom in their choice of stand builders and ancillary type of contractors. From the viewpoint of the exhibitor there is no doubt whatever that it is very much to his advantage to have exhibitions organized by completely unbiased and impartial promoters. For this reason, the trade and professional associations and federations are the ideal exhibition organizers, but there are relatively few of them in existence. No matter who organizes the exhibition, the manufacturer who takes space has a right to expect a reasonable service from the organizers who must keep the hall clean and attractive and also to provide adequate publicity for the promotion of the exhibition. Some organizers take their responsibilities in these directions very seriously, as indeed they should, but others are extremely negligent.

THE THEME OF THE EXHIBITION

To ensure the success of any trade exhibition, the manufacturer should have a clearly defined objective. In other words, there must be a sound commercial reason or justification for spending money – a lot of money – on a stand. Every exhibition is, in essence, an exercise in sales promotion and, as such, it needs to be carefully planned and organized. In other words, there must be a plan of campaign. It is useful at this stage to think of a typical theme which might be developed by a manufacturer, say, an engineering firm engaged in building diesel engines to be used as power packs in industry. He might be interested in taking part in, say, the Public Works and Municipal Services Exhibition, for the following reasons:

(1) To open up new market possibilities in the municipal engineering fields.
(2) To provide a platform for the promotion of his selling slogans of 'Reliability, Durability and Economy'.

Although not able to show any new models at this exhibition, he could achieve a great deal by (a) showing the range of models available (b) illustrating their sterling qualities by case histories which demonstrate reliability, durability and economy. It should not prove too difficult for the manufacturer of these engines to demonstrate by means of photographs, models, etc., installations throughout the world that have given excellent service under particularly strenuous conditions. The point which the writer is trying to make here is that unless the objective is carefully thought out at a very early stage, then the finished exhibition stand is bound to reflect something of this vagueness.

Success is by no means automatic, just because the exhibition stand looks well and satisfies the management. Publicity leading up to the show has to be organized well in advance . . . invitations have to be sent out both to the Press and also to trade contacts. Press releases describing any new development or sensational price movement need to be prepared. Actually the trade exhibition itself should be regarded as just another form of presentation alongside public relations and advertising, all of which are designed to put over the sales message. Capitalization of an exhibition commercially is impossible unless energetic measures are taken to see that all inquiries received on the stand are followed up immediately and the appropriate literature and information passed on to the interested party. If the inquirer's enthusiasm is allowed to wane through lack of attention, then a potential customer might well be lost. Overseas visitors to a trade stand usually want all kinds of facts and figures, and these should be provided in a matter of minutes if the right impression is to be given.

CHOOSING A DESIGNER

How does a potential exhibitor choose a designer? Usually from personal knowledge of his work, or as a direct result of a recommendation from friends or business colleagues. It quite often happens that a manufacturer visiting an exhibition sees a stand that attracts his attention because of the distinctiveness of the overall design, or some unusual feature which it contains, and, having discovered the identity of the designer and satisfied himself about his standing and reputation, gives him a commission. Another, and less direct method, is an introduction to a designer via the technical or trade Press where photographs of the best stands at an exhibition are often featured. There are, indeed, dozens of ways in which a designer's name can be thrown into prominence and lead eventually to commissions. In the writer's opinion, it is unusual for a manufacturer finally to select a designer from a register, no matter how authoritative it may be, without having some prior knowledge of his work or reputation. Registers do, however, serve a most useful purpose in suggesting likely designers to a manufacturer who is new to exhibitions.

In the design world there are men with international reputations who work with associate designers, and there are others, less famous, who operate either alone or with one or two other designers. At the end of the ladder are the young, unknown designers, struggling desperately hard for recognition and also a living! Some exhibition contractors also have designers on their staff or make available to clients a small pool of competent designers. Naturally, the more famous a designer, the higher the fee charged. There is also the risk, which many exhibitors are prepared to take, that if a really top flight designer is commissioned he may not personally carry out the design work himself, but delegate it to one of his associates, the choice depending on the size of the job, its probable financial return and the name of the firm for which the work is being done.

The kind of designer that needs to be avoided at all costs is the one that designs for design sake in order to impress his contemporaries. This kind of man fails entirely to appreciate the real function of an exhibition, which is to provide a platform for selling. The designer's basic function is to present the product and the message in a powerful, dramatic and compelling manner, remembering that the stand is only the vehicle used to achieve these ends. No matter what designer is chosen, he must be original in his approach to the problem, able to understand and appreciate the manufacturer's purpose and his objective and also an efficient organizer. A man may be an artist of quite outstanding merit, but a hopeless organizer. The result is that he is completely unable to co-ordinate the work of the stand contractor and all the other people responsible for various aspects of the work, such as display artists, window dressers and other specialists who may be called in for a particular job.

BRIEFING A DESIGNER

The briefing sessions, particularly the first one, are critical, as upon its completeness depends the designer's overall conception of the stand, and the manufacturer's real objective. Briefing for a new designer should take place in two easy stages, first of all, there should be a general introduction to the company, its personnel and its products. He should be given all reasonable facilities for seeing over the factory, offices and laboratories and talking to those technical and commercial members of the staff who can put him into the full business picture. If the company is a very large one, its organization extremely complex and its products highly technical, then two days may be required for this introduction. Actually the time spent on educating the designer depends largely on his experience and the size and type of stand. When considering this preliminary reconnaissance, which can be expensive in terms of time spent by company personnel, it could be wasteful and frustrating if it had to be repeated too often. That is why it is always a sound policy not to change designers too frequently, but as far as possible to use a few 'regulars', who know from past experience sufficient about the company's business to be reasonably knowledgeable. With these trusted few it is a sound policy to switch the product or theme quite frequently so as to avoid all risk of staleness.

The second stage of briefing a designer consists of a full-dress meeting with all the people in the organization who have to be consulted on the exhibition. If the meeting is too large, then it tends to become unwieldy, and the poor designer leaves it in a completely bewildered state of mind. On the other hand, if it is too small, then it stands a chance of being unrepresentative. The ideal meeting is one attended by, say, 6–8 people representing the commercial, technical, publicity and marketing interests of the company, with the managing director or commercial director taking the chair. Before engaging a designer he should be asked to name his fee, or at least to disclose the basis on which the fee will be based. Some designers adopt a rather silly attitude of mock modesty when approached on this subject, but it is important that the client should know at the outset what kind of a price he is expected to pay. He can then come to terms.

DESIGNER'S FEE

To many exhibitors this is something of a mystery. Broadly speaking, designers usually charge from 10–20 per cent on the actual cost of the stand, that is, the cost in terms of United Kingdom standards. For overseas exhibitions, where the building cost is greatly inflated, such as in the U.S.A. and Soviet Russia, a price has to be negotiated based on United Kingdom equivalents. Freightage charges, which may be exceptionally heavy for some foreign exhibitions, are never included in the costs of the stand upon which the designer calculates his fee.

There is a scale of fees which forms the basis of most calculations, but few exhibition designers keep to this rigidly. The designers in the top bracket, that is, those with internationally famous names, arrive at their fee by patient negotiation with the client; the middle strata, i.e. the reasonably well-known practitioners, usually price themselves slightly below the recognized fee level, depending on the size and reputation of the company engaging them, whilst the independent and comparatively unknown newcomers in the field are ready to offer their services at cut-price fees. It is not unknown for some contractors to offer a free sketch to clients in an effort to secure business, and it is not unusual for an enterprising but unscrupulous publicity manager to secure four or five of these from various contractors, all free and without obligation, and for him to show these to his management as 'free designs', but these methods are to be deprecated as they merely increase the contractor's overheads, thereby making the job more expensive in the long run.

ENGAGING A CONTRACTOR

It should be realized at the start that when a stand is built by a contractor it is hired and not bought outright. This stems from a realization that once an exhibition stand is dismantled it has little real value, and if delivered to the client it could be a serious embarrassment unless he was blessed with unlimited storage facilities, and also was assured that he could re-erect the stand on exactly the same size site at the next exhibition. The term is therefore hiring and not purchasing a stand. But if specific items are required when the stand is dismantled, then special arrangements have to be made with the contractor so as to compensate him for loss of the recoverable material which the exhibitor has taken away. If, of course, the exhibitor wants to buy the stand outright for use on some future occasion, that is supposing he is assured of obtaining exactly the same site again, then terms have to be agreed with the contractor who normally would break down the stand and recover all materials likely to be of value on another occasion.

In looking for a contractor the chief qualification is his ability to give first-class service. Unless this is assured, then difficulties and a great deal of worry are bound to arise. There are various levels of contractors ranging from the very large organizations, who are able to tackle any kind of assignment from making a replica of the Kremlin, to a life-size model of a satellite in orbit. On their staff they have every kind of craftsman – signwriters, metal-workers, woodworkers, model makers, electricians, paper-hangers, painters, etc., all first-class men at their jobs. The middle men in the exhibition business have a somewhat telescoped organization and tend to sub-contract out work requiring special skills. The very small contractors are a kind of super Jack-of-all-trades, e.g. the signwriter is also expected to be able to paint and to do any paper-hanging that is needed and the electrician may be required to turn his hand to simple metal forming. The time is fast approaching, if it is not already here, when Trade Union regulations will be making the life of the small contractor extremely precarious as Union Leaders frown upon and, indeed, forbid any interchangeability of jobs. One man, one craft, is the rule of modern trade unions. This ruling is, of course, rigidly adhered to in all work undertaken at nationally organized exhibitions, say, at Olympia and Earls Court.

Choice of contractor also depends on the nature of the stand, its area, complexity and the time available for building. Small contractors with their smaller overheads can provide good, simple stands very economically, but the big contractor with a modern workshop and a staff of highly skilled craftsmen can, if he is well organized, build a small stand at a reasonable price, provided he has a sufficient number to build to make it worthwhile. It has to be realized that sometimes small jobs, even if built at cost, help to fill the work programme gaps in between two major exhibitions. Another point to bear in mind is that if the job is large or complex, it is desirable to erect the prefabricated units in time for a preview so that the management is given an opportunity of seeing what they are getting for their money. It is only the large contractor with his spacious workshops who has sufficient floor space to put on a dress-rehearsal.

When considering the appointment of a stand constructor the following factors should be taken into consideration:

(1) How large is the stand and how complicated the design?
(2) Is there a great deal of display which requires specialist treatment?
(3) Is the stand to be entirely prefabricated in the shops?
(4) How much time is being allowed for pre-site work?

Simple types of stand, such as one finds at engineering exhibitions where most of the area is taken up with machines or furniture exhibitions, where the furniture itself is expected to take up practically all space, are well within the capacity and capability of small- or medium-sized firms, but for complicated stands requiring very detailed display treatment, such as those found at chemical, pharmaceutical and medical exhibitions, the larger contractors are able to give a better service because they are self-contained.

COST OF EXHIBITING

This can vary a great deal, even for two stands of identical area. Some designs are complex, elaborate and take a long time to build. Others, perhaps no less attractive, are relatively simple and inexpensive to construct. A figure of £2 5s. per sq. ft. can be quoted as a rough guide for exhibition costs in the United Kingdom, but it should be appreciated that this is only an approximation, e.g. a double-decker stand might well cost £8 10s. per sq. ft. to build. The determining factor in this vexed question of cost is the standard of quality which the manufacturer is out to achieve. A prestige stand with its thick pile carpeting, expensive furnishing and well equipped display area, must cost a great deal more than a stand designed and built for hard selling. The former might cost £5–10 per sq. ft., and the latter £4 or less. As much as £25 per sq. ft. can be charged for stands with elaborate displays involving giant colour transparencies, working models and other forms of animation, especially when the complexity of the animation demands constant supervision of technicians. Apart from the actual cost of building the stand and providing the required display material, there are a number of ancillary services to be included in the final bill, such as telephone and electrical services, cleaning, flowers and catering, staff and entertainment.

For overseas exhibitions there is the additional charge of freightage and customs charges, which may be highly expensive, particularly if some of the material is sent by air. Then, for overseas exhibitions, the cost of labour, whether it has been provided by the United Kingdom contractor or hired locally, always costs a great deal more than it does at home. The experience of exhibitors at the British Exhibition in New York in 1961 threw into high relief the fantastically high cost of U.S. exhibition labour. In some cases the actual cost of hiring trade union labour to re-erect the prefabricated stand costs much more than the original building costs incurred in the United Kingdom in the first instance.

TRAVELLING EXHIBITIONS

There is a growing interest in mobile exhibitions that are able to travel from one industrial site to another and special vehicles are made for this purpose. One such unit consists of a powered section built on an A.E.C. chassis and a larger trailer. On site the two sections reach together and open out sideways to provide a total covered area of about 50 ft. × 20 ft. This contains exhibition rooms, conference room and a fully equipped kitchen. An independent power supply is built in. Sleeping accommodation for three is provided. A vehicle of this type suitable for travelling exhibitions in Europe costs about £20,000, but it can be hired for a month or so on terms to be negotiated with the agents. A less ambitious unit suitable for small exhibitions can be made available via an exhibition caravan of the maximum size permitted on the roads in the United Kingdom – this is 22 ft. long × 7 ft. 6 in. wide. A specially designed trailer, reinforced to withstand heavy usage, can be built at a cost of about £850 for the shell, and fitting up is extra. This unit can be towed from site to site with a Land Rover or any reasonably high-powered car.

ORGANIZING AN OVERSEAS EXHIBITION

In organizing an exhibition to be held overseas, the one important commodity that is needed above all else is – time. It takes longer to plan, longer to build and longer to erect an exhibition in Stockholm than it does in London. At the outset, it should be realized by the manufacturer that if United Kingdom standards are to be maintained, costs will be very high and it is advisable at a very early stage, to compromise on quality so as to keep costs down to a reasonable level. Foreign exhibitions generally are much below United Kingdom standards and it seems unrealistic to try and go one better than the Swedes or the Dutch, or any other national.

There are three ways of approaching an exhibition overseas. The first, and most obvious method, is to prefabricate the stand in the United Kingdom, ship it to the country where the show is being organized and erect it on the site using either British labour from the home contractor or locally recruited labour. This is an efficient and economical way of building a stand depending, of course, on the country. In some countries, for instance, British labour cannot be used, except in a supervisory capacity. The second method, which is quite frequently successful, is to arrange for the stand to be built by a local contractor, but to supply all display material from the United Kingdom. This approach has the advantage of saving considerable sums on freightage, but against it must be reckoned the fact that supervision of the construction work is required, and this can necessitate visits to supervise the local work. This is essential if the local agent is unreliable. The third and last method is to allow the local agent or overseas company to be wholly responsible for building the stand and providing all the displays. This procedure may work out very well in some countries, depending entirely on the territory and the standards that are generally acceptable. Obviously, the advice of the man on the spot has to be carefully considered.

A new and promising approach to overseas exhibitions which appeals to many British manufacturers is participation in what are termed 'combined stands' organized by trade federations. These composite stands, which may represent the interests of 12–20 member companies, and perhaps the trade Press, are very economical and represent the simplest way of participating in a foreign exhibition. The space allotted to each manufacturer varies according to the total area and number of firms taking part, but usually it is in the region of 100–150 sq. ft. Members who take part are responsible for their own particular sections and are required to provide staff to be in attendance throughout the period of the exhibition.

For an expenditure of less than £500 a British manufacturer can have his own little stand operating under the umbrella of his trade association. It should be possible to carry this idea still further, and for British manufacturers who are not members of trade confederations to group together, say, under the auspices of the Board of Trade, to show in various overseas exhibitions. Adequate representation could thereby be achieved at comparatively low cost.

INTERPRETERS

Where the manufacturer's own staff is deficient in the languages of the country, then interpreters have to be hired. Usually arrangements for securing the services of really first-class people have to be made well in advance of the opening of the exhibition. Advice on finding and selecting interpreters is usually available from the Commercial Attaché of the British Embassy or the organizers of the exhibition. The difficulty usually experienced by manufacturers interested in a trade exhibition is to find technically competent people. There are generally plenty of interpreters available who are conversationally competent, but very few who have a knowledge of chemistry or engineering. These have to be recruited from the Universities. This is particularly the case in the Iron Curtain countries.

FOREIGN EDITIONS OF COMPANY LITERATURE

The full impact of an overseas exhibition is lost unless ample supplies of technical literature printed in the language of the country are made available on the stand. All translations need careful checking, particularly at the proof stage, to make sure that the printer has not omitted or dropped in a few extra characters. Some mistakes can cause very serious consequences, particularly in the Communist countries where they are apt to be hypersensitive. At one exhibition which the author helped to organize in the U.S.S.R. an elaborate and expensive brochure was translated into Russian and, owing to a minor typographical mistake, one normally inoffensive word was made to assume a meaning which, whilst permissible in the latest edition of *Lady Chatterley's Lover*, is still regarded as distinctly odd in a technical publication. The Soviet authorities took a most serious view of the mistake, pointing out that the brochure was pornographical and they decreed that unless all supplies were burned in their presence, then the stand would have to be closed down. Faced with this alternative, and the possibility of being ordered to leave the country, some thousands of the offending brochure went up in smoke.

WORKING TO A TIMETABLE

It will be readily appreciated that time is a vital factor in all pre-exhibition work and success on the opening day is only achieved by careful planning and co-ordination of all related activities. To ensure that important items are not overlooked, it is essential that progress schedules should be drawn up. Examples of the type of schedule which the author has found most useful are given below. One advantage of the combined stand is that much of this routine organization work is handled centrally but, even so, the manufacturer is well advised to make his own arrangements regarding publicity by means of Press announcements and contact with the local Press.

REMINDER SCHEDULE

Space booking – before accepting, check site for hazards, i.e. manholes, pillars and access doors for reserve supplies, overhead clearance and floor loadings.

Briefing meeting – provide designer with ground plan, site dimensions and detail of hazards – rules and regulations – details of shell scheme if obligatory – construction budget and theme and overtime script.

Appointment of contractor and/or sub-contractor.

Water and waste requirements.

Electrical requirements (both light and power load factor).

Gas requirements.

Lifting requirements (cranes, trolleys – include provision of labour).

Catering requirements including waitresses and bar staff.

Floor coverings and furniture (chairs, tables, desks, cabinets, ashtrays, waste-paper baskets, refrigerators, air conditioning units).

Staffing arrangements (include interpreters, lapel badges, etc.).

Inquiry forms or cards.

Literature (provision of right quantities and right languages).

Telephone requirements.

Insurance (include public liability).

Fire extinguisher requirements.

Cleaning requirements.

Floral requirements.

Record photographs of stand structure and display (include V.I.P. photography).

Catalogue entry and Press notice for organizing press officer and trade Press.

Ticket requirements (exhibitors, workmen's service passes, complimentary tickets).

Liaison with agents and sales offices (? reception for customers).

Liaison with overseas company or agents (? reception for customers).

PROGRESS SCHEDULE

Company meeting to determine theme and products to be shown.

Briefing meeting with designer.

Submission of designer's sketch plans and outline of scheme. *Allow 3 weeks.*

Agreement of structural proposals and display details in principle. *Allow 2 weeks.*

Provision of final caption schedule, photos, references, etc. *Allow 2 weeks.*

Agreement of finalized display layouts. *Allow 2 weeks.*

Caption schedules for translation.

Caption schedules for translation to designer.

Working drawings of structure and displays.

Approval of drawings by organizing and local authorities. *Allow 2 weeks.*

Specification to contractors for tenders.

Acceptance of tender and appointment of contractor. *Allow 1 week.*

Building of stand at contractor's works commences. *Allow 8–12 weeks.*

Exhibits and references to contractor.

Preview and/or customs clearance. *Allow 1 week.*

Packing and shipping. *Allow 1 week.*

Shipment and transit. *Allow 1–4 weeks.*

Arrival on site and clearance through customs. *Allow 5 days.*

Installation on site. *Allow 2 weeks.*

Completion of stand 24 hours before opening day.

Press day (stand partially manned).

Exhibition opens (stand fully manned).

Exhibition closes.

Dismantling of stand and shipment back.

Returned material distributed to original supplier by contractor.

Final contractor's invoice and settlement of design fee.

16

MANNING AN EXHIBITION
STAND

ONCE AN exhibition stand has been built and everything is ready
for the opening morning, the publicity manager would normally
expect to hand it over to his opposite number on the commercial
and/or technical sales side for occupation or manning. It is of importance that not only should there be adequate staff available on
the stand to provide a satisfactory service, but the calibre of the
individual members should be reasonably high. An expensive
stand staffed with junior or inexperienced representatives is a bad
investment for any company.

CHOICE OF REPRESENTATIVES FOR STAND DUTY

This depends on several factors, notably availability of the right
men at the right time; the type of exhibition (public or trade or
both); the audience and inquiries that are expected; the nature of
the products being shown and the purpose of the enterprise. If the
stand is non-technical and designed essentially as a prestige
exhibit, then it would be a waste of valuable technical manpower
to have technicians in attendance. On the other hand, if the purpose is to sell industrial goods, then staffing becomes much more
complex. To cater for the buyer or potential buyer who wants to
discuss performance or properties as well as price, the representative should be chosen who is sufficiently well versed in his subject
as to be able to answer all but the most highly technical questions. These should be referred to the specialist, who should
either be available on the stand for consultation or on call,
i.e. very hot queries can be referred to him over the telephone.

For shows such as Ideal Homes, Food Fair, Do It Yourself, etc., making a strong popular appeal where great emphasis is placed on demonstrations, it is possible to hire from agencies very competent demonstrators, both men and women. They can quickly be taught the right kind of patter to accompany the actual demonstration, which is usually quite simple. These people, although invaluable for such occasions, are of little value as assistants on trade stands because they lack the technical background and commercial experience so necessary if really intelligent answers are to be given to trade inquiries. Only as a last resort should assistants be hired from an agency and then only as a temporary measure, until members of the staff (even retired employees) can be recruited.

Appearance is important and representatives on stand duty should be quietly dressed and give the appearance of efficiency without flamboyancy. Flashy looking representatives tend either to scare away the more sober minded visitors, or to irritate them. In any event, they are a liability to a manufacturer with a good solid reputation and a worthwhile product. The ideal age for a representative on duty on a trade stand at a technical exhibition is about 30–45. If too young, an impression of immaturity is given and if too old, the firm stands in danger of appearing old-fashioned. It is, of course, realized that manufacturers with only a small staff have to make use of personnel that is available at the time, but if any choice exists then the younger man is generally preferable, provided he is acceptable physically and capable of doing the job. Attractive young women are seldom selected for duty on highly technical stands, e.g. you would hardly expect to see a pretty girl acting as representative on the stand of a chemical engineering firm, but she would not appear out of place on the stand of a firm specializing in office equipment or business machinery. Whilst one acknowledges that there are a number of highly qualified chemical engineers who are women, it is still very difficult to reconcile this fact with the general trade acceptance of female representation on a chemical engineering stand. In the eyes of the chemical manufacturer a chemical engineer is always a man.

STAND MANAGER

A large stand of 1,000 sq. ft. or more, where possibly the technical and commercial representatives may total fifteen, requires a manager to act as administrator and organizer. It is his responsibility to ensure that all members of the staff arrive in time and only finish when the exhibition closes in the evening. The manager would also be required to see that representatives were reasonably well turned out and that they behaved themselves when on duty. His responsibility would also include the co-ordinating and the logging of all information likely to be of value to the company, and running the office. Discipline has to be maintained on a stand and representatives have to work to a strict rota for lunch and tea breaks. Nothing causes more dissatisfaction than unfair treatment and the manager must be scrupulously careful that everyone on duty is treated the same – there must be no favourites. Organization of the office is not usually part of the stand manager's duties, this being left to the person responsible for running it.He has to ensure that reports are made out every day and that efficient communication is maintained with head office.

The manager is also expected to be there to welcome important visitors, and where necessary, arrange for a chairman or director to be available, and to escort them round the stand, explaining the various features. To do this competently he must, of course, be thoroughly familiar with the business. The gathering of intelligence about competitors and the market generally is the responsibility of the manager and he would be expected by his superiors to be reasonably knowledgeable on these matters. Another responsibility of the manager, or the person in charge of the stand, is the distribution of trade literature including, of course, the stocking of supplies and replenishment when these run low. This can be quite troublesome on a large stand, particularly if there are many types of literature and price lists, and it is often worthwhile to keep simple stocksheets.

BRIEFING MEETING

An hour or so before the exhibition opens the manager, or

whoever is in charge of the stand, should hold a meeting with his staff and tell them the domestic arrangements which he proposes to make for the efficient running of the stand. After the meeting, which need only take 10 minutes, he should escort the representatives round the stand, explain its theme and describe the exhibits in some detail. This is a very important exercise because when the exhibition actually opens to trade buyers, another opportunity may not arise for a briefing, and without it the staff would be kept in ignorance for the whole purpose of the stand. In addition to a live briefing, which is absolutely invaluable, each person doing duty on the stand should be given a written brief. This need only be a simple document setting out quite briefly the company's objectives, describing the main exhibits and providing extra information in the way of appendices or notes. Here is an example of a brief which could conceivably be useful to representatives on the stand of a leather manufacturer.

Wilson, Trowton and Silbeck Limited

Objective. To show the footwear and allied industries (including the clothing trade) the wide range of light leathers manufactured by W., T. & S. and, in particular, to focus attention on the extensive colour range, especially in suèdes and smooth-finished clothing leathers, now available.

Displays – Leathers. Impressive array of shoe leathers in glacé and calf and clothing and gloving leathers in suède and grain finishes.

Finished Goods

Women's shoes.	*Name of supplier given*
Men's shoes.	*Name of supplier given*
Children's shoes.	*Name of supplier given*

Clothing

Women's wear.	*Name of supplier given*
Men's wear.	*Name of supplier given*

Gloves

Women's gloves.	*Name of supplier given*
Men's gloves.	*Name of supplier given*

SPECIAL NOTES

Points to stress when talking to customers:

(1) High reputation of the firm.

(2) Technical excellence of leathers produced – mention significant advances made by W., T. & S. chemists in the dyeing and finishing of shoe leathers and development of new suède finishes for clothing leathers.

(3) Style and fashion rating of finished goods made from W., T. & S. leathers – mention names of leading firms in the footwear, clothing and gloving trades who use the company's products.

(4) In comparison with cheaper imported leathers, those made by W., T. & S. are better suited to the requirements of the home market and have a higher acceptance value in the more exclusive British stores – give names of shops where merchandise made from W., T. & S. leathers are featured. (The stand was designed by Herbert L. Stalkley-Ross and built by Glasser and Kennedy (Shopfitters) Ltd.)

ENTERTAINMENT OF CUSTOMERS

The standard and degree of entertainment in the form of alcoholic refreshments that is made available to customers at a trade exhibition varies a good deal depending on the type of show, the size of the stand and the nature of the business conducted. Even on stands that are classed as 'dry', there is often in the office the odd bottle of gin or Scotch which is held in reserve for the real die-hard customer who would be mortally offended if not offered a drink. On large stands at important national or international exhibitions, the entertainment is frequently planned on quite a lavish scale and a number of stands are equipped with well-stocked bars manned by professional barmen who are kept busy throughout the period of the show.

Without wishing to underrate the value of alcohol as a means of breaking down sales resistance, a great deal of money can be wasted on entertainment unless it is properly organized. This is

190

where the stand manager can play a vital part. It is his responsibility to see that alcoholic drinks are not dispensed too liberally and that a close control is kept over the liquor store and the amount of spirits consumed each day. On 'wet' stands at every exhibition there are the occasional incidents when visitors are entertained too lavishly and make a nuisance of themselves. If this happens it can be extremely embarrassing and may even lead to a disruption of good relations with an important customer. The manager and his staff should be quick to spot likely trouble-makers and try, before it is too late, to coax them off the stand. This requires the exercise of both tact and diplomacy mixed with firmness. The penalty of leaving a potential inebriate to develop into a drunk is trouble, spelt with a capital 'T'. It is noticeable that some large companies and organizations are now excluding hard drink from their stands and serving only soft drinks and lager. This is an excellent move and removes all possibility of unpleasant incidents occurring and leads to greater efficiency in the running of the stand, with a saving in entertainment costs.

HOW TO DEAL WITH INQUIRIES

Every company has its own system of reporting back and a good deal of ingenuity has been shown in designing suitable forms for use by representatives. If a company has found by experience that its own particular procedure gives good results, then obviously it would be foolish to try and change this. In these days of mounting competition, particularly from overseas manufacturers, it is worthwhile taking a critical look at the way in which inquiries are dealt with by staff. There are, of course, several different kinds of inquiries, some are urgent and require immediate action on the spot, others are more complex and need to be passed to headquarters, and finally there are the large mass of simple inquiries, many of an indefinite nature, which may be dealt with directly by the staff present on the stand. All inquiries, irrespective of their sales, should be logged. It not infrequently happens that the rather trivial inquiry of today is the order of tomorrow.

It is usually assumed, and quite rightly so in the United Kingdom, that if an inquirer refuses to give his name or the name of his company, then there is little purpose in reporting this, or trying to pursue the inquiry any further. This, unfortunately, is a common state of affairs in Eastern Europe where one has to deal through the official organizations and where there is a great reluctance on behalf of individuals to become personally identified with any inquiry. If by chance they do volunteer their names and business addresses, the literature and technical data when it is sent to them from the United Kingdom, seldom reaches them, being re-routed by the censor.

If we take an actual example of a firm showing on its stand a range of machine tool controls for milling, routing, boring and drilling machines, the pattern of inquiries might look something like this:

Inquiries (General)

40 per cent casual inquiries about price and availability from unknown people who decline to disclose their identity or that of their company.

Action Taken

All answered on the spot and simple explanatory price list handed out.

Inquiries (Specific)

40 per cent serious inquiries from known firms who want information about:

(*a*) Limitations of the controlling device.
(*b*) Ease of operating.
(*c*) Type of worker employed.
(*d*) Life of controls.
(*e*) Price and delivery.

Action Taken

All queries answered on the spot, but where the representatives were pressed for very precise or detailed information the questions were referred to headquarters. The latter only happened occasionally and most visitors to the stand were satisfied with the general information provided. Appropriate literature distributed.

Inquiries (Special)

20 per cent inquiries about firms in the United Kingdom and the U.S.A. who have already installed such controls; request to contact them for a first-hand account of their own experience, including cost of operating, etc. Also inquiries about maintenance of control mechanism, details of guarantee and conditions of sale, etc.

Action Taken

These are difficult questions, most of them posed by acknowledged experts in the field who represent important big potential users. In general, the representatives provided the basic information, and failing the presence of a high executive of the company on the stand, referred back to headquarters the particularly difficult or tricky queries. Literature made available when requested.

This analysis takes no account of the flippant questions that are asked from time to time, such as who supplied the flowers, or who designed the stand – all of them nothing whatever to do with the hard selling of controls for machine tools.

It will be seen from the analysis given above that the actual pattern is somewhat abstract in its form and, of course, it may alter radically from one product or machine to another. The important lesson to be learned in every instance is that where possible, the visitor should be satisfied on the spot. Somehow or other, the information he requires has to be given to him before he leaves the stand. This is absolutely vital. Only in the most exceptional cases should he leave without the required information. If this cardinal rule is made known to all representatives at the opening of an exhibition, then both management and trade visitors will be kept happy.

LITERATURE

The appetite for literature at a trade exhibition appears to be insatiable. The most casual inquirer expects to be given a well printed and nicely laid out leaflet or brochure and would be most disappointed if handed a duplicated sheet providing exactly the same information. The larger the firm the greater the volume and the higher the quality of literature expected to be made available. The trouble-makers from the literature angle may be divided into four main classes. First of all, the exhibition magpies, the people who wander from stand to stand collecting samples, booklets and, indeed, anything lying about. Added to the adults in this class are, of course, the schoolboys and young students who, on special days, descend on the exhibition like a plague of locusts. Next in importance are the awkward trade buyers who never seem to know what they want in the way of literature, and the more you try to satisfy them, the farther you appear to drift away from their ill-defined requirements. Then there are the very fastidious visitors who complain that the company's literature is inadequate or non-informative or inaccurate and compares unfavourably with American, Italian or German equivalents. Finally, there are the business tycoons, or would-be tycoons, who never take away any literature, but ask for it to be sent to their office, 'Marked for my attention, please!' When it arrives, sometimes by special messenger, it invariably turns out to be the wrong brochure or price list and the whole tedious process starts all over again.

Printed literature can be very expensive, especially as much of it is now illustrated in four colours and is very well produced. Five shillings to ten shillings a copy is not by any means an excessive price to pay for a 24-page brochure, and if it is given away indiscriminately the total cost can be considerable. In the writer's opinion, trade literature should be prominently displayed on the stand – behind glass, and only given away to bona fide inquirers. A very useful method of controlling the issue of expensively produced trade literature is to issue inquirers with printed cards on which they can tick the items required. The cards are then sorted at headquarters, and after analysis designed to discover likely trade prospects, the appropriate literature is mailed. This practice certainly saves on brochures and helps to conserve valuable storage space on the stand. It can, however, irritate the trade buyer who may reasonably expect to take away with him all the relevant pieces of literature. For policy reasons it is sometimes decided to make available a cheap, give-away leaflet to meet the needs of the general inquirer, but there is a growing feeling that even this is rather unnecessary and encourages the exhibition 'magpies'.

OVERSEAS PROBLEMS

When staging an overseas exhibition many problems are likely to arise, particularly in connection with accommodation, group transport and entertainment. All these matters need careful organization well in advance of the actual date of the exhibition. In the case of International Exhibitions or British Trade Fairs it is advisable to book accommodation at least 3–6 months ahead, and this should be done by the local agent on the spot. He is in a far better position to know the most suitable hotels and restaurants than even the best-informed travel agency. Where entertainment of trade visitors is thought to be desirable this requires very tactful handling – choosing the correct venue, menus, wine lists and invitation cards. In Eastern Europe great importance is attached to protocol and rank must be matched with rank. Offence is easily caused by the failure to provide hosts of the appropriate status, and the Russians are particularly touchy on questions of seniority. The Commercial Attaché at the Embassy is usually very willing to give advice on this vexed question of protocol.

Where possible, hotels for staff accommodation should be chosen fairly near the exhibition hall, or within walking distance. This is very important because foreign exhibitions often keep open until quite late at night, and taxis may not always be available to take tired Britishers back to their hotel, and they may be obliged to walk. Group transport can save the company a great deal of money, and it is quite simple to arrange if steps are taken well in advance of the exhibition date – at least three months notice is usually required. It is stressed that with all foreign exhibitions very careful and detailed planning is essential and it needs to be done several months before the exhibition takes place.

17

OPEN DAYS, SYMPOSIUMS AND CONFERENCES

IT OCCASIONALLY falls to the lot of the advertising or sales manager to organize an open day, conference or symposium for the purpose of promoting a product or service, or making known some new technical development. The objectives in this kind of exercise can be set out as follows:

(1) To increase the prestige of the company or organization in the eyes of the customer or potential customer.

(2) To promote the sales of a specific product, or range of products, or a service.

(3) To provide the opportunity for an uninhibited free discussion on technical problems which are common to the supplier and the purchaser in a prescribed industry.

(4) To enable the company's own executives to meet customers on the home ground and so profit from a frank exchange of views, not only on the subject under discussion, but business in general. It is possible in this way to gain a good deal of useful information about the customer reaction to the firm's selling organization, delivery system, packaging, complaints, competitive activities and overseas markets.

Looked at coldly and clinically, an occasion of this kind pays off handsomely in a number of directions, and from a public relations standpoint it would be difficult to think of any better and cheaper method of improving customer relationship. It is, however, no use organizing a convention or open day, or any other type of get-together with customers unless there is sufficient justification for such an event taking place. In other words, the company must have something useful to impart to the customer.

One way of approaching the problem is to organize the event in collaboration with some scientific or technical association or institute, or to aim the conference at a body of experts, say production engineers or works engineers, or analytical chemists, etc. With this method the papers that are read at the conference can be fairly general in scope, e.g it would be appropriate to read a paper to production engineers on 'New Developments in Work Study Methods' and to the works engineers one on 'Preventing Corrosion in Boilers and Cooling Systems'. No matter how the affair is approached, the ulterior motive is a commercial one – but it is, of course, necessary to coat the commercial pill as cleverly as possible.

If we take a specific example, say a manufacturer of a new type of armchair control for cranes, having master-controllers for the operation of contractor gear, there would be no better method of bringing this device to the notice of building contractors, demolition firms, etc., than inviting them to see a demonstration of the control actually operating under normal working conditions. The visitors, who would consist of actual customers and potential customers, civil engineers and different types of contractors, as well as the appropriate Trade Press, would have the opportunity of examining the control system and seeing for themselves how simple and foolproof it was to operate. Having seen the contrivance in operation they would be susceptible to a certain amount of sales talk by the company's executives, and be ready to put forward questions to the engineers present. Provided this particular control was new or represented some improvement in speed or safety, then the get-together with potential customers would be certain to achieve a worthwhile result. On the other hand, if it were already well known and could claim no novelty, either of design or operation, then it is highly probable that the results achieved would be disappointing.

Just as a Press conference should never be called without having a really good news story to hand out, so too a convention or open day should not be organized unless it had something to give – a new idea, a new design, a revolutionary development of some kind. It does not seem to be fully appreciated by manufacturers that in order to build up interest and a possible sales potential on such an occasion, it is necessary to give something in the form of useful intelligence that the guest will think makes his presence worthwhile. If business or professional people go away from the convention or open day with the uneasy feeling that they have been hoodwinked, then any amount of gin will not wash away this impression; moreover, it is likely to prejudice future good relationship with the company. Those responsible for planning the event should therefore be very careful to ensure that visitors are not only given the impression that it is of real importance, either technically or commercially, but in organizing lectures, demonstrations and displays there should be a preoccupation with the thought that basically people are only attracted by three primary considerations:

(*a*) What they will learn.
(*b*) Whom they will meet.
(*c*) Degree of entertainment offered.

IMPORTANCE OF DEMONSTRATIONS

Purely static shows tend to become rather boring, although their technical merit may rank very highly. Business and professional executives who spend most of their working days either talking to their juniors, or listening to their seniors, like to see something happening. Well staged demonstrations can transform what would otherwise be a very dull conference into something that is both interesting and stimulating. It is emphasized, however, that demonstrations need a good deal of stage managing to make certain that they run smoothly and are clearly seen by all the people present. Dress rehearsals are always advisable and large parties need to be broken down into manageable groups, each group being in the charge of a guide. Attention to detail is definitely worthwhile, because visitors to a plant, laboratory or office, frequently arrive in a somewhat critical state of mind and they are eager to score off their hosts by noticing examples of bad housekeeping, such as untidy workshops, dirty overalls and machines that have not been freshly painted.

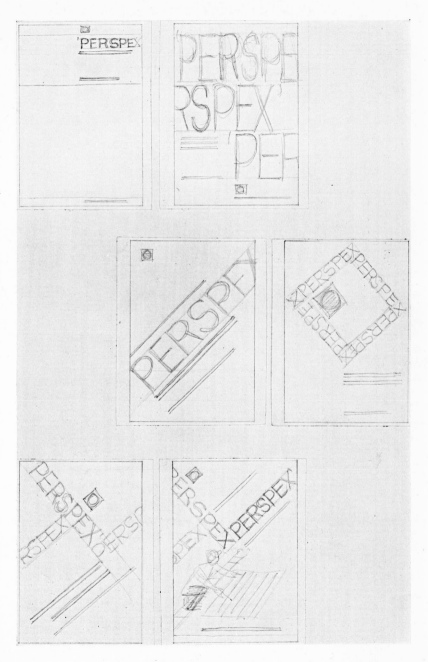

Rough ideas for the cover design of a technical brochure
(*see overleaf*)

Choice of demonstrator is important; he should not only be efficient in his work, but look efficient and smart. There is no denying the fact that a pretty girl, provided she is reasonably intelligent, contributes substantially to the success of demonstrations involving the use of relatively small or delicate pieces of machinery, or where it is desirable to show that finger-tip control is effective in certain operations. A man is obviously recommended for the heavier or clumsier machines, such as working a giant crane, but he would appear to be rather out of place operating a brush-filling machine or an automatic silk screening device.

OVERSEAS VISITORS

Where opportunities exist to invite overseas visitors to symposiums or open days, etc., these should not be neglected. The company's agents in foreign territories should be kept fully informed and their advice sought on the general advisability of extending invitations to potential customers abroad. The Central Office of Information can sometimes be of assistance as this organization is responsible for arranging officially sponsored tours so that specially invited guests from overseas can see for themselves British industries. The C.O.I. point out that, in practice, only a few of these sponsored foreign visitors have any real technical knowledge and, language difficulties apart, the most they can be expected to assimilate is a broad picture of the organization, together with impressions of items of outstanding interest.

In addition to these general tours for specially invited guests from abroad, short tours centred on London or provincial cities are also arranged by the C.O.I. for members of the various associations of overseas Press correspondents based in Britain. Programmes are also arranged for British Government officials on leave from overseas or about to take appointments abroad and for influential overseas visitors who wish to see various aspects of the British way of life. The British Council is normally responsible for official visitors whose main interests lie in cultural subjects, or in studying specific subjects such as medicine, engineering or the chemical industry.

Selling in export markets is now receiving such a high degree of priority that every effort should be made to widen the scope of any function organized by the company. When invitations are sent they should be accompanied by an explanatory note so that the recipient knows exactly what it is all about. For instance, if the occasion was to demonstrate a new design of machine to pre-form polyester glass fibre reinforced plastics, making possible the production of sailing boat hulls in one operation, quite an interesting little preamble could be compiled that would be bound to attract the attention of the plastics technician, the boat builder and the manufacturer interested in the commercial production of large moulded shapes. Accompanying the invitation the following text would be quite adequate.

> 'Although primarily designed as a pre-forming machine of special interest for the mass production of boat hulls, this unit is capable of modification to produce any type or design of large moulding. Many new technical devices have been incorporated in this machine and it represents the most advanced technique available to the plastics industry. Visitors to the Open Day will be able to see for themselves the machine in operation under normal works conditions and to follow the laboratory tests carried out to determine the quality of mouldings produced.'

It is believed that this kind of notice would stimulate interest far more than a formal invitation stating that a demonstration was being carried out. By taking the trouble to develop the idea in this way the company makes quite certain that the person who receives an invitation knows exactly what is going to happen on the day and the information he is likely to secure by being present.

PLANNING AN OPEN DAY

On all occasions when customers or potential customers are invited to a conference, convention or open day organized by one of their suppliers, representation of the host needs to be at the highest level. Visitors should, on arrival, be welcomed by the chairman or managing director and introduced to those executives of the company who will be responsible for the actual organizing and running of the event. All members of the company, which is acting as the host, must be identified by means of lapel badges giving their names and positions, e.g. Norman L. Ellis, Chief Engineer, or Miss Margaret Bond, Personnel Department. To the newcomer, this introduction is of supreme importance as his day will be made or marred by the way in which it is carried out. Whilst effusiveness and over-done cordiality are undesirable and suspect, even more harm is done by coldness and indifference. Guests should be treated in a warm and friendly manner and made to feel welcome.

On arrival, all the guests should be divided into workable or manageable parties, not larger than 20 and not fewer than 10, and a guide appointed to each. These guides need to be very carefully selected from the commercial or technical sides of the organization. Essential qualifications for a guide are – enthusiasm, pleasant and engaging manner, technical or commercial competence, and a flair for organization. It is no use choosing members of the staff who become excited and distraught if the programme is thrown out of gear for one of a hundred reasons. Actually, the guide is not dissimilar to a first class non-commissioned officer, say a company sergeant major, who in the army is seldom put off his stride and is quick to improvise.

Whilst conferences or conventions that are over-engaged are liable to appear 'stagey' and artificial, those company officials whose responsibility it is to organize the affair must be prepared to do a great deal of homework. First of all, a programme based on actual experience obtained as a result of 'trial and error' experiments needs to be evolved. It is useful at this stage to look at a fairly typical programme.

10 a.m. Arrival of party by coach from the station accompanied by a fairly senior member of the firm who travelled from town with the visitors. After de-bussing, visitors should be shown to the reception office and there introduced to the chairman or commercial director of the company.

10.10 a.m. Coffee and biscuits served.

10.25 a.m. Party divided up into groups of 10–20, and a guide allocated to each group. Ten is the ideal number for a group as it is easily manageable.

10.30 a.m. Tour commences, which includes visit to the factory and laboratories. Time allocated to each stop depends, of course, on the number of groups and the total time to be devoted to the tour. Supposing that this ends at 12.30, and if the party is made up of 100 people, it should allow for a maximum of 20 minutes at each of 5 stops, with 20 minutes in hand for walking from one location to another.

12.30 p.m. Assembly of visitors at some central point.

12.40 p.m. Cocktails.

1 p.m. Buffet lunch.

2.30 p.m. Reassembly of visitors in main hall or canteen to listen to a talk by some senior executive of the company on the main topic of the day. This talk should be illustrated by means of a short technical film or projection of slides, the latter being accompanied by a lively commentary.

3.30 p.m. Question time.

4 p.m. Tea.

4.30 p.m. Party leaves for station and return journey home.

FORM OF INVITATION TO AN OPEN DAY

There are, of course, many differences of opinion on the kind of invitation that is to be sent out to the trade or to selected groups of technical or business-men. First of all – timing; this is very important. If the invitation is sent out too early, then the recipients are liable to forget all about the actual date until it is too late. On the other hand, if the invitation is held back too long, it may become crowded out of the calendar. About three weeks' notice is just about right for most occasions of this nature.

Some companies, who have a reputation for organizing events of this kind, make what may be termed as a three-pronged attack. First of all a letter, signed by the managing director and addressed to an individual, goes out to the firm or organization. This letter, which is quite brief, invites the person to the open day and explains very briefly the purpose of the occasion. Accompanying the letter is an invitation card to which is attached a reply paid postcard and a programme. If a reply is not received within a week, then a further letter should be sent out, also signed by a high executive of the company (but not necessarily the managing director), gently reminding the recipient that no reply has been received and requesting an answer before the end of the week. Finally, a week before the actual event takes place, the delinquent should be contacted on the telephone and the final round-up made so that at least five days before the function the organizers know the actual number and identity of those visitors who will be present. This permits the company to make all the final arrangements in adequate time.

PRESS PUBLICITY

It is advisable to keep the trade Press fully in the picture when organizing an open day or conference, and this may be done at small cost and inconvenience by sending the editors of the relevant trade papers an invitation and programme at the same time as it is sent out to the trade. It is highly desirable that reputable journalists representing the trade and technical Press should always be given reasonable facilities so that these events can be well covered. Where dates clash with Press dates, then advance information and photographs should be provided so as to meet the deadline. Occasionally, the city editors of the national Press will give space to occasions of this kind and they should always be invited to come along.

THE COST OF AN OPEN DAY

The main items of expense are:

Printing	Travelling
Drink	Marquee or tentage
Food	where under-cover
Photography	facilities must be
	provided for out-
	door demonstration.

If we take the hypothetical case of an open day staged at a printing machinery firm's premises for 100 guests, it is reasonable to assume that the total bill might work out at approximately £800, which can be broken down as follows:

> Drinks and buffet lunch for 100 visitors and 25 of the company's own staff – £375
> Travelling and expenses, including railfare from London to the site and hire of coaches – £75
> Printing – £135
> Photography – £50

The hire of a marquee might cost £50, depending on the size and period of hiring.

All these purely fictitious items of cost can, of course, be made to vary according to the level of hospitality, the quality and quantity of print and the general standard of the other facilities made available. It would not be too extravagant, however, to consider £8 per head as reasonable for a modestly organized show. Viewed in terms of value for money, this would appear to be a worthwhile investment when compared with expenditure on advertising or exhibitions. It might, of course, be argued that beyond a certain figure, an open day becomes difficult to justify, and certainly if the cost per head were more than £10, then one would be justified in being suspicious of securing value for money. Whilst it is necessary to look at expenditure in this cold-blooded manner, it should be appreciated that, although it may be very difficult to assess the value of an open day, the long term benefit could be quite considerable.

FOLLOW-UP TACTICS

Well-timed and discreetly designed follow-ups can do a great deal to keep alive the memories of an open day. At small cost and the minimum of effort it is possible to exploit the initial advantage gained. Follow-up print material needs to be carefully planned, however, and designed so that it appears a logical reminder of progress made since the meeting. If we refer to the photosetting machine demonstrated by the printing machinery manufacturer, it would be worthwhile sending out a stop-press bulletin giving the latest information on delivery, price or recent case histories. Obviously the pitcher should not go to the well too often, but at least two follow-ups could be planned at intervals of a month after the actual open day.

PLANNING A SYMPOSIUM

Manufacturers of industrial goods and machinery can profit a good deal from meetings organized for specific bodies of people, e.g. works' managers, purchasing officers, medical officers, etc. These are best organized on rather different lines to the open days, and the meetings can be held in hotels, halls or any convenient venue, provided it is strategically situated. A manufacturer with headquarters in Derby could, for instance, arrange for a series of such gatherings to be held in the north-west region at, say, Manchester, Liverpool, Preston, Bolton. The time allotted to each meeting need not exceed $2\frac{1}{2}$-3 hours and it could be held either in the daytime or evening, depending on the kind of audience being catered for by the sponsors of the meeting. A very popular method of presentation makes use of three or four speakers, each one a specialist in his own particular subject, and allowing a maximum of 10 minutes for each talk. Each meeting would have a chairman, obviously a member of the company, chosen preferably from the commercial side of the organization. The procedure is for the talks to be given in succession after brief introductory remarks of welcome, by the chairman. Then follows a short interval for refreshments and the viewing of displays with a period of half an hour to an hour devoted to questions. These are of vital importance and in arranging these meetings it is not unusual for the chairman to ask for written questions or to have one or two in reserve in order to start off the discussion period.

Staffing of meetings of this kind needs a great deal of thought and a ratio of 1:5 of the sponsoring company's staff is usually adequate. Company personnel should wear lapel badges. In addition to senior staff, there should be two secretaries in attendance to check off visitors' names against the invitation list and to obtain signatures of guests in the Visitors' Book. These secretaries should also take notes during the discussion period.

A typical meeting might take the following form:

SYMPOSIUM ORGANIZED FOR CHEMICAL ENGINEERS

6.30 to 9.00 Friday, 20 July. Tilbury Hotel, Coniston Street (West), Liverpool.

CHAIRMAN: Mr. L. Kaufman, Sales Manager, Towston and Breeley Ltd.

AREA ORGANIZER: Mr. S. Jones (Liverpool Sales Office).

TALKS: New Developments in High Vacuum Distillation
(L. K. Temple, M.Sc., Ph.D.)
Filtration Problems in Effluent Disposal
(T. Tenby, B.Sc., F.R.I.C.)
Advances in Centrifugal Pump Design
(L. D. Wanstead, M.A., Ph.D.)

(Towston and Breeley Ltd. is a chemical engineering firm specializing in the manufacture of equipment for vacuum distillation, filtration and pumps, and the speakers are members of their technical and production departments.)

The detailed programme should look something like this:

6.30 p.m. Assembly in the Coronation Room at the Tilbury Hotel.

6.35 p.m. Formal welcome by chairman and introduction of speakers.

6.40 p.m. Mr. Temple reads his paper.

6.50 p.m. Mr. Tenby follows.

7.00 p.m. Mr. Wanstead concludes.

7.10 p.m. Chairman sums up and invites questions.

7.30 to 8.30 p.m. Questions and discussion.

8.30 to 9.00 p.m. Refreshments and dispersal.

GENERAL NOTES FOR ORGANIZERS

Copies of the three papers should be duplicated and made available to the visitors at the end of the meeting, together with relevant literature describing the company's products. Displays, preferably animated, should be arranged in the room where the lectures are to be given and these need to be designed so as to provide fundamental technical information about the apparatus being described. Blown-up photographs of actual installations with case histories also prove of interest to specialists.

EDITORIAL PUBLICITY

Even if the technical Press is not invited, and sometimes it is not possible for policy reasons to extend such invitations, a note about the meeting with copies of the talks should be sent to the relevant trade journals. This is always a sound scheme and, at a fractional cost, secures good publicity for the company's products.

STANDARD OF ENTERTAINMENT PROVIDED

At meetings of this kind lavish entertainment is not expected and beer and sandwiches are quite adequate for most of these gatherings. An alternative to beer could be made available in the form of coffee and soft drinks.

18

DISPLAYS

In THINKING of displays one automatically associates them with the selling of mass products in stores and supermarkets. Yet industrial goods sometimes require promotion at the point of sale, for example, agricultural implements need a great deal of promotion in the highly critical farming market which spends something like £900 million on the tools of their trade. Here the manufacturer has to capitalize on his general Press advertising in the farming papers and press forward with his technical claims for the particular machine, remembering all the time that farmers as a class are extremely knowledgeable. This is, perhaps, a rather obvious example, but if one takes any other type of machinery, such as an industrial water-softener for use in laundries, there often arises a need to demonstrate in some way the main principles of the machine, its advantages and the economics of operating it. A cleverly designed display is often the most convenient and effective means of providing the laundry manager with the basic information. It can, for instance, show by means of a diagram, animated if desired, what happens when hard water enters the apparatus and the average rate of flow of softened water which can be expected as the normal return. Then again, the display could also illustrate the average life of the apparatus and the cost of upkeep. In other words, the display, if it is to be an effective sales weapon, tells a technical story in words and picture. It does not sell the water-softener, but it acts as a reminder, supplementing the general promotionary efforts made by the manufacturer in the form of literature and trade advertising. Displays can sometimes be used effectively to illustrate technical data at lectures or business facts at sales meetings. The managements in some large concerns often favour this way of dressing-up such occasions and realize that well designed and attractive displays can often help to put over even the most boring statistics.

The use of displays in overseas markets can be of great importance as it is often not possible to provide the actual goods and well designed displays can sometimes fill the gap. Special care is necessary here to ensure that the display tells the story in the language of the country and the design is in harmony with what is normally acceptable in the particular market. It is important to remember that in certain overseas territories there is a marked preference for certain colours and a prejudice against others. Although unreasonable, it is a fact that there is in some countries a distinct tendency to associate particular colours with specific types of goods. It has, for instance, been pointed out that in the U.S.A., pastel blue and pink are the accepted colours for cosmetics and beauty preparations generally and appear out of place if associated with other types of merchandise.

Colours can also have racial, religious and political and even mystical associations, for example, yellow is very unpopular in Israel and also in many Moslem territories in India and Pakistan. The reason for this prejudice is not difficult to find. Yellow has for centuries been the hideous colour of discrimination against the Jews and in the East, as it is the colour of the robes worn by the Brahmin priests, it is detested by all devout followers of Mahomet. Red is the traditional colour of China, and was popular long before Karl Marx was born, being associated with good luck and happiness. White is the symbol of death and a mourning colour and blue is associated with sorrow. It is very important that the colours to be used on displays should be carefully examined from the viewpoint of national or local associations. Of course, colour prejudices are, in most cases, quite illogical and often ridiculous, but unfortunately they can seriously affect the popularity and acceptance of an expensive and attractively designed display. For this reason, some research is advisable and this can only be carried out on the spot by the local representative.

DISTRIBUTION AND PLANNING

Before a display is designed, and as a preliminary to any creative work, careful thought has to be given to the distribution. Many ambitious schemes have failed in the past because no advance plans were made to determine what to do with the displays once they were produced. It is sometimes airily presumed that because displays are necessary as part of the selling effort the sales organization will be able to place thousands of these with suitable distributors. This is, unfortunately, rarely the case, and unless a well thought out distribution plan has been worked out in advance of production, then sales representatives and agents are embarrassed when large quantities of displays are suddenly dumped in their offices. With point of sales displays for retail products there is a well recognized distribution procedure based on a very accurate analysis of the market. This kind of approach is also necessary in the case of displays for industrial products. If, for instance, we take as an example the industrial water-softener produced initially for laundries, three questions have to be answered immediately:

(1) How many displays are needed to cover market outlets (a) at home, (b) overseas?
(2) What opportunities are likely to exist for distributors to make good use of these displays?
(3) What is the basic information which has to be provided on the displays?

Dealing with the first query, the laundry industry is a relatively small one. There are about 4,000 laundries in the United Kingdom and supplying these are 225 engineers and machinery manufacturers and some 55–60 miscellaneous suppliers. It is apparent therefore that the number of displays required to meet the needs of this industry is a small one. On the other hand there are many likely users of industrial water-softeners, such as public institutions, hospitals, colleges, hotels, passenger ships, etc., making up a very formidable total. The buyers catering for the requirements of all these places are likely to be sensitive to the kind of publicity provided by well designed displays, but the snag is that opportunities to show them off are relatively few as the distributive outlets are restricted. Therefore, before finalizing on a number, a certain amount of research is necessary in order to discover who are the people in hospitals, public institutes, etc., authorized to purchase expensive equipment, such as water-softeners, and what opportunities exist for showing displays to such people. It could be that an excellent commercial case could be made out for ordering displays, only to find out that no one quite knows where to show them off. There is, of course, a laundry exhibition and there are conferences, symposiums and meetings, but very few actual showrooms exist where such displays could be shown off to advantage.

It might well be that for such a highly specialized piece of equipment as an industrial water-softener, a run of 250 displays could well meet all reasonable requirements in the United Kingdom. In fact, this might well be a top figure. Rounding it off, a production of 500 would possibly be sufficient to meet the requirements of home and overseas markets. It has to be remembered that in order to secure the most advantageous terms for production an economic figure has to be chosen, and for silk screen work 500 is about a minimum quantity. This kind of reasoning may sound a trifle 'woolly', but it is presumed the publicity manager responsible for the production of the displays would have available all the statistics relevant to the particular industry. The important thing is to carry out the exercise objectively. It is easy to be influenced by the magnitude of the market, which can be most misleading, the important factor is that relating to opportunity for showing the display.

DESIGN

There are two ways in which this subject can be approached. In the first place, the publicity manager can secure the services of an independent designer or studio, or he can go to a recognized and reputable display manufacturer and commission him to prepare suitable designs with a view to eventual production. The advantage of the first method is that the independent designer has much more freedom than the designer who is tied to a manufacturer, but, on the other hand, the free-lance usually suffers from a lack of knowledge of display processes and is liable to produce designs that are impractical or excessively expensive to manu-facture. Where it is possible to employ a really gifted artist or studio with a flair towards display work this is always preferable, but as a general rule it is advisable to allow the display organi-zation to be responsible both for design and production. A good display firm will employ competent artists capable of preparing or adapting every kind of finished artwork promptly, compe-tently and intelligently. In addition, the company will have avail-able photographic and printing facilities so as to be able to provide a complete service to the client.

Designs should be so contrived as to make the maximum impact and to convey at a glance the sales message. It is a waste of time and money to produce 'arty' designs that satisfy only the designer and cannot be justified commercially. After all, a display is an advertisement which sets out to promote a product or service and the maximum impact is required. It would be asking too much to expect an industrial display to sell an expensive machine or product, but it plays its part in 'softening up' the market. Eventually, a sales representative will effect the actual sale, but his efforts will certainly be made easier by any advance publicity put out by the manufacturer.

If the designer is to produce the right kind of design he has to be adequately briefed, i.e. told exactly what the display is intended to convey and the type of audience to which it is required to appeal. Citing the case of the industrial water-softener it is immediately obvious that the audience will be an informed one, consisting of laundry managers and engineers. They will naturally expect the display to be informative, giving both technical and commercial information – how the apparatus functions – output – economy – maintenance, reliability and price. These are points which need to be graphically presented on a display. Where displays have proved to be ineffective the reason can often be traced to the inadequacy of the briefing – the designer just does not know what he is supposed to portray! Having been provided with the brief, it is the responsibility of the designer to translate this in the form of a display.

The usual procedure is for the designer, first of all, to prepare a rough drawing showing the kind of treatment he has in mind. This is shown to the client and discussed in detail. Usually modifications are needed and these are put in hand. On the basis of the modified design, a mock-up or prototype is prepared so as to show the client what the real thing will look like. Once this has been approved the actual production is put in hand. What is rather tragic is to allow production to begin and then to insist on further modifications half-way through the work. To avoid this kind of thing from happening, the commercial departments should be given the opportunity of commenting on the prototype before it is passed over to the display manufacturers for bulk production.

THE RIGHT KIND OF DISPLAY

In planning the design the following factors have to be considered at an early stage:

(a) The type of display most suitable for the subject matter.
(b) The process to be used for reproduction.
(c) The story to be told.

The first two must, of course, be reviewed in relation to cost and usually the budget for displays is a very tight one.

A display can be any size and shape from a simple show-card to a very large free-standing unit. Indeed, it is sometimes very difficult to define the difference between an exhibition and a display. What really determines the dimensions of the display is the use to which it is to be put once it leaves the manufacturer. For instance, it could be a show-card in a dealer's window or showroom, a counter display or strip on a builder's merchant's counter or a free-standing unit in a warehouse or showroom. Then again, the display can be designed specifically for some kind of private exhibition or demonstration or to illustrate a lecture.

Knowledge of the purpose for which the display is intended will help to answer such queries as – 'Will the display be illuminated?'; 'Can it be sent by post or must it be specially packed so as to travel by road transport or rail?' Another vital consideration is the durability of the unit. Should it be built to last for years, or is the display only intended to have a seasonable use? These questions are vitally important if money or time is not to be wasted in production. Where the display is intended for overseas markets, packing, freightage and customs dues, etc., have all to be taken into account. It may, in some instances, be more economical to place the production with a contractor in the territory where the promotion is being planned.

When a number of similar displays have to be produced a good deal of thought needs to be given to the most economic means of reproduction. Here a competent display manufacturer will be able to plan his design so as to achieve maximum economy. Type setting, photographic enlargements and silk screen printing can all be expensive if used indiscriminately, but when the display is carefully planned then a large measure of economy can be effected. For example, an additional and often quite unnecessary colour on a show-card could add perhaps a third to the price of the finished job. One very economical method of producing displays is to use current Press advertisements mounted on stout card and strutted so that they will stand up on a counter or table. To give extra impact the advertisement can be 'blown-up' photographically and perhaps colour added.

The kind of story to be told or the sales message which has to be communicated needs to be very carefully thought out so that it is unambiguous. An additional point concerns readability. The printed matter should consist of sharp and crisp statements in a non-serif type face, such as Grotesque No. 9. Other excellent type faces for display work include Gill Sans Bold and Headline Bold, both of which are extremely readable. It should not be inferred that the serif faces such as Caslon Titling, Garamond Bold, Perpetua Bold Titling, Falstaff and Fournier do not have their place in the production of displays, but undoubtedly for providing information about industrial goods in a clear and incisive manner, the non-serif type faces seem preferable. Type faces such as Matura and Othello, Klang and Shadow Titling, Figaro and Goudy, all seem to be ill-fitted for technical sales displays, although they are often used with telling effect in the vast consumer market.

A general view of the Plastics Division's part of the I.C.I. stand at the British Trades Fair held in Stockholm on 18 May to 23 June 1962

View of the I.C.I. Plastics Division stand at the International Plastics Exhibition, Olympia, held from 21 June to 1 July, 1961

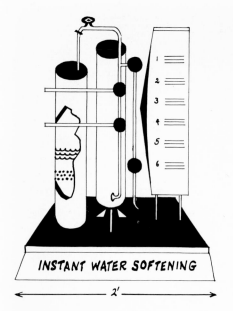

INSTANT WATER SOFTENING

Suggested design for counter display intended to illustrate commercial water softener. Estimated price for display £6 for fifty displays

Display for industrial product intended for showing at trade exhibitions and agricultural shows. Estimated price for construction – £25 for ten displays

ACME - THE SUPREME WATER SOFTENER!

PACKING AND DISPATCH

It is a good plan to make the display manufacturer responsible for packing and dispatching. The success of any promotional scheme involving the use of displays is largely dependent on the efficiency of the supply service. In other words, the display must be provided when it is needed, and not afterwards. An efficient display producer will realize this and make sure that this important service is provided.

19

DIRECT MAIL

A CONVENIENT DEFINITION for this form of direct advertising is that it is a method of bringing to the notice of an individual in a specified trade, professional category or class, an advertising message addressed to him through the post. Direct mail, to be successful and economical in use, must not only be highly selective, but personal. A high percentage of waste is bound to occur unless the mailing is to an individual, e.g. a brochure describing a new type of centrifugal type of pump, which could be of considerable interest to the textile industry, would quickly find its way to the waste-paper basket if the letter containing it was merely addressed to the chief chemist at the textile mill. The letter would, however, stand an excellent chance of being considered sympathetically if addressed to Mr. J. L. Hines, B.Sc., F.R.I.C., Chief Chemist, Messrs. Bloggs and Bloggs, etc.

Direct mail, although considered to be mainly applicable to consumer goods, can be exploited to good purpose for selling both goods and services of a highly technical nature, or it may be designed and directed towards the development of a market. On the Continent, the smaller manufacturers with a limited sales force make liberal use of direct mail to test and to prepare new ground for attack by their salesmen. A manufacturer of electrical appliances in, say, Western France might be unable to extend his sales territory in Northern France and Belgium because of shortage of staff. He could, however, carry out a mailing campaign in these territories and, having located potential customers, deploy some of his representatives for a special drive to capture new business. Here, direct mail could do the initial canvassing and so save the manufacturer the salaries and expenses of his salesmen.

216

Direct mail can also be used as a tool for market research and some of the practitioners in this line of business make generous use of postal questionnaires as a means of securing basic information that would cost a great deal of money, and take a long time to accumulate in any other way.

The outstanding value of direct mail is its versatility, flexibility and selectivity. It can be accurately timed to reach customers on a particular day or at prearranged intervals throughout the year. It may consist of a simple, well phrased sales letter with follow-ups in the form of brochures and catalogues, or advertising novelties designed to attract attention. Every trade and profession can be reached via the postal service and some 89,000 postmen are available to carry the sales message to the potential customer. The fact that this form of advertising is private and confidential can be important, particularly in launching a new product or starting a new service.

The selectivity of direct mail deserves a little attention, because buying in some trades may be largely governed by the calendar. A farmer is unlikely to buy a new tractor or a piece of farm equipment in the middle of his harvest, but he might be susceptible to some sales persuasion through direct mail in the late autumn when some of the cheques for the harvest have been paid into the bank.

The importance of selectivity can play a most important part in a number of campaigns, e.g. a manufacturer might want to explore the sales potential in a particular part of a region, but not the whole region. This can easily be organized and most reputable mail houses offer breakdowns in all territories. For certain types of pilot schemes it may become desirable to try out a product on a very limited scale, e.g. a manufacturer of gelatine capsules specializing in pharmaceutical products might want to extend his business into the food field, but be unwilling initially to carry out a national campaign. He might want to feel the pulse of the market by approaching all the food manufacturers and canning houses in East Anglia. This he could do very easily via direct mail.

Although it is common to regard direct mail as a means of selling, the long-term advertising value of this medium cannot be ignored. If inquiries from a campaign only result in 5 per cent inquiries and 1 per cent actual sales, and these figures are on the low side, it is unreasonable to suppose that the 95 per cent of promotional material has served no purpose. A high proportion of this must have been read and the company or the product's name will be remembered. This apparently unresponsive and unprofitable audience can, however, be looked upon as an untapped reservoir of possible sales. It is unfair to judge the value of direct mail campaign solely on inquiries received, and yet this frequently happens.

Last in this look at the significance of direct mail there is the public relations aspect of a well directed campaign which is not designed to sell but to attract and to stimulate the recipient's interest in the company's products or services. One excellent example of this is afforded by the happy enterprise of Wiggins Teape, who send out to 20,000 customers and friends a charming little pannier of primroses. This arrives on the paper buyer's desk in the early spring of each year and has a greater prestige or public relations value than any amount of printed paper. This well-timed gift draws a 70 per cent response in the way of a little note of thanks – who says there is no sentiment in business?

ATTITUDE OF THE ADVERTISING AGENCY TOWARDS DIRECT MAIL

The agency attitude towards direct mail is a cautious one. Generally speaking, account executives are seldom very enthusiastic about the benefits to be derived from this form of advertising, and only a small percentage of agencies employ experts in direct mail, that is, people on the creative side who are able to plan and prepare complete mailing campaigns from start to finish. There is also a lack of interest shown by the agencies into any form of research to determine not only the degree of readership of mailed material but, more important still, the level of readership. In other words, what is of growing importance to the manufacturer is the basic 'readership value' of direct mail and an assessment of this value in terms of selling and advertising, both short-term and long-term values.

Probably the indifference shown by some advertising agents towards direct mail stems from the fact that the mailing house is regarded as a kind of poor relation of the advertising business. It is true, of course, that it is only during the last fifteen years that direct mail has become really important and has organized its own business on efficient lines. Now it has its own trade association and is highly respectable and reputable. There are very few agencies that actually do their own direct mail, although some have associated companies to carry out this work. Generally speaking, direct mail is usually sub-contracted out to specialists, that is, mailing houses catering for the specific job in hand. One cannot divorce financial considerations from the attitude of agencies towards direct mail, but it is a fact that in terms of profitability, the agency finds it more worthwhile and a lot less trouble to handle Press advertising for a client than direct mail. To be scrupulously fair, this consideration does not, and, indeed, should not weigh too heavily with reputable agencies, but high principles are all very well, but the agency business is, after all, organized to operate on a profit basis.

HOW CAN DIRECT MAIL HELP THE INDUSTRIAL AND TECHNICAL ADVERTISER?

In almost every sphere of industry and commerce direct mail is helping to sell and to advertise both goods and services. There is practically no product, no matter how technical, that cannot be sold or its sale promoted through the medium of the postal service. Manufacturers of such specialized pieces of equipment as electron microscopes can profit from a mailing campaign to 644 research associations, institutes and organizations, and the 548 major industrial research laboratories.

In the same way, sign-makers who want to bring to the notice of shopkeepers a new kind of fascia sign could promote interest by a campaign aimed at Britain's shops, or a section of this vast collection, say, the 2,583 china and earthenware retailers. The lists prepared by direct mail houses are very comprehensive and include every known trade, profession and occupation. Even the

219

most obscure trades, such as anchor chain manufacturers and makers of bagpipes, are all listed. Within these classified sections the direct mail house can break down the trades still further to meet the specific requirements of a client, e.g. he might want to contact only the largest manufacturers in a particular category or the manufacturers in a certain closely prescribed geographical area.

It is, however, important to look upon direct mail as a form of advertising that has to be integrated into a well-planned publicity scheme. Only in this way can the best results be achieved. Before any reasonable return can be expected from a direct mail exercise some preliminary advertising or extensive editorial publicity must be done so as to prepare the ground. The exception to this general rule is where the company or the product is already well known, such as Shell, Esso and I.C.I. Recipients of sales-promotional material through the post are generally suspicious of the claims made for a product, unless they have already seen it advertised or written up either in the trade or national Press. For this reason it is most important that when a direct mail campaign is being launched it should be timed so that the impact of a complementary advertising scheme is fully exploited. A great deal of money is wasted by manufacturers carrying out independent mailing schemes without regard to the advertising that is taking place. Integration is the keynote of success in this business. If, for instance, an explosives manufacturer had perfected a new type of blasting cartridge for use in quarries, the logical sequence of events in the promotion and sale of this would be for him to supply the relevant trade journals with an editorial note on this new development, supplemented with some dramatic photographs of blasting operations. Then, logically, he could profitably follow this up with advertisements in the trade journals. Only after the first advertisement has appeared should he carry out his mailing campaign to 1,323 quarry owners.

It can, of course, be argued that in some instances solus schemes pay good dividends and, indeed, this may be the case with highly specialized products made by long established and highly respected manufacturers, although they may not be known nationally. An example of this could be the sales-promotion of a new kind of pesticide which a manufacturer might want to sell to farmers in, say, Wiltshire, where they were suffering from a plague of the particular kind of vermin sensitive to the pesticide.

THE COST OF DIRECT MAIL

Unless properly planned and co-ordinated and carried out by experts, direct mail can be wasteful and expensive. In an ordinary business house it costs about 1s. 6d. just to type and post a letter, if one includes in this a proportion of the typist's wages, but not the overhead charges, which might conceivably add on another 3d. or even 6d. Direct mail houses with their high-speed addressing machines, automatic enclosing machines, stapling machines, collating machines and stamp affixing machines, to mention only some of the modern equipment used, can reduce the cost of the sales letter to a small fraction of that accepted as normal by the manufacturer. However, with all the aid of the latest business machinery, direct mail is still expensive and the cost must be carefully assessed before undertaking a campaign. First of all, advising, planning and organizing are not usually charged for by the direct mailing organization unless this is extremely complex and takes a long time, then a charge may be made. Normally, however, this preliminary work is undertaken for the client free of charge, at least that is what he has a right to expect.

Apart from the actual postal charge, which is an unalterable figure, the main cost items are as follows:

(1) Folder or other promotional material, letter and reply-paid card.
(2) Envelope of the correct size to hold the printed matter.
(3) Charge for type addressing labels, including the supply of labels, affixing, enclosing and mailing.

Dealing with the first item, the expense here is, of course, determined by the quality and volume of print matter and the grade of paper used. The manufacturer may supply the direct mail house with the printed matter, except the sales letter; he may arrange with his advertising agency to handle production in collaboration with the direct mailing company or let the latter do the entire job, i.e. the creative work and the printing. The last-named course can often work out the most economical and the large mailing concerns are now fully organized and equipped to handle every type of print requirement. It is most important to remember that the quality of both print and paper has a very important influence on the reaction of the recipient, and it is false economy to think that quality does not really matter in a mailing campaign. With industrial accounts it is more important than ever that the folder or brochure should be of high quality and designed to make an immediate appeal to the potential buyer. Emphasis is placed on the word 'immediate', as unless the folder or brochure attracts the person's attention immediately he glances at it, then it has no possible chance of being read. Some manufacturers mistakenly think that any kind of surplus printed matter, if available in sufficient quantity and on the right selling lines, is suitable for mailing campaigns – nothing could be further from the truth. It is only quality in direct mail print that will really pay dividends.

An actual example of a mailing exercise can be quoted.

> Mailing to 7,981 chemical engineers, including supplying and type addressing labels to the above; affixing 3 advertisement pulls (no fold), one pre-folded letter and one leaflet, tucking in double fold, bundling for franking and mailing at printed matter rate

	£232	0	0
Cost of advertisement pulls, leaflet and letter	£165	0	0
Postage	£150	5	4
Envelopes	£ 83	5	0
	£630	10	4

As regards mailing charges, the supply and type addressing of labels is at a standard rate, but the insertion of printed matter into envelopes may vary slightly depending upon the actual number of pieces of paper to be included. The price of envelopes is a variable factor dependent upon the size of envelope and the quality of paper.

In the writer's opinion there is still not enough attention being paid to the presentation of the actual sales letter. This is usually a standard multigraphed letter with the name and address matched-in. Unless this is expertly done the letter has an obvious 'phoney' look about it and immediately puts the reader on the defensive. Very much greater care needs to be taken in securing a more accurate facsimile reproduction of a pleasing and modern typewriter face and the matching-in of names and addresses and salutations in exactly the same face with the same weight of ink. It is worth taking this extra care and paying a little extra for the greatly improved finished result.

HOW RELIABLE ARE THE MAILING LISTS?

Users of direct mail often complain bitterly about the high percentage of letters that are returned by the postal authorities because the addresses are either incorrect or the recipients have died or gone away. Generally speaking, clients are expected to stand the loss of 1 per cent of all letters mailed, but above this, most reputable mailing houses undertake to refund the delivery and return postage on all undelivered letters exceeding 1 per cent of those posted up to 4d. per packet.

It would be unreasonable to expect classified lists, no matter how carefully compiled, to be 100 per cent accurate. All direct mail agencies take great pains to keep their lists up to date, but it should be remembered that they are not collated from personal knowledge of any particular trade. It is impossible to find anyone in the direct mail business who is prepared to guarantee the accuracy of the classified lists they use. On this question of accuracy, there is evidence of some uneasiness both among direct mailing houses themselves and their clients, both of whom realize that the information upon which the lists are based is obtained from a number of sources by relatively low grade workers. It is therefore open to some doubt whether these people, who are responsible for seeking and sifting the basic facts, are sufficiently discriminating. If they are not, then the lists must necessarily become less useful and reliable.

RESPONSE FROM A DIRECT MAIL CAMPAIGN

There is a good deal of misunderstanding about the percentage of replies that a manufacturer might reasonably expect from a mailing campaign. There is no comfortable average that can be quoted, everything depends upon the type of exercise being undertaken. If, for instance, a rubber manufacturer had developed a special formulation of particular interest to golf ball manufacturers, he could quite reasonably expect to receive almost 100 per cent return from the 18 companies in this line of business. This is, perhaps an extreme case, but if we take fruit canners, and there are 203 of these listed, a mailing shot giving details of a new piece of canning machinery might draw replies up to, say, 80 per cent provided, of course, that the product being described offered outstanding practical advantages over existing equipment. On the other hand, a piece of promotional material about a new kind of fertilizer mailed to some 52,000 farmers in the Midland Counties might only result in a return of 1,560, or 3 per cent, of which perhaps only 1 per cent resulted in actual sales. The response from direct mail depends upon several factors, only some of which are controllable:

(1) The size of market being attacked.
(2) The appeal or novelty of the goods or service being offered.
(3) The way in which the exercise is carried out.
(4) The timing of the mailing.
(5) The reliability of the lists used.

PLANNING A DIRECT MAIL CAMPAIGN

It is always advisable to do this in collaboration with both the advertising agent and the mailing house. The agent can contribute a great deal because of the importance of integrating the actual mailing with Press advertising, and because he understands the client's general promotional and sales policy. If we take an actual example it is, perhaps, easier to see how a campaign can be launched. First of all the problem. This is to promote the use of a new and greatly improved type of rigid polyurethane foam as a thermal

224

insulant in building. The material has a good sales potential as it is not only technically superioi to its Continental equivalent, but is offered at a competitive price, moreover, it is made by a company, which, although relatively small, enjoys a high reputation in the building and allied field for entirely unrelated products, mainly glazed stoneware and plumbing accessories.

The first query that arises is the actual market to attack – builders, builders' merchants, architects, heating and ventilating engineers – a tremendous field. This is where the advice of the advertising agent is needed. After consultation it is decided that to attempt to cover the whole market would be too ambitious and that the promotion of the product should be attempted in two stages; first of all, as much editorial publicity in the trade Press as possible, followed up by a modest advertising campaign in the architectural Press and building material journals. Then, in the middle of this advertising, a direct mail scheme should start and be directed towards a section of the market, initially the builders' merchants, of which there are listed just over 5,000. This is a manageable scheme. The direct mail is planned on the following lines:

(1) Sales letter, multigraphed on the firm's notepaper with matched-in name and address and signed by the managing director of the company. This letter would set out very briefly the salient technical as well as the economic advantages offered by the product.

(2) Alongside the sales letter would be folder No. 1, combining a reply-paid postcard. The folder might be printed two-colour offset on 65/70 D/Med. smooth white cartridge and designed to slip easily into a good quality white envelope, 12 in. × 5 in., hand-typed and addressed to the head of the firm of builders' merchants. This folder could be well illustrated with suitable line drawings and diagrams and contain just sufficient technical data and price ratios to attract and sustain attention.

The letter and the folder would be mailed, say, in February, and followed up in March and May with two further pieces of promotional material, each progressively more technical and each containing a reply-paid card. The fourth and clinching mailing shot could be sent out in September. Refinements of this scheme could be made by giving each mailing shot a distinctive colour, say, red to start with, green in March, blue in May and lemon yellow in September. Colour does play quite a significant part in helping to increase the force of the initial impact, and this is what is needed in a campaign of this kind. Another idea which could increase the effectiveness of the mailing shot would be to attach to each folder a sample of the material so as to give the appearance that it was actually *in situ* in a roof as an insulating membrane.

20

FILMS – AUDIENCES, USES AND COMMENTARIES

THE AUDIENCE

BEFORE A FILM treatment is started and the film actually commissioned, the sponsor should have a clear idea of the kind of audience he is trying to reach. It not infrequently happens that a film is decided upon by the management without anyone having a very clear idea of what to do with it when it is finished. There exists, of course, a hazy notion that the film may eventually serve a useful commercial purpose in promoting the sales of a product or a process, or add to the prestige of the company, but no one has a clear idea of its purpose or destination. It is not only necessary to have a well defined objective for the film, but to know precisely the kind of audience to be invited to see it, and even the size of this audience. The last-named piece of information is important. If only small groups are to see the film, and this usually happens in the case of instructional films, then possibly 8 mm. gauge would prove satisfactory. On the other hand, if very large audiences are being planned, then 35 mm. gauge may be required in order to secure the highest standard of definition and the finest colour values on a large screen.

A film is, after all, a story on celluloid and its readership needs to be known before the story is written. Reputable film companies always make a point of trying to find out why the film is being made, and where and to whom it is to be shown at an early briefing meeting with the sponsor. This kind of information is vital as it affects the treatment, the production and the whole economics of film production. Woolly thinking at the briefing stage leads inevitably to a poor film which no one really likes and which serves no commercially useful purpose.

To design the film so that it makes the most effective impact on the audience, the actual breakdown of the audience should be known and studied. The manufacturer of mechanical handling equipment, let us say, fork-lift trucks, may want a film in order to demonstrate the versatility, robust construction and ease of handling of a new model or design. A film can do this kind of thing very well. Once having decided upon the aim of the film, then the audience has to be considered very carefully. First of all, let us look at the manufacturer's order book and find out where he sells these trucks. There we find that his sales are roughly 40 per cent United Kingdom and 60 per cent overseas, the bulk of the overseas sales going to Australia, South Africa, Rhodesia and Ghana. On consultation with the export manager of the firm, it is disclosed that competitors make wide use of this kind of film, not only to interest potential buyers, but also to instruct factory personnel. This complicates the issue, as sales films are usually different in scope and treatment from instructional films, particularly if the latter are intended for native audiences.

There now arises some kind of a picture, not very clear as yet, but still most useful, of the kind of audience one might reasonably expect for a film on fork-lift trucks. A great deal more information is still needed to complete this picture – the type of audience to be invited to see the film in the United Kingdom, i.e. their status and the probable size of each gathering and where such showings are to take place. Then overseas, it is essential to know the probable locations for the film showings, the type of projector equipment available, the size of audience expected and its composition.

The question has to be considered as to whether a film that appeals to prospective buyers in British industry makes the same kind of appeal to overseas viewers. If not, then possibly the answer is to make two editions of the film, one for the United Kingdom and a specially edited version for overseas with extra sequences of a purely instructional nature added. Here the 8 mm. gauge, which is admirably suited to small groups, would serve this purpose very well. One suggestion might be to use mute copies bearing magnetic stripe for local operators to prepare their own sound tracks. If, of course, the film were to be shown in the

European market to try and open up new fields in Holland or Germany, then it is very doubtful whether the overseas edition would be suitable as audiences in the Common Market are somewhat more sophisticated than those found in the Commonwealth.

It is obvious from this example that audience can and does affect treatment and ultimately the cost of the film. Nowadays it is a fairly general policy to prepare, say, one or two films giving general background, and then to break these down into, say, three films – one designed for sales-promotion and the other two for showing operational techniques and perhaps maintenance. Where the films are made within the company, this kind of approach to film-making is economically possible, but if outside contractors are used, then such an operation is not only very expensive, but extremely lengthy and time-consuming.

It is emphasized that successful film-making cannot be haphazard, but needs to be carefully planned at each stage of production.

USES

There are many uses to which a film can be put by a sponsor. Probably the best known are advertising, information and status. A film can help to create a favourable atmosphere for selling in much the same way as a page advertisement. This kind of film is, in fact, an animated advertisement which is designed to interest an audience and at the same time to 'put over' a sales-promotion story. The information film sets out to explain processes or techniques which an audience could not otherwise see. Considerable use is made of such films to tell a technical story to a specialized body of people, e.g. a film showing stage by stage the erection of a prefabricated pre-stressed concrete bridge would be of great interest to civil engineers. It would give them an opportunity of seeing an operation denied to the majority of them and provide information that would normally only be found in technical reports.

The status film is a public relations piece of promotion designed to improve the general acceptability of a company, a brand name, a process, a principle or an institution. It attempts to create a favourable image and is usually an expensive, elaborate and often somewhat flamboyant production. Many films are, of course, made which do not fall neatly into these categories, and are in the nature of a compromise, i.e. they try to convey information and yet have a strong commercial bias, or they attempt to cover two distinct purposes, e.g. public relations and sales-promotion. A compromise film is very often a mediocre affair.

Some films are, of course, made to sell goods, particularly in certain overseas markets. In long-distance selling there is no doubt that a film can pay handsome dividends in the hands of energetic overseas representatives. It not only supplements the publicity created by literature and advertisements, but demonstrates in a convincing way the product or machine that is offered for sale. As films can be made quickly, particularly if produced internally, topicality can be ensured and the customer in the Lebanon or Turkey is able to see for himself the latest machine or technique only a few weeks after it is released for sale in the United Kingdom. The 'selling' film has, however, a restricted use and is mainly confined to showings in those parts of the world where it is difficult to demonstrate the actual commodities.

In making the industrial film there is always a strong temptation to try and pack into it so much technical data that it can be claimed to be an accurate picture of the process or product. Unless this temptation is resisted, the film is almost certain to be extremely dull and will defeat its purpose by having a soporific effect on the audience. The film is not the right medium to use to put over detailed factual information; this should be printed in a brochure. The primary purpose of a film is to create a favourable impression and to sustain the interest of an audience in a subject.

THE MECHANICS OF FILM DISTRIBUTION

Apart from the distribution of a film by the sponsor's own organization there are other means of ensuring that it is seen by a wider audience. These means include film libraries, some of which cater for the documentary or industrial film. There is also the

Central Office of Information which, through its network of contacts in British Embassies and Consulates overseas, is able to give a very wide coverage.

If an industrial film is well made and gives a clear picture of some important facet of British industry, then it is almost certain that the C.O.I. will be interested in having copies for distribution. When shown abroad through the good offices of the Commercial Attaché or Consul, industrial films can do a useful selling job apart, of course, from adding to the prestige of British industry. If the C.O.I. is interested in a film it may want as many as 50–100 copies and with commentaries in the language where the films are to be shown.

In addition to film libraries and the Central Office of Information, there are many organizations throughout the country who are interested in technical films, provided they are not too highly specialized. For example, a film on steel-making, work in a pottery or the manufacture of footwear, are all subjects that might usefully be shown to Women's Institutes, Town Guilds and similar kinds of audiences. The sponsor has, of course, to decide whether the publicity gained is of any commercial value to him.

THE RIGHT COMMENTARY

The commentary is the translation of the actual shooting script into words and the choice of these words is of great significance. A poor commentary can ruin a good film. Professional commentary writers know instinctively the proper relationship between the spoken word and the picture, but the amateur is unaware of this and usually tries to pack in as many words as possible. The result is that the viewer often suffers from verbal indigestion by the time the welcome word END is thrown on the screen. Commentary writing is a highly specialized and skilled art and success depends on the use of the right descriptive words and the right number of words. The best advice one can give to the tyro in this business is to try and keep the commentary both factual and simple and to be as economical as possible with the use of words; where the picture requires no explanation, then words are unnecessary and merely serve to irritate the viewer. Some technical audiences detest music and effects in technical films, but most people tolerate music to play in or play out the picture.

PROFESSIONAL OR AMATEUR COMMENTATORS

It is rare, indeed, that the amateur commentator can compete with the professional in voice quality, audibility and general oral acceptability, although he may possibly score when it comes to the pronunciation of long or awkward technical words. However, with a little coaching the professional commentator should be able to get his tongue round almost every kind of word, even such a tongue-twister as polytetrafluoroethylene. The only advantage of the amateur commentator is economy but this is rather doubtful advantage when one looks at film production as a whole. In the writer's opinion the professional commentator scores every time and it is usually false economy to try and save the odd 50 guineas or so that is paid for his services. Apart from having a good voice and one well suited to the film, the professional is able to tackle the whole tricky business of recording with efficiency and speed, thereby saving a great deal of production time.

FOREIGN COMMENTARIES

If a film is to do a workmanlike job overseas, then the commentary has to be available in the language of the country where it is to be shown. Experience tends to show that it is always advisable to have the commentaries prepared and recorded by nationals. Where the languages are unusually difficult, say, some obscure Eastern dialect, it generally pays to provide mute copies of the film with a magnetic stripe so that local representatives are able to prepare their own sound tracks on the spot. This practice can be recommended as it speeds up the whole process of film-making and ensures that sales representatives in the Malay Peninsula or other far-distant territories have full control over the recording. It also saves the publicity manager a great deal of trouble and even embarrassment. Faulty commentaries not only irritate viewers but tend to give a poor impression of the efficiency of the company who sponsored the film.

The writer has had some experience of the difficulties of making films for showing in the Soviet Union using White Russians resident in the United Kingdom for writing and recording the commentaries. Such people do an excellent job, but unfortunately their use of archaic phrases betrays the fact that the commentaries were written outside the U.S.S.R. Audiences in Moscow and Leningrad tend to be highly critical of such films. The making of foreign commentaries presents a number of difficulties, the least of which is the editing of the English script so that the foreign version fits the picture – German and many other languages take up far more space when written and far more time when spoken than the equivalent text in English.

21

FILMS – PRODUCTION AND COSTS

THE RIGHT GAUGE

IN THE professional film world there is general unanimity of opinion that the best technical films are taken on 35 mm. stock and where 16 mm. material is eventually required, then reduction copies should be made from the 35 mm. original or copy. Whilst few would care to dispute the fact that for high definition and true colour values there is nothing to touch the 35 mm. Eastman print, the cost of making a film of this gauge is high and often beyond the reach of many industrial concerns. It is, however, possible to make satisfactory and commercially acceptable films direct on 16 mm. stock, thereby saving large sums of money on equipment, lighting and all the auxiliary services, as well as labour and, of course, effecting a very substantial economy in film stock, which in 35 mm. size is very costly. For most purposes in industry 16 mm. film production is an attractive proposition and many thousands of excellent films are sponsored every year. Such films can meet all the reasonable requirements of the average publicity department.

A very interesting development is the emergence of the 8 mm. as a direct competitor to the 16 mm. film as a gauge suitable for many commercial and educational purposes. Advances in technique now make possible the production of good quality 8 mm. prints and high quality sound on magnetic stripe. Demonstrations have shown that it is possible to project an 8 mm. colour print so as to fill a screen 12 ft. × 9 ft. to give an acceptable picture. This means that the film is magnified some 600,000 times in area.

The advantages of using 8 mm. film are, of course, economic

ones. Copies are very cheap to make, projection equipment is less costly and certainly less bulky. On the question of cost, it is claimed that complete 8 mm. colour prints with magnetic sound-track can cost less than 40 per cent of the cost of equivalent picture material in 16 mm. gauge. It is not suggested that the 8 mm. film copy can replace the 16 mm. for large audiences, but it is certain to find fairly wide acceptance where only a limited screen size is required to meet the requirements of small groups. There is also a growing interest in the use of silent 8 mm. films for educational purposes where the commentaries are provided by local instructors.

Although interest in the 8 mm. film is mainly centred on the production of reduction copies from either 35 mm. or 16 mm. original negative material, there is a growing awareness of the potentialities of the 8 mm. film as an original gauge. So far no great enthusiasm has been shown on the part of professional film-makers to take films on 8 mm. negative stock, and there appears to be a number of technical difficulties to be overcome before this becomes generally possible. Apart from the limitations of camera equipment, most of which is designed for the amateur, there are still difficulties of processing and sound recording which have to be overcome before professional film-makers will be willing to consider seriously the 8 mm. gauge for the original negative.

COLOUR OR MONOCHROME

It should not be assumed that every worthwhile film has to be made in colour. There are, indeed, a number of subjects that are more suitable in black and white than colour, for example, a film relating to a civil engineering project, such as building a bridge over a railway, could advantageously be shot in monochrome. This would enable quite substantial reductions to be made in the cost of the film, as much as 50 per cent less, and also permit greater latitude in film-making owing to the higher speed of black and white material as compared with colour stock.

For instructional films, such as the working of a lathe, there are few advantages to be gained by using colour as the machine itself, and the steel being processed, are largely devoid of colour. It is true, of course, that nowadays audiences are colour-conscious and tend to regard the black and white film as somewhat old-fashioned. On the other hand, people are well reconciled to the black and white picture they see on their television screen! Where the subject matter is itself colourful and a certain amount of prestige is associated with the film itself, then, if the budget allows, the film should be taken in colour.

CHOICE OF FILM-MAKER

The sponsor who is new to film-making presents something of a problem, and one not easy to solve. If he has had no previous experience of a professional film-making company and is in doubt about a producer, then his wisest plan is to contact the Association of Specialized Film Producers, whose membership includes practically every established British company, both large and small. The A.S.F.P. will, on request, provide names and addresses but, of course, cannot make recommendations.

The only sensible way to choose a particular film-maker from a list of companies is to see some of the films already made, selecting subjects not entirely dissimilar to one's own business. A machine-tool manufacturer might, for instance, gain quite a lot if he saw a film on the work of a tabulating machine, but very little if the film were concerned with the benefits of life insurance. Having seen several films and being given an idea of their cost, then he might reasonably ask the film company to be allowed to approach one or two sponsors so as to learn at first hand whether they were satisfied with the treatment given them. Only in this way can the new or potential sponsor be reasonably certain that he has chosen wisely. It may seem a rather involved procedure, but as some hundreds, and maybe thousands, of pounds, are involved, then the precautions suggested do not seem unreasonable.

Although a film can hardly be put out to tender in the same way as the purchase of a piece of equipment for the factory, sufficient background information may be gained from this kind of investigation to ensure that money will be spent wisely. The one-man-band type of film producer seldom gives value for money even though his prices may be very tempting. Unless the sponsor is willing to prepare the script, write the commentary, supervise the editing and generally 'wet-nurse' the whole production, then the one-man-band type of film producer can seldom be recommended. It is far better for the newcomer to films to go to a reputable film company who can provide him with a complete service at an agreed price, rather than to try and save money by employing just a cameraman. There are, of course, notable exceptions, but as a general rule the above observations seem justified.

MAKING ONE'S OWN FILMS

There are powerful arguments in favour of making one's own films, speed being one of the most important. Where a film is required to do a selling job and to demonstrate the working of a machine or the operation of a process, then the film needs to be topical. There is little purpose in sending out a film to describe a new type of electronic computer if it is 9–10 months old by the time it is seen by the customer. It is the writer's opinion that speed of film production offers the greatest practical advantage to the company that makes its own films. At a time when long-distance selling is becoming increasingly difficult in the face of intense competition from Japan, Germany and Italy, not to mention the U.S.A., topicality is a vital factor in all demonstration films.

Only when film production is under the control of the sponsor himself can the flexibility of this media be fully exploited.

It is not suggested that do-it-yourself films can be as good as those produced by outside units who, on the whole, will make better sales-promotion and public relations films than those made internally. On the other hand, where films are required to demonstrate and to take the place of 'live' demonstrations, then some sacrifice can be made in quality provided the films take only weeks instead of months to produce.

THE COST OF FILM-MAKING BY PROFESSIONAL FILM-MAKERS

It is very difficult to arrive at even an approximate cost for a film unless a treatment has been prepared, and this involves a good deal of work. Factual films with sound commentary, involving only one location and showing a process or a project, are the cheapest to produce, but these serve only a limited purpose. Such films are mainly produced for educational or instructional purposes and have little real publicity value. Working with a reputable, although small film company, a 10-minute, 16 mm. film showing, stage by stage, and mostly in close-up, the manufacture of a toothbrush, might cost about £800–£1,000 in colour and £500–£600 in black and white. This film would involve a small production team and the minimum of equipment.

Lighting would be fairly simple as no long shots need be included. When the script becomes more involved, the number of locations increased and the lighting much more extravagant, then costs mount rapidly. The use of interior long shots and succession of camera angles, introduction of animated diagrams and such devices as stop-motion sequences all add considerably to the cost. Some film producers quote £1,500 per reel for the lower limit of 16 mm. industrial colour film and £6,000 for the higher limit, but these figures can be very misleading.

There is no such thing as a cheap film – film producing is expensive and it can be taken as an axiom that the more complicated the subject matter, particularly where a number of locations is involved, then the more expensive is the film. One way of approaching this question of cost, although not usually acceptable to the accountant, is to earmark a given sum of money, say, £5,000 and to have the film rigidly made within this budget. There is a lot to commend this type of approach and for most 16 mm. industrial films designed to have a reasonably high prestige value, it should be possible to produce a satisfactory 16 mm. colour lasting, say, 20 minutes. This is not likely to be an epic, but at least it will be adequate. Once the sponsor has disclosed his upper limit in this way, the film company can prepare the type of treatment that can be accommodated within the budget.

If the film is to be taken on 35 mm. material, then costs are likely to be at least 25 per cent greater than with 16 mm., and some of the larger film producers are wedded to this particular gauge for the original negative. The sponsor has, in considering costs, to take into consideration the advantages offered by the 35 mm. technique and to decide whether he is willing to pay an extra premium for the higher quality. In the writer's opinion, there is only a fractional benefit to be derived from making the film on 35 mm. stock and then reducing to 16 mm. for showing, as compared with the cost of shooting directly on to 16 mm. stock and making the print from the 16 mm. negative.

If, of course, the film is to be shown in the public cinema or to a very large audience then a 35 mm. film may be desirable. It is, however, rather rare for an industrial film to be shown in 35 mm. gauge as very few 35 mm. projectors are readily available in industry. A modern 16 mm. projector fitted with arc lamps can meet the needs of very large audiences, up to about 1,000 but the picture, although adequate, is not as good as that projected from 35 mm. material. Referring briefly to 8 mm. prints from either 35 mm. or 16 mm. colour negatives, via a colour duplicate positive and colour duplicate negative, the cost is likely to be at least 40 per cent less than with 16 mm. prints produced from the same negative material. This is presuming, of course, that at least 20–50 copies of the film are needed.

THE COST OF MAKING FILMS INTERNALLY

Wild claims are often made about the low cost of films made internally and these can be very misleading. It is unfair to compare a price based on film stock, processing and commentator's fee, etc., but excluding overheads with a price quoted for the same length of film made by a professional contractor. The overheads, although not usually disclosed with internal films, still have to be paid for and it serves no useful purpose to delude one's self that films can be made internally at only a fraction of the price charged by outside film-makers. To quote one example, three 16 mm. colour films were made by one large industrial concern mainly for staff recruitment and the instruction of process workers in a new plant. The total footage of film shot was 4,000 ft. and the production costs, i.e. stock, processing, editing, music and spoken commentary, etc., amounted to £650. The overheads amounted to some £2,000, this figure including depreciation on equipment purchased for £5,000, lighting, heating, office amenities, etc., plus labour charges incurred by use of a team of five senior members of the firm for three weeks. The total cost of the film was therefore £2,650 for three 10-minute films, each one costing £883, which is almost comparable with the price likely to be charged by an outside concern.

In the writer's opinion, film-making to professional standards is expensive no matter whether it is carried out inside or outside the company. Where internal films can score is on speed of production and this is very important.

EQUIPMENT AND STAFF NEEDED FOR AN INTERNAL FILM UNIT

The basic equipment required by any newly recruited 16 mm. film unit consists of a camera, projector, screen, editor and ancillary equipment, means of lighting and a tape-recorder. The camera must be a precision piece of apparatus, easy to handle and simple to operate and have available a range of high definition lenses. For an expenditure of a thousand pounds or so it is possible to purchase a camera that can be used to record synchronized sound as well as picture, and this may be required for certain types of advanced work. Highly specialized kinds of filming, such as works study and process research, may necessitate the use of a high-speed camera, but this hardly comes within the province of publicity work. Lenses sufficiently versatile to deal with all the situations in film-making are expensive, but it is foolish to attempt any economies in this direction. As regards the projector, a good 16 mm. sound projector fitted with, say, a $f1.4$ lens should meet most of the normal requirements of industrial audiences, but other lenses may be necessary. Screens, amplifiers and loud-speakers are also required and where the blackout of rooms cannot be made effective, then special types of screens, or back projection units with a translucent screen might become necessary.

Without going into details, it can be said that a capital investment of £5,000 is required to set up a modest little 16 mm. filming unit. Added to this a cameraman is required and his salary could easily be in the £1,200 bracket. There is no such thing as cheap filming; the equipment is expensive in itself and the cost of operating this equipment is also fairly high. Added to this is the fact that a cameraman, although highly proficient at taking the picture, editing and even working the projector, is usually not qualified to write the treatment, script and commentary. This work has either to be contracted out or other members of the company have to be persuaded to undertake these tasks. Their time, and therefore a proportion of their salaries, must be put on to the production costs of the film. Film stock itself is expensive and a great deal of it is inevitably wasted in making a film, particularly one in colour. Added to this are the processing charges which can be high.

THE PLACE OF THE FILMSTRIP IN PUBLICITY

Although the filmstrip lacks many of the possibilities of the cine film, particularly loss of movement, it can nevertheless play an important part in the demonstration of a product, machine or even a technique. The advantages offered by the filmstrip include, of course, low cost, ease of handling and flexibility of picture sequence and the ability of an audience to study each individual frame for as long as required. Filmstrips are usually produced on a standard width of 35 mm. in two types – single frame strip, in which the individual pictures measure 18 mm. × 24 mm. and are arranged across the strip with their long edges adjacent, and double frame, with pictures 24 mm. × 36 mm., arranged with their shorter edges adjacent.

There is no doubt that the filmstrip is very suitable for the presentation of static subjects, particularly machines and equipment generally, in fact, all goods where close examination of detail is essential. Not only can colour transparencies be projected, but also black and white negatives can be converted into positive transparencies for use in the projector. The filmstrip is also excellent for showing diagrams and charts.

Sound filmstrips are now in general use and these help to fill the gap between the 16 mm. sound film complete with spoken commentary and silent filmstrip. The equipment required for sound filmstrips consists of a 35 mm. filmstrip (single or double frame) with a standard gramophone record or magnetic tape carrying the associated commentary and dialogue. Incorporated with the disc or tape is a sound signal which informs the operator when the picture has to be changed, either manually or automatically.

First-class filmstrips are invaluable to illustrate lectures and for use on exhibition stands where products not actually available on the stand can be shown in the office on a back projection screen. Apart, however, from the value of the filmstrip as a publicity aid, it serves its most useful purpose for the instruction of staff.

22

PHOTOGRAPHY

PHOTOGRAPHY AS AN AID TO BUYING AND SELLING

IT IS UNFORTUNATELY true that British industry has for years neglected many of the possibilities offered by photography for the vigorous pictorial promotion of goods and services overseas. This sentiment was expressed some little time ago by Mr. Hubert Davey, past president of the Institute of British Photography, who complained about the short-sightedness of British industrialists. There is a reluctance on behalf of many sections of industry in this country to spend adequate sums on commissioning first flight photographers to show to the world the products made in Britain and to reveal something of the background of their manufacture. In contrast, America, and also it seems, unlikely countries such as Japan, spend vast sums on promotional photography. It was reported a few months ago that the American photographer, W. Eugene Smith, was commissioned by a Japanese industrial concern, Hitachi, to take a series of pictures in and around about their manufacturing plants for a fee amounting to about 25,000 dollars.

Photography can play a vital role in public relations and is one of the most effective and economical means of telling an industrial story. In the projection of British goods and services overseas there is no doubt that it can play a vital part, particularly if the right kind of photographers are commissioned and they are given the right kind of opportunities. Unfortunately, the curtain of secrecy falls so readily that these opportunities, in so far as they apply to industrial processes, are frequently denied. It is possible, we are so often told, for photographs of manufacturing techniques to disclose 'know-how' and trade secrets, and therefore security taboos must be imposed. Yet in contradiction to this one finds the same kind of photographs published in American trade journals and issued quite freely by leading American companies. In the interests of sales-promotion abroad and the development of new markets, it is surely time that this curtain of secrecy was drawn back and a much more liberal attitude taken towards photography in industry.

PHOTOGRAPHY UNDERTAKEN BY THE ADVERTISING AGENCY

Here one is in danger of treading on very thin ice. Advertising agencies, as a general rule, like to undertake what they term the 'creative photography' used in the client's advertising. This work is seldom done in the agency and is usually farmed out to studios specializing in a particular type of work. It might involve the use of models, elaborately built sets, trick photography or even photo-micrography. There are on the books of the art director in every agency at least fifty studios and free-lance photographers who can tackle competently almost every kind of assignment from puppets to blast furnaces.

Most reasonable clients agree that if the photography required for a certain advertisement is highly imaginative and has to be integrated with artwork and copy, then it is obviously to the advantage of the account for the photography to be under the control of the agency. On the other hand, if the photography is fairly straightforward and is merely designed to provide a squared-up half-tone or colour set, then it is questionable whether the agency needs to be involved. The company's own publicity department should be competent to supervise and to produce most of the photographic illustrations required both for advertisements and public relations work.

Not only do agencies have a habit of choosing the most expensive studios, but two lots of overheads are involved – the photographer's and the agency's. The net result is that the client has to pay heavily for the luxury of routing his photography through the agency. The alternative is for the company's publicity department to be responsible for the work and to supply the agency with black and white prints or colour transparencies. Where possible this is recommended as it saves money and also gives the publicity manager complete control over the picture, i.e. subject matter, angle, impact and technical quality. It does mean, of course, that he has to be prepared to supervise the photography and to approve the picture to be used as an illustration either for an advertisement or editorial material. In other words, by taking the work away from the agency, the publicity manager takes on more responsibility but reaps a reward in the form of greater control over the advertising and reduced production costs.

NEWS VALUE OF PHOTOGRAPHS USED IN PUBLIC RELATIONS WORK

Good industrial photographs with fairly full explanatory captions are of the utmost value in any present-day publicity campaign. Not only are such pictures welcomed by many national newspapers in their City columns, but also the more specialized financial papers and the provincial Press are always anxious to see photographs that tell an industrial story. It may be the visit of a foreign delegation or mission to a factory, a new apprenticeship scheme in operation, the installation of a giant electronic computer, indeed, the subjects are legion, and provided they are topical and have even a restricted value, then they are certain to be welcome. The trade and technical journals always claim to be starved of good factory pictures and by feeding into them a steady flow of newsy prints, one is certain of achieving useful and, indeed, quite valuable editorial publicity. What are the requirements of a good news-worthy photograph?

(1) Technically the picture must be good, i.e. sharp and clear, and the story or event obvious.
(2) It needs to be topical. A photograph of an event which took place a week before its receipt by the editor is of little value.
(3) The caption on the back of the print should be just long enough to give all the relevant details and yet not so long as to be wearisome to read; moreover, it must be accurate.

Whole plate glossy prints, with or without white borders, are acceptable for all public relations work and for block making generally.

THE COST OF PHOTOGRAPHY

In paying for photography one pays for a service. The better the service – that is, the higher the photographer's professional skill, knowledge or experience – then the higher the price. Although the Institute of British Photographers provides a most useful guide on the question of conditions of engagement and scale of professional fees it is, after all, nothing more than a guide. It is pointed out that 'when the services of a specialist photographer are obtained, fees in excess of those shown in their guide will normally be payable, since specialized skills and creative ability of a high order must and do require higher remuneration'. This proviso makes possible wide differences in the fees charged by different photographers. For example, the basic fee given in the Institute's scale of fees for professional services, attendance and taking and providing one photograph in monochrome at the studio or on site is £3 3s. A small and comparatively unknown photographer might charge this sum if he were commissioned to take a series of pictures, say, three or four, but a well-known West End studio would probably charge a minimum of £5 5s. With colour work the discrepancies in fees between different photographers is greater still. The Institute gives £8 8s. as the basic fee for taking and providing one transparency to the client's instructions either at the studio or on the site in daylight, but £10 10s. to £15 15s. is a more usual price to pay. To safeguard the client, and also the photographer himself, it is recommended that the terms of the remuneration are agreed before any commission is undertaken.

Where photography is carried out by the works photographer, then costing can be a little deceptive as not only must material and processing be charged, but also salaries and overheads. It is very doubtful whether any works photographer could produce a picture at a price charged by the average outside operator!

OWNERSHIP OF NEGATIVE AND COPYRIGHT

It is accepted in law that the negative is the property of the photographer, but the copyright of all photographs taken is

246

vested in the client who commissions the work. If the photographer surrenders the negative, then he is entitled to make a substantial charge for it and the sum asked may, in fact, exceed the actual sum charged for the initial photograph. Some industrial concerns like to purchase the negative from the photographer and to file this alongside the print in their photographic library, then further prints can be made as required. This practice seems hard to justify commercially as such a heavy premium is paid for a print and negative, and whilst in some instances a large number of prints may be needed, in others, and these constitute the majority, only one or two prints may satisfy all requirements.

A rather tricky situation exists where multiple copies are made from photographic prints by one of the modern duplicating systems and the photographer, who owns the negative, is not immediately involved. This practice is frowned upon by the photographic professional organizations as it deprives the photographer of a certain amount of revenue and seems somewhat unfair. It is recommended therefore that where this kind of work is likely to take place, the owner of the negative is paid a fee as a measure of goodwill and some recompense for loss of business. Two or three guineas is adequate in these cases.

As regards colour work, the transparency represents the finished work and is, of course, surrendered. When the negative/positive system is used, then clients are normally provided with one finished whole plate colour print. The negative is retained by the photographer and from it further prints may be obtained or, if required, colour transparencies can be made from the negative.

WHERE TO FIND GOOD PHOTOGRAPHERS

The only reliable yardstick one can use in judging the value of a photographer is his photography. That is why an unknown photographer should, before he is commissioned, be asked to provide evidence that he has the necessary skill and experience to undertake the work. His portfolio should substantiate all his claims. The fact that a photographer is a Fellow, Associate or Licentiate of the Institute of British Photographers is no proof that he is suitable for any particular assignment, but merely indicates that he possesses certain qualifications indicative of his knowledge of the profession. On the other hand, the list of incorporated photographers supplied by the Institute provides a very useful guide and enables the business-man who wants to have some photography carried out in the provinces to contact a likely man on the spot.

Apart, of course, from an acquaintance with the photographer's work gained by examining his prints and colour transparencies, it is possible to obtain a useful impression of the quality of a photographer's work by seeing his pictures in exhibitions, magazines and advertisements. It is easy to make a mistake in the evaluation of a photographer who may be brilliant in one field, but quite hopeless in another. The general practitioner in photography usually gives the best all round value.

COLOUR PHOTOGRAPHY

Not all industrial subjects are equally well suited for colour, indeed, a large proportion look more dramatic and have a greater impact in monochrome. The lavish use of colour may be justified if the subject matter is highly colourful, for example, it would be foolish for a manufacturer of printing inks to produce brochures in black and white. Similarly, the maker of machine tools would derive only a marginal benefit from using colour. It is all a question of suiting the technique to the subject.

In most types of technical literature there is room for a well balanced mixture of both colour and monochrome reproductions, but to justify the lavish use of colour throughout a publication then it must have a high sales value. Colour is expensive, not only to produce initially either as transparencies or prints, but also in the form of blocks and, of course, the actually printed page. It is, therefore, emphasized that where colour photography is justified on the grounds of greater sales impact and to increase the prestige of the company, then it should be superb in quality. The idea that money can be saved by using 35 mm. colour originals taken by the managing director, who is very keen on photography, instead of recruiting the services of a professional is entirely false. In the first place, irrespective of whether the 35 mm. transparencies are good or bad, any block-maker will tell you that much better blocks can be made from 5 in. × 4 in. transparencies than those of postage stamp size and, as block-making is a highly costly business, then it is sound common sense to start off with the best possible originals.

COLOUR PRINT OR TRANSPARENCY

When considering the respective merits of the negative/positive system and the colour transparency a number of factors need to be taken into account. Generally speaking, the colour print is not as popular with photographers or, indeed, with customers as the transparency, it being contended that the latter gives better definition and truer colour values. On the other hand, there are a number of advantages attached to the use of the colour print and these can be summarized as follows:

(1) Colour prints in number can be produced quite economically from a negative, whereas it is a very expensive exercise to obtain copy transparencies from an original.

(2) It is also possible to have colour prints made to size for a layout, whereas this is not at all possible when using transparencies.

(3) Flat copy gives greater latitude in block-making than colour transparencies as the colours to be reproduced are those seen and approved by the client and if alterations are required, such as intensification or alteration of colour or removal of defects, then these can usually be effected in the studio. When working with transparencies there is always some doubt as to the validity of the colour values as seen by transmitted light, these depending on viewing conditions. Alterations to the transparency, when they become necessary, are difficult and costly to undertake. On the other hand, of course, one must remember that some process engravers have geared their works to the use of transparencies and these fit neatly into their conveyor-belt system.

(4) Transparencies are sensitive both to handling and storage and, if spoilt, replacements cannot be obtained. With colour prints there is also the possibility of securing further prints from the original negative.

VALUE OF THE POLAROID SYSTEM OF PHOTOGRAPHY

It sometimes happens that an instant photographic print is required for publicity purposes, and here the Polaroid Land apparatus can give excellent service in providing a print within half a second or so of taking the picture. Not only is it possible to obtain a first-class photographic print direct from the camera, but by use of the Neg/Pos Type 55 a usable negative of the conventional type can be made available as well as the print. The photographer is not nowadays restricted to the use of a special Polaroid camera involving quite considerable extra expense and also additional apparatus; he can, at reasonable cost, fit a special back to the standard 5 in. × 4 in. back of his Graphic camera to accommodate 5 in. × 4 in. Polaroid Film Sheaths. The speed of the black and white Polaroid film material is sufficiently high to meet practically all conditions of exposure and the quality of the finished print is superb.

In some concerns the Polaroid system is being used very successfully to photograph members of the staff whose pictures are required for immediate editorial purposes, also to cover certain events in the organization which have to meet Press deadlines. It might happen, for instance, that an extension to the factory is opened by some V.I.P. and that the time factor hardly allows for adequate Press coverage using normal photographic apparatus. Here the Polaroid system enables prints to be made available in seconds instead of hours, and for them to be on their way to newspapers or journals in a few minutes after the actual event has taken place.

BUILDING UP A PHOTOGRAPHIC LIBRARY

It has often been said that a photographic library is the cornerstone of any good publicity department, and this is no exaggeration. Apart, however, from being comprehensive in scope, the library needs to be organized in such a way that it is easy to find a photograph quickly when it is wanted. The system breaks down completely if it is so complicated that you have to study a page of instructions before you can get what you want.

In the early planning of a photographic library there are a number of points to consider:

(1) Size of photographic print to be filed.
(2) Desirability of captioning each print or merely giving it a key number so that the full caption is available on request.
(3) The number of different subjects or categories to be covered.
(4) The ease with which any particular photograph or selection of pictures may be found.
(5) The simplest system to adopt for obtaining further copies of each print in the library.

Once the size of photographic print has been decided upon, and this should be either half-plate or whole plate, preferably the latter, then suitable folders should be ordered, and cabinets provided of the correct size to hold such folders. A good method is to attach a print to the back of each folder for identification and reference. The photographer's name, business address and his negative reference number are also essential pieces of information that should be on the folder.

If the prints are to be individually captioned, the required descriptive material could be written or typed on gummed labels, one of which can be stuck to the top front of the folder and the others on the reverse sides of the prints. In addition, each print should carry the negative reference number and a specimen acknowledgement to the company owning the copyright, e.g. 'Photograph by courtesy of Leonard and Tutton Sawmills Ltd., Brancaster.' The name of the photographer could be added alongside the negative reference number, but this is not essential as his name appears on the master-file.

Heading cards should be made out for each subject or category, and the folders which come under that heading can be filed behind it. These sections can then be further subdivided as, for instance, architectural applications, bakery equipment, medical, etc., headings specially applicable to the subject matter. These sections must, of course, be in alphabetical order, and the folders in each of these sections can be numbered from 1 onwards so that each folder has its own particular reference both to the subject and the file number.

In order to find a particular photographic print it is necessary to have a card index system. This is made up of small cards upon which are entered all the relevant details about any particular photograph. The photograph may illustrate one single object or a number of objects, and a card would have to be made out for each of these so that complete coverage of the entire picture is assured. Let us take an actual example from the photographic library of a manufacturer of sanitary fittings. The photograph of a bathroom set shows a number of items – bath and fittings, lavatory and cistern, wash-basin and mirror. There should be individual cards for each of these items, so that a person who was looking for a photograph of a bathroom with a number of the firm's fittings could find (a) a bathroom picture, (b) a bathroom showing a bath, (c) a bathroom showing a lavatory, etc. Other index cards could be prepared by listing the reference numbers of photographs which come under main headings, these being, of course, dependent upon the nature of the business of the company.

An alternative system to the one described revolves around the use of albums, allowing a separate album for each product or category. Each photograph could still be given a reference number within the category, and this could be written beneath it together with brief details about each picture. Further details, including the name of the photographer and the negative number, could be made available in a reference book. Where the photographic library contains up to 10,000 prints, then the album method might well prove easier to operate.

If we take again the example of a sanitary goods manufacturer whose stock lines are

Baths;
Fittings for baths;
Shower fittings and trays;

Lavatories, cisterns and all the necessary fittings
Wash-basins and taps, etc.;
Mirrors and fittings,

then a separate album could be devoted to each of these categories of goods or, in the case of a large range of a particular line, then possibly two or more albums might be reserved for these.

CLEARING PHOTOGRAPHS FOR USE IN ADVERTISING

One grave pitfall into which an advertising manager can readily fall is the unauthorized use of photographs showing recognizable individuals. These may be people in the street, operatives working machines, demolition gangs, road-sweepers, chimney sweeps, Boy Scouts and even the Brigade of Guards. If their faces are shown and they can be identified, then they will have to be approached for permission to use their photographs in any type of advertisement. It is assumed that, if a person's photograph is used in an advertisement, then it can be said that he or she is endorsing the product or service offered for sale. Unless the person shown gives his or her own personal release, which usually involves acceptance of a fee, equivalent to a model fee, then there may be sufficient grounds for him to bring an action against the company for substantial damages.

Agencies take this question of clearance very seriously and some of the large agencies employ a couple of 'chasers' whose job it is to secure releases from all people shown in pictures to be used for advertising purposes. Indeed, in some advertising agencies, there is an inflexible rule that failure to secure a release from everyone shown in an advertisement can mean instant dismissal for the executive responsible.

In industrial advertising it is often taken for granted that, because official sanction is given by the advertiser for the use of a photograph taken in his works, clearance is automatically given for the reproduction in an advertisement of all the operatives shown in the picture. This is not so. If the men or women can be recognized, then they have a legal right to complain, and, indeed, they might conceivably sue their employers for damages. Whilst it is undoubtedly true that there is usually less grounds for complaint, as regards implied endorsement of products in most forms of industrial advertising, permission must still be obtained from all the persons shown in the advertisement. Occasionally, it is possible to block out or to remove the faces of extraneous individuals who may appear in a photograph, and this, of course, solves all problems.

INDEX